# The Chief

# THE CHIEF

## Field Marshal Lord Wavell
### COMMANDER-IN-CHIEF AND VICEROY
### 1939–1947

## *Ronald Lewin*

'The brilliant chief, irregularly great'
LORD LYTTON, *The New Timon*

Hutchinson
London Melbourne Sydney Auckland Johannesburg

Hutchinson & Co. (Publishers) Ltd

An imprint of the Hutchinson Publishing Group

3 Fitzroy Square, London W1P 6JD

Hutchinson Group (Australia) Pty Ltd
30–32 Cremorne Street, Richmond South, Victoria 3121
PO Box 151, Broadway, New South Wales 2007

Hutchinson Group (NZ) Ltd
32–34 View Road, PO Box 40–086, Glenfield, Auckland 10

Hutchinson Group (SA) Pty Ltd
PO Box 337, Bergvlei 2012, South Africa

First published 1980
© Ronald Lewin 1980

Printed in Great Britain by The Anchor Press Ltd,
and bound by Wm Brendon & Son Ltd,
both of Tiptree, Essex

British Library Cataloguing in Publication Data
Lewin, Ronald
    The chief.
    1. Wavell, Archibald Percival, *Earl Wavell*
    2. Generals – Great Britain – Biography
    3. Great Britain. Army – Biography
    4. Viceroys – India – Biography
    I. Title
    355.3'32'0924        DA69.3.W37
ISBN 0 09 142500 X

*In Memoriam*
John Connell
and
Brigadier Michael Roberts, DSO

# Contents

# Illustrations

# Acknowledgements

The late John Connell and the late Brigadier Michael Roberts, to whom this book is dedicated, were my cherished friends at different times and in different circumstances. But all students of Wavell must owe a particular debt to the biography that Connell, before his sadly premature death, so nearly completed, and for whose conclusion Roberts's exceptional experience of Indian affairs was so apt: even though, since its publication, much new material has become available and new perspectives have opened.

To Wavell's daughter, Lady Joan Robertson, I am grateful for much kind consideration.

For access to their private papers and for information I am indebted to the late Major-General Sir William Abraham, Mrs Philip Astley (Joan Bright), Brigadier the Lord Ballantrae, Lieutenant-General Sir Thomas Hutton, Major-General J. D. Lunt, General Sir James Marshall-Cornwall, General Sir Richard O'Connor, Brigadier John Shearer, and Brigadier the Rt. Hon. Sir John Smyth. Air Marshal Sir Thomas Elmhirst kindly allowed me to quote from his correspondence and shared his recollections of events and personalities. Major-General David Belchem was indefatigable in our joint efforts to clarify certain events in the spring of 1941. Anthony Quayle most helpfully produced and allowed me to quote a characteristic letter from Wavell. Grahame C. Greene, Managing Director of Jonathan Cape Ltd, placed at my disposal the file and statistics relating to *Other Men's Flowers,* whilst J. H. H. Gaute provided some enlightening facts about the publication of Wavell's *Allenby*.

I am grateful to the Trustees of the Liddell Hart Centre for Military Archives at King's College, the University of

London for access to the considerable file of correspondence between Wavell and Liddell Hart, and to the Public Record Office for material gathered from the files at Kew.

For further advice and assistance I am indebted to Brigadier Shelford Bidwell, Lieutenant-General Sir Clarence Bird, Major-General R. L. Brown, Professor Raymond Callahan, Field Marshal the Lord Carver, Dr Charles Cruickshank, D. M. Davin, General Sir David Fraser, Sir Rupert Hart-Davis, Major David Horner (Australian Army), Lieutenant-General Sir Ian Jacob, Gordon Lee, Philip Mason, Lieutenant-Colonel Brian Montgomery, Mrs Mary Pain, Lieutenant-General Sir Reginald Savory, Lieutenant-Colonel Antony Simonds, the late Marshal of the RAF Sir John Slessor, Aileen Viscountess Slim, Dr I. McD. G. Stewart, and Mrs Rosalind Warren.

*Ronald Lewin*

# 1

# Forethoughts

The General . . . repeated nearly the whole of Gray's elegy . . . adding,
as he concluded, that he would prefer being the author of that poem to
the glory of beating the French tomorrow.
*Account by J. Robinson of Wolfe at Quebec, 12 September 1759*

In a profound sense, Wavell is one of the unknown soldiers.
This is not because he is numbered among those missing
millions anonymously honoured in national memorials. It is
rather because the basis of his decisions and actions during his
peak period as a commander – from 1940 onwards – is ob-
scured partly by his own shrouded personality, and partly by
an encrusted overlay of misunderstanding, misinterpretation
and myth. To see Wavell plain is not easy. The military analyst
is always at a loss with a general who keeps his thoughts to
himself. Wavell's career has a countenance of great nobility,
even though it is pitted with marks of failure, yet in triumph as
in defeat the lineaments are enigmatic. There is a penumbra of
uncertainty – of contradictions to be resolved and incon-
sistencies to be explained. To indicate some of them may
provide a useful backcloth for the chapters that follow.

When his former ADC, Bernard Fergusson,* wrote a book
about the regiment to which both he and Wavell belonged, he
called it *The Black Watch and the King's Enemies*. Wavell, in his
introduction, quoted a description of the type of Highland
soldier inducted into the Black Watch when William Pitt, after
the 1745 rebellion, decided to trammel the hillmen by putting
them into uniform. The Highlander, wrote one Stewart of
Garth,

> acquired a hardihood which enabled him to sustain severe priva-
> tions. As the simplicity of his life gave vigour to his body, so it

---

* In 1972 Brigadier Fergusson became Lord Ballantrae.

fortified his mind . . . he was taught to consider courage as the
most honourable virtue, cowardice the most disgraceful failing; to
venerate and obey his chief, and devote himself for his native
country and clan; and thus prepared to be a soldier, he was ready to
follow wherever honour and duty called him.

This is how Wavell himself is mainly remembered.

The image constantly returns of a sturdy upright figure
apparently hewn from weathered oak. With an elusive but
endearing smile, it stands at a point of slight detachment from
the rest of the universe, inspecting the scene in a manner
which, because of its single eye, seems quizzical and even
sardonic but in fact is mercilessly penetrating. Like the Highlander of '45 it is in an absolute sense loyal, enduring and brave:
not to be subdued by circumstance, menace or self-interest and
utterly devoted to a lifetime's service against the King's
Enemies. The qualities are such as to be instantly recognized.
At a London party during the summer of 1943 Harold Nicolson ran into Wavell, and noted in his diary for 1 June:

> A stocky man with one blind eye. I am reminded of the day when I
> was writing in the ante-room of the Quai d'Orsay and there entered
> a square little man clasping an enormous portfolio. I thought, "That
> must be a sergeant in the Ordnance Department come with stat-
> istics for his chief." I then thought, "My God, it's Foch!"

Like another remarkable Wykehamist, Marshal of the RAF
Lord Portal, Wavell was self-contradictory. In a public setting,
whether it be in council or merely in his office, the Commander-in-Chief, like the Chief of the Air Staff, could seem
remote and even glacial: inaccessible. Yet each amid his family
or the small circle of his close friends could be warm, out-
going, stimulating, human. The sense of delight in Wavell's
company and of reverential respect for the personality there
disclosed has been naturally, but often uncritically, dis-
seminated by those who shared it. What has so far been written
about Wavell has to a large degree been produced by people
who were deeply moved by an experience of living, as they
felt, within the shadow of a Great Man.

Yet of all the enigmatic features which Wavell's career presents to the student this is the most puzzling. For there are
indeed marks of failure on that noble countenance. In his final

Despatch as Commander-in-Chief, India, Wavell wrote:

> During the present war, in just under four years, from September 1939 to June 1943, I have directed some fourteen campaigns in the Western Desert of North Africa, in British Somaliland, in Eritrea, in Italian Somaliland, in Abyssinia, in Greece, in Crete, in Iraq, in Syria, in Iran, in Malaya, in the Dutch East Indies, in Burma, in Arakan.

No Allied commander in the Second World War could flourish a list of operations comparable for their range or for their almost unqualified difficulty. Nevertheless, as Wavell commented on his own campaigns, 'some have been successful, others have failed'.

It would be facile to observe that the successes were against Italians or Vichy French whereas every campaign conducted by Wavell against Germans or Japanese ended in disaster. History disdains such black-and-white contrasts. Wavell himself knew well that circumstances alter cases. On 23 October 1942, the day of Alamein, *The Times* printed the first of two contributions by the distant Commander-in-Chief India on the subject of Military Genius and the qualities that make a great general. In these he pointed out the dangers of such comparative assessments and of placing commanders in a pecking-order. 'Was Mynn a better cricketer than Grace, Grace than Trumper, Trumper than Hammond? The difference in conditions of pitch, bowling, outfield, etc., make any comparisons most difficult.' 'Suppose Hannibal had possessed 50 more elephants', he added. 'Would he have marched direct on Rome after Cannae and changed the face of history?' In weighing Wavell's failure to change history's face in his own campaigns against the Germans and the Japanese it is, of course, vital to remember that elephants were always in short supply; that the bowling was often masterly and that the pitch was rarely of his own choosing. Still, the resulting failures stand on record and, as W. H. Auden wrote,

> History to the defeated
> May say Alas but cannot help or pardon.

The enigma therefore persists. Was it merely the effect of wartime propaganda and the eulogies of his intimates that, in spite of his failures, placed Wavell on a pedestal from which he has never been effectively dislodged? Or was it that the ineffaceable charisma of the man himself, and a distinctive style of conducting war, properly and permanently enshrined him? Only a strict and unabashed examination of his generalship can answer such questions. The precise circumstances of each campaign, the force and relevance of political pressures, the resources available to him, the character and power of his opponents, the manifest qualities that led to success and, where he erred, the technical and temperamental causes of his mistakes must all be held in balance.

Such is the purpose of this book: and Wavell's own reaction, no doubt, would be a wry patient smile. He experienced too many clumsy post-mortems on his own affairs not to know that such probes can never reconstitute the living reality. At the same time, his deep historical sense would inform him that men of a certain scale are perennially and inevitably exposed to re-appraisals. But in the end any student who seeks to analyse his career must remember that from some niche on Valhalla an unwavering if single eye is watching, and that in its dispassionate way the spirit of Wavell will be reflecting: 'My case rests. It is all there, in the words I uttered at Trinity College, Cambridge, long ago.' For in those famous Lees-Knowles Lectures of 1939 Wavell indeed composed an epitaph for himself at which none can cavil. 'This is the first and true function of the leader, never to think the battle or the cause lost. The ancient Romans put up a statue to the generals who saved them in one of Rome's darkest hours, with this inscription: "Because he did not despair of the Republic." ' In 1939 the lectures were attended by between twenty and thirty undergraduates, but when war followed and he carried in his hands the fate of millions, when battles were lost and the cause was fading, Wavell of the Black Watch still found that, like his predecessors, he had 'acquired a hardihood which enabled him to sustain severe privations'.

Throughout that later period of his life during which he achieved a national and, indeed, an international reputation adversity was usually his familiar. But like a good general he operated from a firm base – from a series of bases, in fact, organized in depth. And the first citadel and stockpile on which he relied for assurance and reinforcement was his own mind. As the story of his career unfolds it will be seen that his mode of conducting affairs, whether as a commander or as Viceroy, has a distinctive character because it is the direct expression of a *Weltanschauung,* a set of mental categories studiously derived by Wavell from his personal experience and articulated into a trusted but idiosyncratic version of 'the principles of war'. The performance of remarkable commanders often reveals an identifiable calligraphy; we can read a battle and recognize the style of a Rommel, a Patton, a Montgomery, a Napoleon or even a Genghis or a Scipio. So it is with Wavell. Indeed, an objective analysis of his defeats is liable to disclose as a main reason some departure from his innermost convictions. Exhaustion, injury, distracting voices from his political masters, misconceptions about the enemy, misplaced trust in his subordinates, stubbornness that hardened into obstinacy, over-confidence and undue depression – all the hazards and distractions to which a commander is prone affected Wavell during those fourteen campaigns, and his arduous years as Viceroy. Stress sometimes warped, though it never snapped, the shaft of steel. He was his own sceptical critic, as mordant as one of Conrad's characters; and when he does attempt self-defence it seems like the instant reaction of a mind drained by exhaustion which reason later qualifies. Certainly the self-awareness of *The Viceroy's Journal* would have pervaded the diaries he refused to write while he was a military Commander-in-Chief.

The contours of his mind were essentially classical. Indeed, their outlines were traced during his schoolboy studies of Latin and Greek. It was a classical scholarship that took him to Winchester, and though he professed to have found Sophocles stilted and Xenophon boring one observes that throughout his life a prehensile memory – as effortless as Macaulay's, but quickened by his partial blindness – discovered precedent, analogy and sometimes comfort among the Greeks and Romans. Military men have often been surprised by the opening section of Wavell's lectures on *Generals and Generalship*, in which he defines a general's qualifications by a quotation from Socrates.

This was not ostentation. It merely indicated that Wavell was civilized – civilization meaning that answers to the problems of war must be found not simply in the narrow solutions of staff colleges but in the larger fields of human experience. And, of all the post-1945 generals, who besides Sir John Hackett (his retirement diversified by his Presidency of the Classical Association)* has had a sense of the past capable of devising the unorthodox exercise which Wavell composed for his 2nd Division in 1936, a period of deadly conservatism for the British Army? 'This exercise,' the brief began, 'is based, very remotely both as regards time and matter, on the legend of the GOLDEN FLEECE, which relates how an expedition of some of the bravest and most expert warriors of the day sailed under their leader Jason, in a ship called the *Argo*, to carry off the GOLDEN FLEECE, from the land of COLCHIS.' At least that was a variant on the sort of setting for a training scheme which began 'Forces of Redland are established on the line ANDOVER – SALISBURY . . .'

His knowledge of classical literature was selective rather than academic – before leaving Winchester he had already transferred to the Army class. In other fields too – history, poetry – the intensity of his concern was perhaps more marked than its width and depth. Indeed, a cynic might observe that the impression he made among his fellow soldiers of being an intellectual was mainly due to the fact that he could read a book or quote a verse while they could do neither. That would be unjust, for his reading, like his friendships, had a range and a sophistication far beyond the reach of most of the generals of his day. Yet though he wrote and thought about military affairs with convincing assurance and a lapidary authority he was entirely unpretentious – and perhaps sometimes seduced by intellectual pretence. How else could he have written of T. E. Lawrence: 'On the theoretical side, he had read more and thought more on military history and the military art than probably any great commander'?

All this is irrelevant. Whatever Wavell read he digested and absorbed. By a kind of osmosis the books he encountered

* In 1948 Wavell similarly became President of the Virgilian Society.

became part of himself and he kept their contents, as the gunners say, like ammunition stacked 'for ready use'. Throughout
his campaigns, therefore, he was always liable to place a problem or consider a situation in perspectives wider in scope and
further-reaching in time than those of the conventional commander. Alexander, when he was conducting his final *Blitzkrieg*
drive down the Medjerda valley to Tunis, reflected that his
predecessor had been Belisarius. When that educated general
'Gertie' Tuker had to assault Monte Cassino with his 4th Indian
Division he personally scoured the shops of Naples till he found
an old volume which described the construction of the monastery.* So Wavell saw things.† Few of the other Allied Generals
were able to look beyond the immediate battlefield into history,
or to direct their commands with an instinctive sense that the
past is part of the present. This was not Montgomery's style, or
Eisenhower's, or Zhukov's. Among Wavell's best qualities was
his grasp of dimensions.

His ideas, like his emotions, ripened in some guarded recess.
It will be seen later that service under Allenby provided him
with a model for generalship, and it is interesting that when
Allenby, like Wavell, contributed to the symposium *T. E.
Lawrence by his Friends,* he should have written about the
'uncrowned Prince of Arabia' in terms which were as true of
Wavell as they were of Allenby himself. 'He depended little on
others; he had his private reasons for all he did, and those
reasons satisfied him.' This self-sufficiency was life-long; at
Winchester one of his masters wrote that 'he has a large
amount of latent power and all his work is strong' but added,
prophetically, that 'he must be a little more communicative as
he grows older.' A mind turned inward can develop great
strength and subtlety. Without a capacity for introspection,
moreover, men in high command are certainly vulnerable.

* Tuker's reproach to his Corps Commander, Freyberg, was indeed worthy of
Wavell. 'When a formation is called upon to reduce such a place, it should be apparent
that the place is reducible by the means at the disposal of that Division and that the
means are ready for it, without having to go to the bookstalls of Naples to find out
what should have been fully considered many weeks ago.'
† 'I said once that I began to feel I was back in Europe on arriving at the Dead Sea,
then a staging-post on the way to Cairo. I suppose this was probably because one saw
holiday-makers sunbathing. But Wavell said musingly, "The boundary of the Roman
Empire." ' Philip Mason, *A Shaft of Sunlight.*

But in Wavell's case the dangers foreseen by his schoolmaster were not averted.

His quelling silences are legendary. In battle, when he flew forward to advise or sustain one of his subordinates, he could be cogent, à propos, and even inspiring. But at base, in Cairo or Delhi, he could listen to the reports or proposals of his staff with the discouraging immobility of a statue. His response was habitual: 'I see.' No comment would follow: no dialogue was generated.* Whereas Alexander and Montgomery in the west and Mountbatten and Slim in the east had an articulate and constructive relationship with their senior officers, Wavell too often maintained a distance that sometimes became an abyss.

Whether this inability to communicate derived from some deep inhibition about personal relations, or whether a genuine mental impediment, destructive of conversation, prevented him from getting on terms with people (except in the stronghold of his private life) is a matter not to be explored by the amateur psychologist: but it cannot be disregarded by the historian. Wavell's reserve, his self-reliance, his independence, his granite stoicism were massive and positive qualities on which his achievements were firmly based, yet in some profound way they were negated by a sort of disdain, a refusal to 'give', a spirit of *noli me tangere*.

This was a limitation affecting his attitude not only towards his staff or the unfortunates who found themselves beside him at the dinner-table, but also towards his troops. In *Generals and Generalship* he made his position plain – on the eve of a world war:

> But does it matter to a general whether he has his men's affection so long as he has their confidence? He must certainly never court popularity. If he has their appreciation and respect it is sufficient. Efficiency in a general his soldiers have a right to expect; geniality they are usually right to suspect. Marlborough was perhaps the only great general to whom geniality was always natural.

Since this is a view which was contradicted by the whole

* 'How well I remember wondering what Archie wanted, for he did not always express his wishes vocally: somehow I got to know without being told – a sort of instinct between friends.' Lieutenant-General Sir Arthur Smith, Wavell's Chief of Staff in Cairo, to Bernard Fergusson, 4 September 1961.

experience of the British Army in the Second World War, it must certainly be kept carefully in mind in any consideration of Wavell's generalship – for it was a view which he did not noticeably modify during the war itself. Was he, perhaps, over-influenced by his experience of the pre-1939 Regular Army? That his doctrine was not tolerable in the mass army of a democracy, comprised in the main of reasonably educated men with minds of their own and there for 'hostilities only', was a fact understood by all the best of the British leaders. Montgomery with his Eighth Army and Mountbatten in South-East Asia courted popularity and displayed geniality as a calculated and necessary policy which others, like Slim, pursued instinctively and consistently. Generals like Gott, or Gale, or Horrocks elicited from their men not merely respect, but affection, which in some instances had even greater warmth. British volunteers and conscripts in the mid twentieth century would obey an efficient leader: but for those they found to be congenial they were more readily prepared to die. In their memoirs the loyal supporters of Wavell refer not infrequently to the impression he made on the troops in his wartime commands. There is little evidence of such impressions from the troops themselves.

Yet in spite of his reservations about charismatic leadership, in spite of his tongue-tied detachment, in spite of his difficulty in establishing a *rapport* man-to-man, it is unquestionable that on occasion – and sometimes on occasions of great stress – his impact on the men under his command was not only direct, but even uplifting. His mere presence could raise morale.*
There was none of the adopted techniques or instinctive methods of other commanders. He lacked the showmanship of Mountbatten or Montgomery or Patton, the cheering and cheerful *bonhomie* of Horrocks or the down-to-earth humanity of Slim. Of all his contemporaries he was perhaps most – though by no means entirely – akin to Alexander: for their soldiers, to see them was enough. The troops at the sharp end in the Western Desert, or in a fetid Burmese jungle, became

* See Connell (Roberts), *Wavell: Supreme Commander*, p. 226, for Wavell's inspiring visit to the 7th Hussars during the retreat from Burma. The account ends: 'General Wavell was always welcome. He was, in himself, a tonic.'

aware of this rocklike figure beside them and simply felt the
better for it. There was nothing specific to remember, no joke
or gesture or effective flamboyance: merely a presence. His
officers spoke of him as The Chief. On these occasions his
great virtue was that he seemed like one. And perhaps it was
because something indefinable then happened to his troops
that so few of them were subsequently able to define it.

It is true that apart from trivial episodes in his early days as a
young officer he never led men into action or knew the personal involvement, and perhaps the heartbreak, of commit-
ting *his* company or *his* battalion or *his* division to the
slaughter. In two great wars he was always either a staff
commander or a commander-in-chief. With the men he sent to
die – sometimes in large numbers – he was not directly identified as he would have been, say, if he had commanded a
battalion of the Black Watch on the Somme or, like Slim,
personally led the retreat through Burma instead of being
restricted – as Wavell was – to a remote control. All the same,
from the first he was an *habitué* of the front line. During seven
months in the Ypres Salient from November 1914 to June
1915, as Brigade Major of the 9th Brigade, he kept as close to
the action as most of the regimental officers. The Staff tended
to hold themselves back, but Wavell felt that 'I did not see how
I could do my job without knowing what the trenches were
like, and soon started visiting them.' He never stopped, until a
splinter destroyed his left eye on the Menin Road. In effect,
therefore, Wavell knew at first hand that necessity which the
author of *Servitude et grandeur de la vie militaire,* Alfred de
Vigny, noted in his Journal: *'il faut toujours exiger des hommes
plus qu'ils ne peuvent faire, afin d'en avoir tout ce qu'ils peuvent
faire'*. Nobody who had shared so intimately the self-sacrifice
of the British Expeditionary Force at Ypres could be ignorant
of the responsibilities, and the price, of leadership.

Indeed, Wavell was far too shrewd not to grasp, intel-
lectually, that if an officer is to demand the impossible from his
men so that they can achieve the possible, efficiency is not
enough. What he called geniality in Marlborough Liddell Hart
defined more precisely: 'The power of commanding affection
while communicating energy.' It is strange therefore, and

perhaps symptomatic, that in lecturing about generalship Wavell should have dismissed so coolly the inspirational factor – a dismissal that says more about his own temperament than it does about the desirable qualities of a leader. For it is surely an odd deduction from military history to assert that good generalship displays its power by communicating energy without commanding affection: even more curious as one observes Wavell himself refuting it in practice. He presents the paradox of a natural leader inhibited by his own nature.

Such a stance suggests a lack of empathy. Indeed, Wavell's conversational paralysis was itself a form of inability to enter another person's mind, for it was not an expression of contempt or (at least not always) of boredom or inattention. Something more integral kept him dumb. He has been compared with Haig because each was able to articulate lucidly in writing and yet, faced by others, could only stutter or be silent. But Wavell had delicate sensitivities and sympathies: he was not merely humane, he was a humanist and with a set of values far more civilized than Haig's. The self-reliance which, in Haig's case, stemmed from Calvin and in Wavell's from the Stoic philosophers helped each of them to shoulder the intolerable burdens of their high commands, yet it still seems both sad and strange that Wavell, so lonely, so cut off but so intuitive, should have been denied the richness of relationships with those under his command by which other generals have been fortified and uplifted. When he went out as Commander-in-Chief, Middle East, in July 1939, John Connell in his devoted biography compared Wavell with Stevenson's Lord Weir of Hermiston: 'On he went up the great, bare staircase of his duty, uncheered and undepressed.' There is something in that.

The most tragic result of Wavell's taciturnity was, of course, his failure to retain Churchill's confidence – a failure so complete that in the end the Prime Minister might well have said to him what he is supposed to have said to de Gaulle: *'Si vous m'obstaclerez, je vous liquiderai.'* Certainly Wavell was liquidated – or at least rusticated from Cairo to Delhi. The tragedy was Greek in the sense that it derived directly from the characters of the protagonists.

Connell thought that its roots ran deep. In an instructive

passage he describes and documents Wavell's outrage at the time of the Ulster Crisis and the Curragh Mutiny in the spring of 1914. (Wavell was then in the Russian section of the War Office Intelligence Department.) In letters to his father, Major-General Wavell, we see him vehemently opposing the readiness of other officers to resign. 'The idea of the officers of the Army going on strike,' he wrote, 'which I think is what it really amounts to, over this business, is to my mind absolutely disastrous. What about the men? They can't resign whatever their opinions are.' More to the point was his feeling that when the dust was settled the Army would close its disordered ranks, but 'it will merely increase their contempt for the politicians.' The politicians meant, in particular, Churchill, whose braggadocio during the crisis was in his worst vein. Connell commented:

> The source of some misunderstanding and mistrust, a quarter of a century later, between two great servants of the state is perhaps to be found in the reactions of an unknown young staff officer to the behaviour of a powerful and famous Cabinet Minister, nine years his senior, in the days immediately following the second reading of the Irish Home Rule Bill.

1941 was not 1914. No doubt Wavell consciously or unconsciously retained a memory of those distant days, but what of the interval? For there is also no doubt that in the thirties he disapproved of appeasement. After the war he recalled that 'I always held that we should have fought at Munich time,' and the vulgar response to Chamberlain's scrap of paper seemed nauseating. 'How can we hold up our heads again?' he said. 'We don't deserve to be great, and we'll end up as a second-rate nation.' It might therefore be supposed that Churchill's lonely stand against Nazism might have effaced any lingering recollection of Ulster and the Curragh. There is no evidence, however, that this occurred.

The truth is more complex. It may be defined as a case of inperfect sympathies. Connell himself has vividly described the disastrous drop in the temperature of their relationship during the very first meetings between the Prime Minister and the Commander-in-Chief, Middle East, at the London conference in August 1940. Of Churchill's own account Connell observed that 'the note of pained bewilderment, of a sense that something (which could not, surely, be his own fault?) went wrong, sounds through sentences written nearly a decade later.' Those sessions with the War Cabinet during which Wavell sat like a mute even depressed his admirers. Then, later in August, after Wavell had returned to Cairo, he put his thoughts on paper – where he was always at ease – with a fatal effect. The issue was the recent evacuation of Somaliland, which Churchill abhorred. In response to 'a red-hot cable' from the Prime Minister protesting at the small number of British casualties sustained during the withdrawal, and demanding a court of inquiry, Wavell answered that 'a big butcher's bill was not necessarily evidence of good tactics.' Afterwards the CIGS, Sir John Dill, told Wavell that 'this telegram and especially the last sentence roused Winston to greater anger than he had ever seen him in before.' Without pre-empting the discussion of subsequent events in later chapters, it may be claimed that for Wavell this episode represented the point of no return.

And the fault was partly – though by no means entirely – his own. There was that lack of empathy which prevented him from entering his Prime Minister's mind – from seeing that in 1940 and 1941 Churchill like Lincoln in the Civil War was desperately seeking for generals who could 'deliver'. Facing the major and central threat of Germany, he needed and demanded at least a success on the periphery. As Lincoln tested and shed one commander after another until he came to rest on Grant, so Churchill tried first Wavell, and then Auchinleck, in an initial mood of admiration and respect which turned to a disillusion that only Montgomery removed. Wavell was never tuned to the right wave-length. His telegrams to London were logical and lucid, but they were not the signals of a man sensitive to the insistent realities which presented themselves daily in Churchill's war room. There was no effective dialogue.

Yet self-interest and his historical studies should have told him that for a commander in a detached and distant theatre an essential requirement is that he should secure a firm political base at home. The lessons variously exemplified in the careers of Marlborough and Wellington and Haig were all familiar to Wavell. He devoted the third of his Lees-Knowles Lectures to

'The Soldier and the Statesman', and touched there on a case of imperfect sympathies so like his own that his words are worth quoting.

> The chief and bitterest controversy centres round Mr Lloyd George and Sir William Robertson, who were, as you know, practically always at odds. A great pity, they might have made a fine combination had Robertson been a little more pliant and Lloyd George a little less opinionated. Robertson made the error of treating the Prime Minister's ideas with scant courtesy, instead of explaining in what respect they were faulty. And where Lloyd George went wrong was not in his strategical concepts, which were often excellent, but in his lack of knowledge of the mechanics of war . . . .

If Churchill is substituted for Lloyd George and Wavell for Robertson the passage has a genuine relevance. In dealings with Churchill it was not impossible to be pliable without surrendering, or to explain without giving offence. Wavell never seized imaginatively on this need to make acceptable responses, to yield a point here for the sake of gaining there, to capture Churchill's interest and make certain of his support. He played it by the book.

The result was that 'pained bewilderment'. In his memoirs Lord Butler recalled Churchill saying of Wavell in 1941, as the Middle East was falling apart, 'I do not understand his intellect. It may be my own fault, but I always feel as if in the presence of the chairman of a golf club'.

That one of Britain's greatest Prime Ministers should speak in such terms of one of her greatest proconsuls captures the tragedy of their misunderstanding. Yet if Churchill could have risen above his anxieties and bridled his arrogance about military affairs he might have seen that Wavell in fact possessed many of the qualities he most admired. For behind the mask that Churchill and others found most impenetrable was a mind original, subtle and daring: quick to note a man's undisclosed promise or to devise an unorthodox stratagem. In 1943 the Prime Minister prided himself on identifying Wingate as the 'Clive of India' who might shatter the Japanese, but it was Wavell who during his 1937 command in Palestine spotted a young intelligence officer – 'an odd creature', as he called him

– and gave Orde Wingate there, and later in Abyssinia and in Burma, the chance of becoming a cynosure. Indeed the first Chindit expedition, which concentrated Churchill's attention on Wingate,* occurred only because Wavell on his own responsibility, and facing the easily calculable risks of failure, allowed it to be launched.

There is a matter of far greater moment. A general consensus would now recognize that the D-Day landings in Normandy might have resulted in temporary or permanent disaster had it not been for the Allies' carefully co-ordinated deception plans which preceded them. Yet it was the far-sighted and unconventional Wavell who, as early as 1940, first drew attention to the need for a centrally controlled and dextrously orchestrated system of deception. It was under Wavell in the Middle East that the techniques and principles, the hazards and profits of this elegant chicanery were first explored and exploited. Such conceptions are not the characteristic output of the chairman of a golf club.

Nevertheless, as Wavell's military career passes under review – for different considerations apply to his years as Viceroy – something seems to be missing: something so rarefied that it is difficult to define. Perhaps its composition is multiple. But it is worth asking from time to time, as his campaigns unfold, whether Wavell really possessed the instincts of a killer. Montgomery's clinical approach to war, and his own ambition, made him a ruthless master of the battlefield. Even when he was controlling the Allied armies in Italy from a royal palace, Alexander's real passion was for the trench and the gunsmoke. But in Wavell one detects – or does one, for the scent is so uncertain? – a hampering sense of diffidence and withdrawal, as though in some final but hardly manageable analysis it might have to be said that this 'son of the regiment' was misplaced as a soldier: as though one might have to

---

* Churchill was first made aware of Wingate in 1938 by Liddell Hart, who described him in a letter as 'playing a Lawrence-like role (in the opposite way) in combating the Arab Terrorist gangs in Palestine.' But when Wavell in India heard of the acceptance at the Quebec Conference of Wingate's ideas about Long Range Penetration he wrote in his diary for 23 August 1943: 'I expect PM will now claim him for his own discovery and ignore the fact that I have twice used Wingate in this war for unorthodox campaigns and that but for me he would probably never have been heard of.'

conclude that his notable qualities of character and intellect, his imagination, his clarity of thought, his broad and penetrating vision, his feel for perspectives and dimensions, his moral courage and his perfect integrity could have been as well, and for him more happily, applied in some other field of endeavour. Surely there is something revealing in a remark he made to Liddell Hart in February 1936, as the clouds darkened over Nazi Germany: 'No nation ought to pass its entrance examination into civilization so long as it has an itch for war or possesses slums'?

This is guess-work: but why is one prompted to guess? Wavell was well aware of himself, and more than once he spoke suggestively. General Pownall was his chief staff officer during the hard times of his ABDA command in 1942. Afterwards Sir Henry wrote in his diary a long appreciation of Wavell which noted that

> he is reserved to a degree – though occasionally there are flashes of self-revelation. "My trouble is I am not really interested in war," he has said to me. Fond of poetry and books, with a fine command of the written word, he has an immense capacity for taking hard knocks. Day after day he would receive bad news due to enemy action or our own failures with just his usual comment, "I see." He carries responsibility unflinchingly, yet he certainly feels its weight.

Five years later Wavell made an entry in his own diary which has a similar drift. On Sunday, 12 January 1947, he was visited in Delhi by another civilized commander. 'Tuker came in to see me before his departure from Calcutta. I like him, he has many more interests than soldiering, in fact his defect as a soldier is probably the same as mine, that soldiering rather bores him and books and history and art interest him more.' Wavell was writing, it should be remembered, of a man who at the head of the 4th Indian Division performed with an extreme distinction in North Africa and Italy. Yet he detected the *faiblesse,* and recognized himself. Does this explain why, during his years of high command, there is something which recalls Wordsworth's lines about the old soldier he met one night, under the moon, resting on a mountain road?

He all the while was in demeanour calm.
Concise in answer; solemn and sublime
He might have seemed, but that in all he said
There was a strange half-absence, as of one
Knowing too well the importance of his theme,
But feeling it no longer.

Why, indeed, when thinking about Wavell does one recall
those famous words uttered by General Wolfe on the eve of his
death and a victory at Quebec?

# 2

# A Thing of Shreds and Patches

I have formed a picture of a general commanding which is not
chimerical – I have seen such men . . . . He should possess a talent
for sudden and appropriate improvisation.
MARSHAL DE SAXE, *Reveries* (1757)

Vast experience of colonial or imperial warfare taught the
British Regular Army that it is not necessarily fatal to be
outnumbered by an enemy. From Plassey to Rorke's Drift,
from Assaye to Mons the lesson was reiterated. But though in
the summer of 1940 Mussolini's armies were less prepossessing
than a Zulu impi or the Kaiser's field-grey swarms, the scale of
their military presence in Africa was sufficiently daunting.
When Italy declared war on 10 June 1940 the approximate
strength of Marshal Graziani's forces, from the Egyptian
frontier westward into Tripolitania, was 250,000. The East
African garrison under the Duke of Aosta was rather larger:
some 300,000. In the whole of Wavell's Middle Eastern theatre
the British contingent, by contrast, fell short of 90,000 – a total
including 27,500 troops in Palestine which were either horsed,
or ill-equipped, or under-trained, and sundry units in the
Sudan, Kenya and British Somaliland which are best described
as miscellaneous. And yet, according to the Official History,
'numbers were almost the least of General Wavell's anxieties.'

The fact is that until the spring of 1941 Wavell's situation
was the one that best suited his temperament. For all his
experiences on the Western Front he was not instinctively at
home in a world of lengthy set-piece battles and wars of
attrition. The *materialenschlacht* was not his preferred mode.
Indeed, as Allenby's staff officer in Palestine (and later as his
biographer, and as historian of his campaigns) Wavell had
watched, studied and applauded the techniques of mobile
warfare. Put simply, it is not easy to imagine him master-

minding Alamein, or the final breakthrough at Cassino, or the Normandy landings. His military scope and aptitudes seem to have been shaped in an earlier mould, that of previous centuries when space, manoeuvre and dexterity were exploited. One more readily envisages Wavell at the side of Marlborough or the early Napoleon, or scintillating in the Indian Mutiny, than replacing Montgomery outside Caen in 1944. In the American Civil War his affinity would probably have been with the Confederates. And so it was that from his Commander-in-Chief's desk in Cairo he surveyed with equanimity the enormous regions for which he was responsible, the enemy's masses and his own few troops. Whatever the external problems, he felt tranquil and confident because the war that faced him was one he knew how to fight.

He struck the key-note from the start. At the end of July 1939, shortly after his appointment to Cairo, he wrote to the CIGS a brief appreciation in which he summarized the strategic aspects of his new command. 'Whether Italy is openly hostile or nominally neutral,' he wrote, 'our only possible counter to the German intention to bring SE Europe under her power is by a domination of the Mediterranean at least as complete as in the Great War *as early as possible*. If not within the first month or two of war, it may be too late . . . . The last war was won in the West . . . . the next war will be won or lost in the Mediterranean; and the longer it takes us to secure effective control of the Mediterranean, the harder will the winning of the war be.' His task therefore was to plan '. . . not merely the defence of Egypt and our other interests in the Middle East, but such measures of offence as will enable us and our Allies to dominate the Mediterranean at the earliest possible moment . . . .'

The point about this memorandum is not that it profoundly misjudges Hitler's purposes or that the epicentre of victory in the Second World War was not, in the end, the Mediterranean. The point is that having, at an early stage, identified the critical importance of the Middle East, Wavell consistently maintained his view (against opposition in London) even while Italy stayed nominally neutral, and then implemented it instantly and vigorously as soon as the neutral became an open enemy. But at first he was working against the grain. The policy of his Government, endorsed by the Chiefs of Staff, was affirmed in the autumn of 1939: so far as a non-belligerent Italy was concerned, 'no attempt should be made to compel her to declare her position if this would be likely to bring her in against us'. Wavell would have been prepared to risk much by way of overt preparation and even provocation. In retrospect he recalled his discontent.

> I thought the policy of doing nothing whatever that could annoy the Italians – appeasement, in fact – quite misguided. I was allowed to send no agents into Italian territory, though all our territories were full of Italian agents, to do nothing to get in touch with the Abyssinian rebels, and so on. Meanwhile stores continued to pass through the Suez Canal to Italian East Africa, and we even continued under a pre-war agreement to inform the Italians of our reinforcements to Middle East.[1]

But on 10 June 1940 the Italian jackal, by taking sides with the great German beast of prey, brought release from this *drôle de paix,* and during the night of the 11th 7 Armoured Division carried out Wavell's instructions 'for offensive action on the Italian frontier with Egypt to be taken immediately on the declaration of war.' Probing relentlessly with their armoured cars, by the 16th 11 Hussars had actually ambushed and captured an Italian general, Lastucci, the Engineer-in-Chief of the 10th Army. (There was a further uncovenanted blessing when, on 28 June, the able Marshal Balbo, Commander-in-Chief in Libya, was shot down at Tobruk by his own anti-aircraft guns.) This instant assertion of moral superiority was paralleled in East Africa.

Since greater audacity was to follow, it is worth pausing before Wavell destroys a whole colonial empire to take a broad view of the situation along the shores of the Mediterranean and the Red Sea, as he saw it during that summer of 1940, and to ask what his decisions and actions tell us about his timbre. The Italians' superficial strength on land was there from the beginning, but until the sudden fall of France it had always been assumed – not least by Wavell – that the Mediterranean could be dominated by Franco-British warships while French divisions and aircraft would provide a strong buttress at either end of the inland sea. Now the French Fleet had been scuttled, sunk, dispersed or immobilized. Morocco, Algeria and Tunisia were in Vichy's control, as were Syria, and French Somaliland. Not only had Wavell lost an ally strong in numbers and in its strategic locations: all countries where France had freely reigned were now open to German infiltration, while the Mediterranean itself was no longer a safe route of reinforcement to the British Middle East. Sadly he noted that 'I had not realised the extent of the moral disintegration of the French since the end of the First War'; but in that respect many others were equally culpable.

In the face of a threat to which there was no logical answer Wavell, like Churchill after Dunkirk, never flinched. It is true that he kept in his desk some sheets of notepaper headed 'The Worst Possible Case' and 'Worse Case Still' – the texts are in Connell's biography – which ruthlessly examined the implications, were German bombing to make Britain untenable and the Empire to be forced to fall back on a line running from Canada through South Africa to Australasia. These should not be taken too seriously. In Africa as, later, in India his 'Worst Possible Case' exercises merely represented the dispassionate conclusions of a highly trained staff officer prudently analysing a theoretical possibility. They were never, ever, defeatist – either in spirit or intent. Indeed, during that summer of 1940 defeatism in Cairo would have been difficult. Of the three Commanders-in-Chief in the Middle East Wavell was only *primus inter pares*. He was their chairman and their representative, with an inherent authority due to the fact that the military arm predominated. But Admiral Cunningham and Air Marshal Longmore were independent in minds and status. Cunningham was a Nelson at heart, yearning to lay his ships alongside the enemy's. Longmore's first thought was for action. And then, of course, there was the growling ardent Prime Minister in London.

In fact Wavell's response to a formidable challenge was aggressive, both in the short term and in its long term implications. He was never a general of unapplied theories. What he preached he practised. In the Lees-Knowles series and other lectures, in his books on Allenby and on the Palestine campaigns, the message had always been the same. Socrates was right: the good general is he who, above all, is meticulous about his administrative arrangements. So now Wavell gave exemplary proof that he had meant what he said and, at the same time, displayed absolute confidence in the long term assertion of British power in his theatre: he set about converting Egypt into a military base with expanding facilities far in excess of current requirements. Authority for accumulation of stocks and preparation of the technical establishments to support nine divisions in Egypt and Palestine had, indeed, emerged after discussion with the Chiefs of Staff during the winter of 1939–40, but the Middle East was a Cinderella for whom mere authority or even money was not enough to effect a transformation. Immense effort, clear vision and sustained ingenuity were required from Wavell and his staff before those great store-houses and workshops could be created in caves hacked out from hills where Pyramids once were quarried; before the enlargement of ports and harbours and the improvement of lines of communication had been set in action: and before (in default of supplies from beleaguered Britain) the myriad essential stores and equipment had been raked in from Australia, India and southern Africa.* This energy and foresight earned its reward. London's initial requirement for a base for nine divisions was swiftly altered to one for fourteen divisions arriving by June 1941 and twenty-three divisions by March 1942, and much is due to Wavell for the fact that the Middle East base was not overwhelmed by this expansion. Certainly the humming activity of the rearward areas at the time of Alamein was an inheritance that Montgomery owed to the acumen and resourcefulness of his predecessor.

These long term schemes were advanced remorselessly after the Italian declaration of war: as though Wavell, having taken the measure of his enemy, felt that it was safe to indulge in capital investment while maintaining the security of the Middle East out of current income – the latter being represented by the meagre forces he was able to deploy along the

---

* 'There was a pleasant windfall of German-made pipes in Palestine, which enabled a water pipeline in the Western Desert to be started.' *The Mediterranean and the Middle East,* vol. 1, p. 65.

western and southern frontiers. And with those forces his short term achievement in the summer of 1940 would seem incredible had it not happened. In spite of every statistical probability, he won a moral victory by keeping the Duce's gross armies in East Africa and Cyrenaica in a state of military paralysis. The paralysis was, of course, partly self-induced, since neither Mussolini nor his generals were in a mood for major offensives. Along the hinterland of the Red Sea the Duke of Aosta took a few frontier posts, attacking always in superior strength, and in August twenty-six Italian battalions with twenty-one batteries expelled five battalions from the exposed British Somaliland – a strategically useless territory, which London had at first been prepared to lose. (Wavell was perhaps too optimistic in trying to hold on, but his contempt for the Italians was boundless.) And that was all. In the Western Desert, meanwhile, the situation was even more remarkable. By their marauding activities the highly trained troops of 7 Armoured Division dominated the no-man's-land, while as yet Marshal Graziani showed no relish for a forward move. 'Thus,' wrote Churchill, 'the first phase in the war which Italy had declared upon the British Empire opened favourably for us.'

But Churchill wanted more. The Battle of Britain was still raging, and he yearned – with every good reason – for news of positive success in Africa. But though Wavell was equally, though less emotionally, eager to attack, he had always known that *major* operations were beyond his capacity, and by the end of July this truth was self-evident. Wear and tear and shortage of spares were eroding his desert spearhead. 7 Armoured Division, whose proper complement was 220 cruiser tanks, was down to 65.* Moreover, though infantry reinforcements had reached Egypt from India, Australia and New Zealand their formations were incomplete, their artillery not always adequate, and their training often sketchy. The long lists sent from Cairo of deficiencies and requirements now produced a summons for Wavell to report to London where, on 23 July, Churchill had passed a menacing minute to General Ismay:

---

* In default of new tanks from England, the only course was to withdraw worn-out armour from the front line for the slow process of renovation.

'What is happening to the concert of the campaign in the Middle East?' In a material sense the discussions that followed were productive and, indeed, of critical significance for Wavell's operations in North Africa. Yet the deeper truth is this: as they sat round the conference table a chasm opened between the Prime Minister and his Commander-in-Chief that the future might bridge but would never close.

Aircraft and Wavell were incompatible. During his wartime service in the Middle and Far East he flew many thousands of miles – and survived: but the log-books of those journeys are diversified with the records of engine failures, emergency landings in the wilderness and other misadventures far beyond the ration appropriate to a Commander-in-Chief. At times it seemed as though Wavell had only to step into an aeroplane for something to fail. In the Middle East, it is true, a wrong sense of values caused the authorities to deny him the personal aircraft essential for a man whose command spanned so vast an area. He had to fly in whatever was at hand. But this is not a full explanation: the truth is that Wavell was something of a Jonah.

Inevitably, therefore, when he set off from Alexandria on 4 August to make for England in a slow Sunderland flying-boat, the passage was far from smooth. He took with him his trusted Director of Military Intelligence, Brigadier John Shearer, who wrote in his private memoir that 'coming over we were attacked, and had to descend to sea-level, in the vicinity of Pantellaria and again approaching Gibraltar. German aircraft also chased us far into the Atlantic the night before we landed at Plymouth.'[2] Wavell occupied himself during the intervals between these avoiding actions by rehearsing until he was word perfect the statement he must make to the War Cabinet and, as Shearer put it, by 'spouting poetry by the yard'.

If the flight was dangerous, its consequences were calami-tous. The *idée reçue* about Wavell's London visit is that he damaged himself by his taciturnity – which was certainly a factor. But from Shearer's account it seems that not enough consideration was shown to the travel-weary party from Cairo by the Prime Minister and the comfortable War Cabinet. Rightly or wrongly Wavell sensed an indifference,

even a growing animosity. Tired and anxious, he may have
expected too animated an attention, about matters of supreme
importance to himself, from men who in that embattled summer took vital issues almost as their daily bread. Yet one mind
was not indifferent. Shearer added,

> Knowing my Chief as well as I did, I could feel the temperature
> rising between him and the PM, whose interrogation seemed to
> me to become increasingly curt.
> Finally, after Mr Amery asked General Wavell to repeat his
> appreciation of Marshal Graziani's probable intentions in the
> Desert, I was aware that the electricity had really built up.
> My C in C rather impatiently repeated his previous statement.
> Now the PM interjected, 'But, Commander-in-Chief, you
> said . . . .' In a flash, General Wavell replied, 'I did not.'
> And the relations between these two magnificent men were, at
> that moment, irretrievably damaged.
> It may sound a petty reason . . . .

Petty, perhaps: but such a reminiscence by the only living
member of that meeting is perhaps symptomatic. At the
House of Commons a couple of months earlier, in June, Lord
Boothby was talking with Lloyd George about Churchill as
the only possible saviour for the country. Lloyd George said:
'You are probably right. But it will be a one-man show. He
has at least one great general – Wavell. I was not so fortunate.
But, mark my words, he will get rid of Wavell.'[3]

Well, Lloyd George, in 1940, was unique in his knowledge
of Churchill's capacities in wartime, and within twelve
months his prediction would be justified. It was in fact a great
misfortune that Wavell's first confrontation with his Prime
Minister should have occurred when Churchill was at his most
imperious, when all was breathless and urgent, and when he
had not yet been trained by the strong team of Chiefs of Staff
under Alan Brooke (compared with whom the 1940 team of
Dill, Pound and Newall was under-powered) that reasoned
arguments from his advisers must be expected and respected.
In August the Battle of Britain was still unresolved, and a
cross-Channel invasion seemed probable. Churchill was at full
stretch, without time for the niceties. For his part Wavell, who
had meticulously mastered his brief, had every reason to feel

wounded by what appears to have been a peremptory and unsympathetic reception. Still, a War Cabinet discussion of strategic issues must not necessarily be conducted with the good manners inculcated at Winchester, and generals who are trained to endure defeat in the field might be expected to show a degree of stoicism in the council chamber. As the perspectives lengthen, it becomes more evident that there were faults on both sides – faults venial in themselves, even trivial, the reactions of tired men, but faults, nevertheless, of great consequence.

For both Wavell and Churchill were wounded. Shearer recalled how, after the first meeting, he and the CIGS, General Dill, walked with Wavell through the streets of Westminster. 'My Chief said that the PM had asked him down to Chequers for the weekend but he would be damned if he would risk further treatment of the kind to which he had just been subjected.' 'I remember so clearly,' Shearer continued, 'General Dill saying, "Archie, no one would deny that you have had unbearable provocation. But he is our Prime Minister. He carries an almost incredible burden. It is true you can be replaced. He cannot be. You must go to Chequers." ' Dill averted disaster, but the temperature continued to rise. On 13 August Eden was noting in his diary: 'Found Wavell waiting for me at 9 a.m. He was clearly upset at last night's proceedings and said that he thought he should have made it plain that if the Prime Minister could not approve his dispositions and had no confidence in him he should appoint someone else.'

As the consultations drew to a close Churchill's own disillusion about a man whom he had sincerely wanted to admire reached the moment of truth.* On 15 August Eden again wrote in his diary:

> More Wavell talks, when Winston told me he must stay another day. I was against this, for Wavell is doing no good here and

---

* 'A year later, when I was honoured to be entrusted with many confidences by the PM, he confirmed to me my earlier belief that his lack of understanding with Wavell was a sadness to him. He had genuinely hoped to establish an affinity with a man who, he knew, combined soldierly qualities of the highest order with exceptional erudition.' Shearer, *Memoir*.

should either return or be replaced. Winston asked me who was a possible alternative. I said Auchinleck, he agreed. But we both felt that he had not sufficient evidence to compel a change which at the moment might have a very bad effect on morale throughout Middle East. At a further meeting of the four of us in the afternoon, Winston suddenly agreed that Wavell should leave tonight.

And so the events of August 1940 foretold what was to happen in the summer of 1941. 'Mark my words', Lloyd George had prophesied, 'he will get rid of Wavell.' Dismissal was already on the *tapis*: Wavell's future successor was already nominated. In *The Second World War* Churchill certainly exercised a remarkable economy of expression when he wrote, 'While I was not in full agreement with General Wavell's use of the resources at his disposal, I thought it best to leave him in command.'

The tragedy was that they lost sight of one another's minds at the outset, for the days of conference disclosed that on the truly important issues Churchill was bold and ardent in his support of the forces in the Middle East. If their minds could have met together on these issues Churchill's confidence in Wavell would have bloomed. Instead, that confidence shrivelled almost instantly, and the Prime Minister's temperament was such that if a general ceased to command his imagination that general was lost: for now small and secondary disagreements would be magnified while suspicions and resentments festered. Once Churchill had decided on his verdict it was difficult to reverse, and in the course of the whole war there are very few examples of commanders recovering his trust once the fatal withdrawal had occurred.

The series of August discussions about the Middle East were mainly conducted at the level of the Chiefs of Staff and the Defence Committee of the War Cabinet, over which Churchill presided in his capacity as Minister of Defence. There were two dominant themes, whose handling by the Prime Minister illuminated in a striking fashion his strength and his weakness as a war leader. Out-of-date ideas, lack of technical knowledge and the passion for action could lead him to nag and rage over matters about which it was obvious, even at the time, that he was wrong. And so it was during those August days as he

probed and questioned Wavell's plans for making use of the
Rhodesians, the South Africans and the troops from East and
West Africa now gathering in the Kenya region. Why could
they not be hurled against Aosta's army? Why could not the
troops in Palestine, Australians, New Zealanders, British
Yeomanry, be brought into line in Egypt? Why not arm the
Jews to replace them? In his memoirs Churchill printed the
texts of the memoranda he addressed to Wavell on 10 and 12
August, vehemently arguing his case, and implied (by
omission) that the opposition to his views had thus been
worthless.

Yet this was unjust. Churchill was perpetuating his pique.
As to the troops in Kenya, General Sir William Jackson has
remarked in his admirable *The North African Campaign* that
'none of them was adequately acclimatised, trained or
equipped; the logistic preparations for a 200 miles advance
across the waterless bush country of Northern Kenya could
not be completed overnight; and the season was wrong for
major military operations.' As to the troops from the Anti-
podes, we observe here an early manifestation of the way that
Churchill thought of them as if they were no more than units
from the Home Counties, utterly subject to direction by the
War Office in Whitehall. Bearing in mind the difficulties that
arose later in the war between the British, the Australian and
the New Zealand Governments, it is interesting to speculate
what the reaction would have been if the troops in Palestine,
still unready and under-equipped, had been deployed by
Wavell piece-meal and without preparation.* He was right to
resist such propositions: but he was not forgiven.

And yet – such was the variety of the man – during the same
conference Churchill is also to be seen displaying those qualities for which he is most honoured: courage, imagination,
magnanimity.

Wavell arrived, inevitably, with a large shopping-list –

* A little later on, Wavell put this problem in a nutshell. Writing on 7 November to
the CIGS about the difficulty of reinforcing Crete, he observed that 'Dominion
Governments are most reluctant to allow their formations to be broken up in any way
or to permit their use in the field until fully trained and equipped or for guards on
internal security duties except in a grave emergency.'

particularly for armour, anti-tank and anti-aircraft guns. An officer of Longmore's staff had come with him to support the case for substantial reinforcements for the RAF: but this was a doomed endeavour, since neither the British nor American production had yet created the kind of surplus that could be spared from Fighter and Bomber Commands in England. Aircraft still had to be despatched to the Middle East in dribs and drabs. But the request for tanks for the desert army produced a more constructive and indeed spectacular response.

On 10 August General Dill, the CIGS, with Eden's assent, placed before Churchill a plan for sending to the Middle East three armoured units, one of light and one of cruiser tanks and a third – the crucial item – of the heavy infantry type, the 'Matildas'. There were substantial extras in the shape of guns and ammunition, technical stores and so on, but the Matildas were the *pièces de résistance* because no Italian weapon could penetrate their armour. Churchill endorsed the proposal with an enthusiasm that persisted in a proud retrospect. 'The decision to give this blood-transfusion while we braced ourselves to meet a mortal danger,' he wrote in his memoirs, 'was at once awful and right.' Awful seems a curious adjective in the context: nevertheless, though the decision did indeed turn out to be right, it demanded great courage and breadth of vision from the Chiefs of Staff, in supporting it, and from the Prime Minister who alone bore the final responsibility. For after the losses at Dunkirk the British Isles were virtually empty of any effective armour, and during the few weeks that had since passed this void had certainly not been filled. Defeat in the skies, and an invasion presaged by many sources of intelligence, could not yet be discounted.* The Chiefs of Staff at this time were undoubtedly of a lesser calibre than their successors later in the war, but in this matter their nice calculation of the strategic possibilities must be applauded, while Churchill was justified in his pride.

But how to get the tanks to Africa? An operation had

* The despatch of armour to the Middle East was approved by the Cabinet on 15 August, *Adler Tag* or Eagle Day, when the *Luftwaffe* was foiled in its first major attempt to destroy Fighter Command.

already been in hand for some time, under the code-name *Hats,* to run the battleship *Valiant,* the aircraft-carrier *Illustrious* and other warships through the Mediterranean from west to east as reinforcements for Cunningham's fleet at Alexandria, but the idea of passing transport shipping under their protection had been rejected as too dangerous. The *Valiant* group was due to leave England on 20 August. Churchill now argued with passionate vehemence that Wavell's tanks should be sent straight through the Mediterranean under the warships' cover instead of directing their transports, as was proposed, more cautiously around the Cape. His chief staff officer, General Ismay, who knew his master's moods so well, recorded that 'he could not bear the idea of this priceless equipment being out of action for three months on a long voyage'. Considering that he was putting the homeland itself at risk, and remembering the urgency of Wavell's requirements, Churchill's attitude is understandable. But he was baulked.

From Alexandria Admiral Cunningham signalled that he could only agree 'if the urgency was so great as to justify the risks of loss of the army reinforcements and of serious damage to the Fleet'. Admiral Pound as First Sea Lord blew cold, and was supported by his fellow Chiefs of Staff. Moreover Wavell, whose interest was the most acute, declared that he would prefer to receive the armour intact but late, rather than risk losing for the sake of speed a precious reinforcement which could hardly be replaced within many months. He was oppressed, of course, by the strong possibility that German armoured divisions might appear in Africa, for it was agreed that their passage from Europe could not be prevented. Three new tank units intact at Suez would then be more use than if they had been sunk off Sicily. And if the Italians were to attack in September, he felt that he could deal with them more cheerfully if he knew that *secure* reinforcements were on the way. In the face of a united opposition Churchill succumbed, and the convoy of armour, under the code-name *Apology,* sailed in due course for the Cape and safety.

Now, it is instructive to compare Churchill's reaction to this rebuff with his treatment of Wavell. His minutes about the use of troops in East Africa and Palestine are petulant and 'nit-picking'. Wavell's carefully weighed rejection of the proposal to send his Matildas through the Mediterranean was coldly received by the Prime Minister. Like a Roman emperor, once he had lost confidence in a frontier general he found reason for suspicion in anything and everything. But how different was his response to the Admiralty's attitude over the tank-transports! He wrote of the First Sea Lord in his memoirs: 'We had gone through a lot together. If he would not do it, no one else would. If I could not make him, no one else could. I knew the Admiralty too well to press them or my great friend and comrade, Pound, or the First Lord, for whom I had great esteem, beyond a certain point.' From that single phrase, 'my great friend and comrade, Pound', one may gauge the irrecoverable damage caused by Wavell's London visit. Friendship, comradeship: he was never to get on these terms with his Prime Minister – and even after his death Churchill was absent from the funeral. The tragedy of imperfect sympathies was complete.

Churchill's growing doubts were later summarized in that single sentence: 'While not in full agreement with General Wavell's use of the resources at his disposal, I thought it best to leave him in command.' Tepid enough: but at the time the Prime Minister used a great many more sentences in an attempt to ensure that those resources were applied as he himself thought fit. Wavell left London on 15 August. It was not until the 23rd that he received in Cairo, in the form of a signal, the unprecedented document which Churchill had issued on the 16th under the heading *General Directive for Commander-in-Chief, Middle East*. Churchill states that his own draft was approved by the Cabinet and the Chiefs of Staff. However that may be, its character was such that had it appeared over the signatures of the Chiefs of Staff alone its tone and contents would have been unsuitable. Wavell observed, coolly: 'It showed clearly that Winston did not trust me to run my own show and was set on his own ideas.'

Military history tends to be written by men of military experience whose training and ethos dispose them instinctively to the view that commanders in the field should be 'left alone' by what they usually call 'the politicians'. The assumption is out-of-date, a hangover from an Imperial past when it might take weeks or months before a message from Whitehall could make its slow way to the battlefront. The perfection of radio has given universal force to a fact which the telegraph and the telephone had already emphasized – that in the twentieth century a theatre commander must automatically expect (and should not think improper) a stream of signals from the centre of government. In any case, such communications are not really a recent development. The sensible CIGS, General Dill, put the matter in a nutshell in the helpful letter he wrote to Auchinleck on 26 June 1941 when the latter succeeded Wavell in the Middle East:

> The fact is that the Commander in the field will always be subject to great and often undue pressure from his Government. Wellington suffered from it: Haig suffered from it: Wavell suffered from it. Nothing will stop it. In fact, pressure from those who alone see the picture as a whole and carry the main responsibility may be necessary.

Everything depends on the nature of the pressure. Churchill's August directive (which fills three and a half closely-printed pages of his memoirs) was certainly ill-judged, though perhaps not wholly indefensible. Even during the anxieties of the Battle of France he had never promulgated so detailed and extensive a set of instructions to his generals. Nor did Lloyd George, in the First World War: but then, neither he nor most of his predecessors as Premier was capable, like Churchill and Hitler and Stalin, of thinking like a soldier. In this sense the character of the directive to Wavell was truly without precedent. It implied a new relationship of authority between the Prime Minister and field commanders which his Chiefs of Staff spent the rest of the war trying – not always successfully – to keep in the right proportions.

Certainly it was unusual for a document *from* a Prime Minister *to* his Secretary of State for War and his CIGS, about the responsibilities of a Commander-in-Chief, not only to survey with an imperious clarity the dispositions and proper objectives of all the Imperial forces in the Middle East, but also to prescribe, for example, the movement of specific units from Palestine, Kenya and India to Egypt; the rendering undrinkable of wells along the desert approaches to the Delta ('a special note on this is attached', said the directive); and the utilization of the Nile's flood waters to create 'no-go' strips whose width is exactly defined as 'four or five miles wide'. Premiers should not usurp a staff officer's functions. Before the long *Diktat* reached its end the Napoleon of 10 Downing Street uttered a firm and summary instruction: 'In this posture, then, the Army of the Delta will await the Italian invasion.'

Mercifully Wavell's response was not contentious, though confidence in his own experience and judgement, a proper pride and the sense that there was now no love lost between himself and Churchill might have impelled him to meet head-on this challenge to his authority. Instead, as he wrote afterwards, 'I carried out such parts of the directive as were practicable and useful, and disregarded a good deal of it.' His Laodicean reaction was tactfully concealed by the device of not making a complex single reply, but of spreading out his carefully calculated answers in four different signals dispatched between 23 and 27 August. Some of Churchill's bright ideas, we can now see, were obviously impossible to implement. Take the case of putting the desert wells out of action and, as was suggested, of rendering the tarmac coastal road from Mersa Matruh to Alexandria impassable 'by delayed-action mines or by chemical treatment of the asphalt surface'. After his return to Cairo ideas were already germinating in Wavell's mind, very private ideas about a forward offensive move, which would have been negated by such a policy: as he wrote later about the coast road, he had 'an inkling all the time that I might want it before the Italians'.* Within months, those ideas would launch the Army of the Nile towards an historic victory.

And yet, though Churchill's directive now seems to consist, in some parts, of presumption, in others of miscalculation and in others of sheer bathos, the historian must remember the circumstances of the time. Day after day, in mid August, the *Luftwaffe* was savaging southern England and bleeding the RAF. Apart from the current uncertainties of the air battle, it was not until mid September that Churchill and his advisers

---

* In the event, a certain amount of sabotage was carried out, but less grandiose than Churchill envisaged.

could reckon that invasion had been postponed, if not cancelled. And there were all the other pressures on Churchill – shortages of equipment, shortages of trained men, the American connection to be nursed, civilian morale: the list was endless. Churchill in those days had an overwhelming need and passion to get things on the move. All felt his lash, to the nation's benefit. If he sought – excessively, indeed – to whip on the Commander-in-Chief in Cairo, some plea in mitigation must be allowed. The unfortunate fact is that even his visit to London, during the critical period of the Battle of Britain, does not seem to have stirred in Wavell any sympathetic understanding of Churchill's mentality. The man who said he was prepared to sup with the devil to save his country was not likely to be chary about badgering his generals. It required much empathy to understand this, and to understand the reasons. Intuitive, intelligent, alert, Wavell nevertheless failed to enter his Prime Minister's mind. If the same is true *vice versa,* it may be felt that Churchill had a good many other things to think about.

And yet, curiously enough, the episode of the August directive was hardly over before a process began which, for a brief but halcyon time, would set Churchill aglow with praise for Wavell and his desert army. The precise point at which the process started is readily identifiable. On 11 September Wavell instructed his Chief of Staff (the subsequent Lieutenant-General Sir Arthur Smith) 'that a study be made of the question of an offensive into Cyrenaica, which he should be in a position to launch by the end of the year or early in 1941, if all went well.' This was the birth-certificate of the dramatic operation, later to be known as *Compass,* which shattered Mussolini's North African empire.

The timing is significant. Wavell's aggressive note to Smith was issued only four days after Mussolini, on the 7th, had ordered his timid Marshal Graziani to begin the long-awaited advance into Egypt. The text of the published diaries of the Duce's son-in-law Count Ciano cannot always be assumed to be authentic, but his entry about Graziani's reaction has the ring of truth: 'never has a military operation been undertaken so much against the will of the Commander.' However, by the

13th the massive Italian *roulement* to the East was in train. Like mosquitoes the light mobile troops of Wavell's outpost line darted and stung, but could scarcely impede. Sometimes this was not even necessary: at Sollum the 1st Libyan Division mounted a formal assault, complete with artillery concentrations and troops drawn up 'in serried array', on the abandoned airfield and empty British barracks. Still, by the evening of the 16th the 1st Blackshirt Division had pushed on to capture the modest mud-brick village of Sidi Barrani, and Mussolini had something to show for a five-divisional advance (the other two divisions of the 10th Army had been left back at Tobruk), for the Italian radio was able to announce that when Sidi Barrani fell the trams were still running! Here, against all expectation, Graziani halted.

Wavell's pugnacious note of 11 September to his Chief of Staff has a richer flavour when one grasps that it was written at a moment when the enemy was about to bear down on him with what at first seemed like an uncontainable superiority. It has almost the quality of a reflex action and is to be compared, as an example of what Connell called 'his indomitably resilient spirit', with another instruction he also gave to a Chief of Staff – the note he composed in Delhi on 16 April 1942, when Slim was leading out of Burma the remnants of a retreating army and the Japanese were approaching the gates of India. 'I want the Joint Planning Staff,' Wavell ordered, 'to begin as soon as possible consideration of an offensive to reoccupy Burma.' There are times when the essence of a commander's quality seems to be distilled into a single remark. Wellington had this flair for pregnant brevity. It was revealed in monosyllable when General McAuliffe made his famous response to the Germans at Bastogne: 'Nuts.' And at such moments Wavell himself, who was not known as the Chief for nothing, showed that oaken strength, that capacity to absorb every kind of punishment and come back fighting, which among his many attributes has perhaps won for him the greatest respect from the professionals and an instinctive admiration from the public.

When Wavell sent his first note to Smith, and for some weeks afterwards, he assumed with good reason that the

Italian mass would continue to move onwards: his purpose, in fact, was to attack if the advance proceeded seventy-five miles eastwards towards Mersa Matruh. But Graziani never stirred. He and his staff were now facing the intractable problems with which both the British and the Germans would struggle in due course: how could men be fed and watered, ammunition be stacked, trucks and tanks be replenished with fuel at the end of a supply line stretching across interminable miles of rock and desert? This was a game at which the Italians were children. So Graziani dug in till his strength could be renewed, improving the defences at Sidi Barrani itself and running a line of fortified camps some fifty miles inland from the coast – first the Tummars, then Nibeiwa, and then a fifteen-mile gap to the great escarpment down which the hinterland of northern Africa falls to the coastal strip: on this higher ground perched the southernmost camps or defensive positions, at Rabia and Sofafi. This loosely strung chain, and Graziani's evident apathy, began to suggest to Wavell the possibility of some more dramatic stroke in which the prime features of his military philosophy would be dominant – secrecy and surprise.

All good generals cherish secrecy as a bodyguard for their plans. So Wavell's studies had taught him and this, above all, was the practical lesson he had learned from his experience of Allenby's campaigns in Palestine. But his concern went deeper and was, it may be thought, obsessional. He brooded long and cleared his mind – for his conclusions were always lucid: yet however freely he might talk off parade about literature or other diversions with friends he trusted, about operational matters his instinct was to veil his thoughts. Certainly operation *Compass,* which he was shortly to launch, was characterized by secrecy to an exceptional degree – but particularly on the part of the Commander-in-Chief. The truth is that behind that formidable and sometimes chilly exterior there lurked a romantic spirit. As a horseman Wavell was mainly notable for the pleasure he took in riding, but it is not too much to hazard that in his imagination he was often a cavalryman . . . nay, a cavalier . . . galloping on some desperate foray: some *secret* affair. Among those who shared his confidence and his conversation he had a way of talking with enthusiastic admiration about that great captain of the American Civil War, Stonewall Jackson. And on such occasions he was liable to quote, perhaps with a tinge of envy, the passage in which Colonel Henderson's famous biography of Jackson describes the departure of his column before dawn for the classic raid on Manassas Junction: 'The men were hungry, and their rest had been short; but they were old acquaintances of the morning star.'

The lines Wavell loved were these:

> Something mysterious was in the air. What their movement portended not the shrewdest of his soldiers could divine; but they recalled their marches in the Valley and their inevitable results, and they knew instinctively that a surprise on a still larger scale was in contemplation. The thought was enough. Asking no questions, and full of enthusiasm, they followed with quick step the leader in whom their confidence had become so absolute.

Mystery: daring: the calculated risk: above all the secret locked in the leader's head. So Wavell liked to conduct war. During the coming months he is to be seen applying his preferred principles with a confident dexterity: with that fingertip-feel which the Germans always admired in a commander and which Wavell would never discover in himself again. But in the winter months that followed his military skills danced an intricate measure with poise and assurance.

The Italians had bulk and mass. Wavell's assets were of a more refined quality. His Western Desert Force, though small, was composed of highly trained regular units – as professional a group as Britain has ever possessed at the outset of war: units more advanced in one vital respect than those of the British Expeditionary Force in 1914, which the Germans christened 'a splendid thing apart'. The BEF came to France unprepared for a static struggle of trench and siege: 7 Armoured Division had been training in desert conditions since long before 1939. Some regiments, indeed, had been members of the Mobile Force exercising at Mersa Matruh as far back as 1936, a precautionary measure during the Abyssinian crisis. The Desert Rats knew the form. And steel was added to skill by the arrival at Suez on 24 September of the *Apology* convoy, containing the heavy Matilda tanks of 7

Royal Tank Regiment whose armour was virtually impenetrable by any Italian weapon.

At the head of the Western Desert Force, moreover, was a
man who matched the hour, Major-General Richard
O'Connor. Wavell had summoned him in June from his
command of the southern district in Palestine to take over in
the desert: a warrior with a brain, whose combat experience
began on the Western Front in 1914 when he was a young
officer in the Cameronians. By 1918 he was commanding a
battalion on the Italian front with extreme distinction. The
O'Connor of 1940 is recaptured in this brilliant vignette from
Correlli Barnett's *The Desert Generals*.

> He was small and neat as a bird. He had a fine head with an
> aggressive rake to it. The high, broad brow suggested great
> intellect; his eyes, large and deep with slightly hooded lids,
> powers of imagination. Command showed in the straight nose
> and mouth and thrusting jaw.

This is exact and just, only missing the quality of those eyes,
which were a pure and limpid blue: but in moments of decision
they turned into pools of ice.

A little man, so it might seem, with a little army, but the
combination was sufficient for Wavell, and he had useful
auxiliaries. His mind still stretched out towards the unorthodox – the devious, the irregular, the clandestine. For such a
soldier the prospect of an enemy like Graziani with a flank
wide open was irresistible, and in Palestine Wavell had long
ago formed an accurate estimate of the part played by
Lawrence's Arabs in distracting the Turks along the vulnerable
inland rim of their defence line. Now he had such a distracting
element ready to his hand – the Long Range Desert Group
(LRDG), whose procedures beautifully illustrated the principles laid down in a passage from the Chinese *Book of War,* of
the fifth century BC, which was well known to Wavell.
' "What is of first importance in operations of war?" Wen
answered and said: "Lightness . . . if the men be free to move,
the fight prospers".'

The long thin strip of territory within which the British
fought the Italians and later the Afrika Korps, with the distinc-

tive marker lines of the escarpment, the coastal road and the cultivated regions, represents but a minute northern appendage attached to the vast sand sea sweeping through hundreds of miles southwards via the Libyan Desert to the Sahara. For years before the war weekend experimenters like Major R. A. Bagnold, Peniakoff who became 'Popski' and their main equivalent on the Axis side, the Hungarian Count Almasy, had been probing this wasteland on private expeditions and learning the sophisticated techniques of desert travel.

After Italy's declaration of war Wavell accepted proposals from Bagnold for a special penetration team which he had hitherto kept dutifully in the pending tray, in accordance with the policy of appeasing Mussolini. Now, with remarkable speed, the first Long Range Patrol Unit was organized from British and New Zealand volunteers. Specialized equipment was begged, borrowed or filched when even the high priority granted to Bagnold was not enough. Soon the men were free to move – and the fight prospered. After inspection by Wavell himself the pioneers set off in September for the inland wilderness: their success was marked by a personal letter from the Commander-in-Chief on their return.[4]

General Headquarters,<br>
Middle East,<br>
Cairo<br>
1st October 1940

Dear Bagnold,

I should like to convey to the officers and other ranks under your command my congratulations and appreciation of the successful results of the recent patrols carried out by your unit in Central Libya.

I am aware of the extreme physical difficulties which had to be overcome, particularly in the intense heat.

That your operation, involving as it did 150,000 truck miles, has been brought to so successful a conclusion indicates a standard of efficiency in preparation and execution of which you, your officers and men may be justly proud.

A full report of your exploits has already been telegraphed to the War Office, and I wish you all the best of luck in your continued operations, in which you will be making an important contribu-

tion towards keeping Italian forces in back areas on the alert and
adding to the anxieties and difficulties of our enemy.

Yours sincerely, A. P. WAVELL

Indeed, it was immediately obvious that the initiative lay with
Bagnold and that the Italians had neither the intention nor the
capability of competing for the freedom of the sand-seas. (Their
air force, however, was always a menace.) And so, in an
October sortie, roads and tracks were mined far inland, enemy
posts were attacked and, on one landing-ground a bomber was
destroyed. By November Bagnold was reaching down into the
remote Free French territory of Chad to organize joint operations with the local garrison. In some ways the ethos of the
LRDG was more that of a scientifically planned Everest expedition than of a characteristic Army venture: a classic example of
how, in the military field, the highly skilled amateur at his best
can surpass most of the professionals. What cannot be doubted
is that for Graziani and his staff their enemy's ability to wander,
apparently at will, past the limits of their defended line and far to
the south and west offered a threat not only to their communications, but also to their morale. It was nerve-racking.* 'Every
commander,' Wavell observed in a note on *Ruses and Strategems
in War,* 'should constantly be considering methods of misleading his opponent, of playing upon his fears, and of disturbing his mental balance.'

The comprehensive term for 'methods of misleading' is of
course deception. It was during these months of 1940 that the
embryo took shape under Wavell in the Middle East of the
organization later known as 'A' Force, which, with the large
central groups based in London, would ramify and expand
until the whole system achieved its finest and most elaborate
coup by total deception of the Germans before D-Day in 1944.
In 1940 means were scarce and experts rare, but in Cairo there
was a Commander-in-Chief who was not just a simple soldier.
His view of war was sophisticated. Indeed, he had himself
observed and described many of the basic methods of deception which, when they were later used before Alamein, were

---

* Decoded Italian signals bore witness to this during *Compass* – and were sometimes
useful in identifying the location of far-flung LRDG units!

greeted with astonishment. In his biography of Allenby Wavell summarized the deceptive techniques employed before the breakthrough at Megiddo.

> Elaborate precautions were made as if to transfer GHQ from the camp in the plains to an hotel in Jerusalem, which was cleared and prepared for it, with telephone lines laid, offices marked, and so forth. This was backed by rumours of a great concentration in the Jerusalem area and the marking of billets. New camps were pitched in the Jordan valley and additional bridges thrown across the Jordan. Fifteen thousand dummy horses, made of canvas, filled the horse lines; and sleighs drawn by mules raised clouds of dust at the times when the canvas horses should have been going to water. Battalions marched ostentatiously down to the valley by day and returned by lorries at night. Wireless traffic was continued from Desert Mounted Corps headquarters near Jericho long after headquarters and nearly all the troops had been transferred to the other flank. . . . Such were some of the measures taken to give enemy observers and enemy agents the impression that another advance east of Jordan was being prepared.

Here, in 1918, are many of the basic stratagems which, whether it be before Alamein or D-Day, or the Germans' Ardennes offensive, or Slim's crossing of the Irrawaddy, or Alexander's breakthrough at Cassino, were later used to deceive: feigned locations of command posts, the covert movement of troops, the manufacture of substitutes for real weapons or transport, fake wireless traffic and the cozening of enemy agents.

Wavell understood them all, and at least a few could now be applied for the discomfiture of the Italians. The more Graziani's concern for his open desert flank increased, the less likely was the 10th Army to creep forward. Agents could at last be infiltrated into enemy territory to spread false rumour, while Cairo, Alexandria and other cities of the Middle East bred a rich crop of malleable Italian spies and sympathizers, some of whom could be 'bent' into double agents whose signals to their masters were henceforward doctored and controlled. Glossy accounts have also been published of how great quantities of inflatable rubber dummies were used to simulate concentrations of tanks and field guns; of dust-clouds raised by

Arabs to represent columns on the move; of misleading roads, tracks and so on. As these gestures tend to be associated with the arrival in Cairo of Colonel Dudley Clarke, who on his own admission did not reach Egypt until 18 December,★ they seem premature and sometimes suggest that Sidi Barrani 1940 is being confused with Alamein 1942. What cannot be disputed, however, is that deception was a valuable preliminary to *Compass,* that simulated threats to his flank kept Graziani off balance, and that Clarke's arrival from England – on Wavell's initiative – gave a great and continuing impulsion to the whole process and to the consolidation under his command of 'A' Force as a potent weapon for the future. (According to David Mure, who served in 'A' Force, its headquarters were established for cover in a brothel in the Kasr-el-Nil in Cairo and the ladies continued their ancient profession. 'On my first visit there, two and a half years later, they were still on the top floor . . . .')[5]

Two further benefits should be noted: one on which Wavell could hardly have dared to count – the absence of German troops – and another which, for all his trust in the Navy, he can scarcely have anticipated – the victory at Taranto.

In the 'Worst Possible Case' appreciation which he prepared on 24 May under the shadow of the Battle for France he had noted as one possibility 'Middle East cut off and attacked by Italy, supported perhaps by German air or troops.' This contingency was ever-present in his calculations, and on 7 October he actually produced an assessment of what might happen. Though no German formations had yet been identified in North Africa, he estimated that within four or five weeks he might have to deal not only with attacks by the *Luftwaffe,* but also with a presence on the Egyptian front of a German expeditionary force on the scale of one armoured and one motorized division. He therefore requested appropriate reinforcements. This paper, as will be seen, caused a flurry in London.

For the time being, nevertheless, his scenario was too dramatic. Rommel would not arrive until 1941. Hitler had

---

★ Private sources suggest, however, that this may have been as early as October. But O'Connor himself does not recall these devices.

indeed accepted his Army's suggestions for an African venture, with the Navy's warm approval, and just before Wavell wrote his paper the Führer had met the Duce at the Brenner Pass. However, his offer there of military support had been coolly received by Mussolini, who claimed that he could reach Mersa Matruh on his own, though some armour and dive-bombers might help a later advance to Alexandria. But the key factor was a report made by that hard professional, General von Thoma, who had been dispatched to Africa to thrust aside Italian bombast and assess the harsh realities. His recommendation was wholly adverse: he saw then what Rommel learned later, that there were 'no laurels in Africa'. Any immediate prospect of a German presence faded. Fortunately: for if the German Navy's pressure had prevailed, or if Hitler had suddenly felt that destiny summoned him to the Suez Canal, the effect on *Compass* must have been disastrous.

Instead, Wavell received a further timely gift. During the night of 11 November the Fleet Air Arm attacked the Italian warships clustered in the harbour of Taranto. At a cost of two aircraft and eleven torpedoes half the main fleet was seriously damaged or, in the case of *Cavour*, eliminated. (Of the Italian battleships at Taranto *Cavour* was beached and never went to sea again, while *Littorio* and *Duilio* were put out of action for a vital six months.) The effect on the balance of sea-power in the Mediterranean was instantaneous, for all the major ships in the Italian Navy that could move were shifted round to the western coast of the peninsula. In naval terms, this retreat was equivalent to throwing the towel into the ring. The propaganda value of so brilliant and unexpected a victory was enormous. From Wavell's point of view, a special benefit was the psychological trauma suffered by Graziani and his troops, already conditioned to an apathetic acceptance of British superiority. It was another step in the process of 'disturbing his mental balance'.

Above and beyond all these shifts of circumstance, moreover, Wavell had an inestimable advantage whose scale and depth have only been documented in detail by the publication in 1979 of the first volume of the *Official History of British*

*Intelligence in the Second World War.* In January 1942 Wavell himself wrote to Liddell Hart: 'The more I see of war, the less I think that general principles of strategy count as compared with administrative problems and the gaining of Intelligence . . . .'[6] Previous students were unable to understand fully what is now plain – that all Wavell's campaigns against the Italians, in both North and East Africa, were buttressed and underpinned by what is generally the most reliable intelligence of all; the cryptanalyst's ability to unscramble an opponent's signal traffic which he confidently assumes to be secret and secure.

British mastery of the contemporary Italian code-system, though not absolute, was maturing effectively at least as early as the Spanish Civil War. Though setbacks followed after the Italian entry into the German war – including the organizational problems on the British side when a service to the Middle East became paramount and, more significantly, the introduction of new codes and ciphers when the Italians became belligerents – nevertheless both the planning and the execution of *Compass* were assisted by cryptanalysis to a critical extent. (In East Africa, as will be seen, the British command of the Italians' secret traffic was overwhelming.)

This facility stemmed from two main sources. At the now famous 'Station X' at Bletchley Park in England the Government Code and Cipher School or GCCS was already well on the way to achieving its dazzling success in breaking the variety of ciphers created mechanically by the Germans on the Enigma machine. Indeed, during the *Compass* period GCCS was already adept at breaking *Luftwaffe* ciphers, so that when German tentacles began to reach out to the Mediterranean in early 1941 a vital source of intelligence was rapidly available. But GCCS also continued to pursue its pre-war preoccupations with the Italian codes and ciphers. Though the by-products were not always supplied to Cairo expeditiously, they constituted an important source for Wavell when matched with the decoded material acquired either at his Middle East base, or in the field, from Italian signal networks. By the end of the Cyrenaican campaign Wavell's cryptanalysts had broken no less than 8000 coded ciphered signals from the Italian Army. Until the higher grade Army cipher was changed early in the New Year, GCCS' at Bletchley had cracked about 2600 further messages. And it was calculated that for much of this period about 80 per cent of the high-grade ciphers of the Italian Air Force could be broken. When to such figures are added the invaluable information acquired progressively from free-speaking Italian prisoners of war, and from an efficient postal censorship, it will be seen that though, in the end, battles had to be fought and men had to die, Wavell was certainly not engaged in a game of Blind Man's Buff.

The calculation in Cairo of advantage and disadvantage was continuous and spread, of course, over many weeks. Still, it was as early as 21 September 1940 (with Matilda tanks in the *Apology* convoy still three days out from Suez) that Wavell sent his first operational instructions about *Compass* to Maitland Wilson, the general with over-all command of British troops in Egypt under whom, in the hierarchy, O'Connor and his Western Desert Force took their place. An amorphous elephant of a man – hence the nickname 'Jumbo' – with a disconcerting habit of talking down his nose or trunk, Wilson later reached the rank of Field Marshal for reasons which are difficult to identify and have never been explained. His endowment for one of the most senior commands seems sparse, in retrospect, and at best run-of-the-mill. Perhaps the very absence of originality or scintillation enabled him to float upwards unimpeded. But in 1940, at least, his recognized qualities as a trainer of troops and as an organizer were strong and evident: O'Connor had nothing but praise for Wilson's contribution during the preparation and planning of *Compass*.

In mid September it was still hard to believe that Graziani had come to a halt. The first outline of *Compass* which Wavell issued on the 21st therefore took the shape of a counter-attack on an advancing enemy rather than a direct assault on an army that had never even emerged from its defensive positions – the theme, of course, of the final operation. Nevertheless that first draft was full of fire. 'I wish every possible precaution that our military training can suggest to be made in order that if the enemy attacks Matruh the greater part of his force shall never return from it.' What he envisaged at this stage was something like a major raid – Jackson at Manassas? – in which the opportunities presented by the disconnected Italian positions, incapable as they were of mutual support, might be exploited with brutal speed. From the first, secrecy was dominant. Nobody was to know what was in the air except Wilson; his Chief of Staff, Brigadier Galloway; O'Connor and Major-General Creagh, commanding 7 Armoured Division.

Cairo and Alexandria were leaking sieves. For long after 1940 British security in the Middle East was too often amateur and irresponsible. There were Axis supporters in plenty, and disaffected Egyptians who loathed a war that was not theirs. It was for good practical reasons, therefore, and not merely because of his personal preference for secrecy, that Wavell imposed so strict a ban. But there was another to be excluded: the Prime Minister. 'I realised Winston's sanguine temperament and desire to have at least one finger in any military pie. I did not want to arouse premature hopes, I did not want Winston to make detailed plans for me, and I knew that absolute secrecy was the only hope of keeping my intentions from the Italians, who had so many tentacles in Cairo.' Only a month or so had passed since that terrible *General Directive*. This was Churchill's way – and it was infuriating. Yet whether Wavell was wise must remain an open question. Assuming that plans for *Compass* had gone ahead with the Prime Minister successfully kept in the dark, it was nevertheless obvious that sooner or later he must hear about an attack by the desert army for which, in the end, he was responsible to people and Parliament. When then? Italian spies were one thing, but to distrust your Prime Minister was another. Would his predictable rage not be justified? Rage there would be, for certain. If the risk Wavell took was finely calculated, it was still grave. But circumstances can alter cases, and things now took a different course.

Wavell's appreciation of 7 October about the likelihood of a German intrusion and his own need for reinforcements produced, not surprisingly, a loud buzz in London and an immediate response from the Secretary of State for War. Eden signalled on the 8th, '. . . have decided with concurrence of PM to pay you a flying visit and hope to arrive Alexandria 14th'. He actually arrived on the 15th. During their opening discussions nothing – it seems curious in retrospect – was disclosed about *Compass* to the War Minister and member of the Cabinet's Middle East Committee. The silence persisted, even though on the 20th Wavell gave Wilson specific instructions to examine at once the feasibility of attacking Graziani's positions in the Sidi Barrani – Sofafi region. 'The operation I have in mind is a short and swift one, lasting four or five days at most, and taking every advantage of the element of surprise.' (The concept is no longer one of counter-attacking an advancing enemy, but of assaulting him *in situ*.) 'I should not propose,' Wavell added, 'to attempt to retain a large force in the Sidi Barrani area if the attack were successful, *but to withdraw the bulk of the forces again to railhead,*★ leaving only light covering forces in the forward areas.' O'Connor, who received the same instructions, commented later that 'neither then, nor at any other time, was an ultimate objective given'. But *Compass* is like several of Rommel's impressive forays, in that when the seed was sown it was not expected to bear so fine a crop.

On 28 October Eden and Wavell were down in Khartoum engaged in discussions with Field Marshal Smuts and the Emperor Haile Selassie about the progress of the war in East Africa. At 3 a.m. that morning, however, the Italians presented Greece with an ultimatum. ('It is a document,' Ciano noted in his diary, 'that allows no way out for Greece.') Within hours Italian troops were on the move across the Albanian frontier – and now Wavell was forced to declare his hand. The scale of assistance that could be spared for the Greeks was minute – a few squadrons of aircraft, an infantry brigade to Crete, and so on – and the instinct of a man like Eden, who thought less in military terms than in those of foreign policy, was to ask for more. Wavell described his dilemma. 'Eden was proposing to sap my strength in aircraft, AA guns, transport etc. in favour of Greece, thinking I had only a defensive policy in mind, to such an extent that I had to tell him what was in my mind to prevent my being skinned to an extent that would make an offensive impossible.' The Official History says of Wavell's plans for *Compass* that he was preparing them 'in a secrecy so great that he would not inform even the Prime

★ Author's italics.

Minister save by Mr Eden's word of mouth'. It is plain, however, that at this stage Wavell had no intention at all of informing either Eden or their master; he only did so through *force majeure*. He was compelled against his will to make the Prime Minister and his advisers realize that since he was actually planning *offensively* his army must not be stripped for the sake of Greece.

The word of mouth was naturally welcomed. Ismay in his memoirs vividly described the meeting of the Defence Committee in London after Eden's return on 8 November:

> Every one of us could have jumped for joy, but Churchill could have jumped twice as high as the rest. He has said that he 'purred like six cats'. That is putting it mildly. He was rapturously happy. 'At long last we are going to throw off the intolerable shackles of the defensive,' he declared. 'Wars are won by superior will-power. Now we will wrest the initiative from the enemy and impose our will on him.' Needless to say Wavell's plan was approved without a moment's hesitation, and even before the meeting broke up Churchill started estimating the spoils. He was always prone to count his chickens before they were hatched, and as a rule his estimates erred on the generous side.

There, as usual, was the rub: and there, above all, was the reason why Wavell had sought to keep his secret from the Prime Minister until the last, the very last permissible minute. He did not want to be hurried and harried. Yet pressure immediately started for him to name D-Day: pressure that was resisted, and that evoked sharp memoranda from Churchill to Eden like: 'General Wavell's telegram to CIGS does not answer the question I put. The last sentence but one leaves everything unsettled.'

Then there was the sense so unhappily conveyed by Churchill that London was seeking to take over the conduct of *Compass* from an incompetent Cairo. His intentions were laudable: he wanted to help and he wanted to win. Yet for a commander in the field who is working incessantly to launch an operation which he himself has devised, a signal like this one of 26 November, which combined the avuncular with the dictatorial, can scarcely have been exhilarating:

I am having a Staff study made of possibilities open to us, if all goes well, for moving fighting troops and also reserves forward by sea in long hops along the coast, and setting up new supply bases to which pursuing armoured vehicles and units might resort. Without wishing to be informed of the details, I should like to be assured that all this has been weighed, explored and as far as possible prepared. . . . One may indeed see possibility of centre of gravity in Middle East shifting suddenly from Egypt to the Balkans, and from Cairo to Constantinople. You are no doubt preparing your mind for this, and a Staff study is being made here.

Such was the tone and content of Churchill's *feu de joie* with which Wavell was now bombarded, during the most intensive stage of his preparations for *Compass* and at a time when the whole region of his concern, from the Balkans to Ethiopia, presented him daily with insistent problems.

His best course was to avoid a war of telegrams and anger between himself and his Prime Minister, which on the whole he managed to do – though if Wavell had been less stiff Churchill might have been more yielding – and to evade every attempt to extract the actual date for *Compass*. This was perhaps as well, for by the beginning of December Wavell had yet another secret in his pocket.

# 3

# The Enemy Encompassed

COMPASS . . . To close round, as a multitude; to surround,
with friendly or hostile intent; to hem in . . .
*The Shorter Oxford English Dictionary*

English land forces cannot survive long in Egypt and in particular
could not operate there. Those which were moved towards our
frontiers at the time of the Abyssinian war were very soon struck
by dysentery and had heavy losses.
*Mussolini to Ribbentrop in 1937, recorded by Count Ciano*

The general leading from the front: his commander-in-chief
directing from the rear. When the two are meshed together in
the actual conduct of a battle, united by absolute trust and
mutual understanding, it is sometimes extraordinarily difficult
to apportion the laurels of victory. The public at the time and
posterity later find it easy, for they are both misled by the
instant stereotypes of the press. 'Haig wins at Amiens,' or
'Eisenhower breaks out in Normandy,' make dramatic headlines whose message endures even though it was not Haig who
in fact *won* the battle or Eisenhower who made the breakthrough. In this fashion *Compass* immediately became known
as 'Wavell's offensive', and it is mainly in these terms that the
operation is usually recalled.

Wavell knew the truth. On 13 December 1940, when the
last Italians were trailing out of Egypt, Churchill signalled
triumphantly: 'I send you my heartfelt congratulations on
your splendid victory, which fulfils our highest hopes . . . .
The King will send you a message as soon as full results are
apparent. Meanwhile pray convey my thanks and compli-
ments to Wilson and accept the same yourself.' Where was
O'Connor's name? Wavell was quick to write from Cairo a
personal letter to the CIGS, drawing attention to the work of
his generals at the front, and this he followed on the 20th with
an explicit signal to Dill. 'Hope that O'Connor's share in

success will be given publicity as well as Wilson's and mine. He played very large part both in making plan and directing battle.'

Two years later, when O'Connor was still a prisoner in Italy, one of his former officers, Lieutenant-Colonel Collingwood, wrote to Wavell in India to tell him that O'Connor was being ignorantly criticized in England. Wavell replied from Delhi on 10 December 1942 with a robust letter which began:

> The detailed plans for the attack on Dec. 9 1940 and for the subsequent operations up to the fall of Benghazi were almost entirely the work of Dick; I and Jumbo Wilson saw him at very frequent intervals and gave him general instructions, but the detailed planning and the conduct of operations were his more than anyone's. I am sure that Jumbo Wilson would bear this out. I sent at least three telegrams home during the course of the operations to the CIGS or Prime Minister, pointing out how much of the credit was due to Dick, and asking that due publicity should be given to him and others, as I felt the limelight was coming much too much on myself who had only done the general direction.[1]

Generosity, integrity and loyalty to his subordinates were Wavell's hall-marks: the careers of some other applauded commanders, from Montgomery to MacArthur, were flawed by their absence.

Yet in that phrase 'the general direction' other truths are concealed. It was Wavell, above all, who had nursed the delicate situation in the Middle East to the point at which *Compass* could even be imagined. It was Wavell who had chosen O'Connor as his instrument. However spectacular its development in O'Connor's hands, it was Wavell who first saw the possibilities and initiated the preparations for 'a raid'. It was Wavell's constant visits to the front, his rapid grasp of O'Connor's needs and problems, his firm endorsement of daring proposals for the advance and, beyond everything, the mantle of confidence in which he swathed O'Connor that sustained the waning impetus of the Western Desert Force as it pressed onward to Benghazi and beyond.

These complementary truths were well understood by O'Connor. After he was captured (as will be seen) and imprisoned in Italy he wrote a full personal account of *Compass* under the date-line 'Prisoners of War Camp, Sulmona, Italy, May 22 1941'.\* As a document it is perhaps incomparable. Certainly there are few cases of a commander writing, shortly after the event and with no official compulsion, a detailed narrative of scrupulous precision which was not formally addressed to the War Office for ultimate publication – like a Despatch, (with all the cautious evasions or half-truths that characterize such compositions) – but as a frank private narrative addressed 'To my Mother or my Wife', who were instructed to keep it in custody until his return† because 'I am particularly anxious that anything I have said in it should not now or at any other time be an embarrassment to the soldiers and politicians whose duty it is to direct our policy. My only reason for writing it now is that events are still fresh in my mind.' Reflecting on Wavell's visits to his forward command-post O'Connor declared:

> It would be impossible to say what great pleasure and assistance these visits gave me, and also to all other commanders and units which he visited. He listened patiently to all our difficulties and made notes of everything; and I always received a wire from him on his return to Cairo, regarding which of my many demands he was able to supply. I felt the greatest confidence in him and knew that he would support me to the full in any bold action. All my instructions emanated from him, and it seemed to me that a further link in the chain of command was unnecessary.

On 15 December, when *Compass* was already well on the move, Wavell jotted down some notes on the preparations for the battle which he forwarded to the War Office. Describing how, about mid October, Graziani's apparent reluctance to advance suggested possibilities for a counter-move, Wavell continued: 'The enemy's defensive arrangements, which I studied daily on a map fixed on to the wall facing my desk, seemed to me thoroughly faulty. He was spread over a wide front in a series of fortified camps, which were not mutually

---

\* Extracts from this report were published in *Against Great Odds* by Brigadier C. N. Barclay. Thanks to the kindness of General Sir Richard O'Connor, a full copy of the text is in the author's possession: an invaluable source for this chapter.

† O'Connor contrived to smuggle the papers out of his prison in the hands of an authorized but well-disposed visitor.

supporting, and separated by wide distances.' Here was the crux: how to unstring that vulnerable necklace of defence-posts stretching from Sofafi in the south to Sidi Barrani on the coast?

Wavell required a weapon and a plan. His weapon was already sharp. The old hands of 7 Armoured Division, who had developed their desert skills under the brilliant General Hobart before the war, polished and perfected them during those summer months of 1940 when Wavell dominated no-man's-land by the self-confident ascendancy of his small mobile groups, who darted and spat fire in the wilderness between the main Italian and British forces like the destroyer screens fighting their private battles in the waters that divided the giant fleets at Jutland. Now, in October, they were rein-forced by the armour from the *Apology* convoy, 3 Hussars with light tanks, 2 RTR with Cruisers and 7 RTR with the heavy Matildas. 'From then until early December,' Liddell Hart noted in *The Tanks,* 'the units practised desert movement by day and night.' The weapon was a bright sword. Yet there were qualifying factors which O'Connor, who combined shrewd judgement with a dynamism no less than Rommel's, had always to take into account. Precisely because of their months on the desert front some of the tanks in 7 Armoured Division were reaching the limits of their effective mileage. This was equally and unfortunately true of some of the armour newly arrived from England, and there were, of course, no tank-transporters in those early days of the desert campaigns. Above all a desperate shortage of supply trucks, so essential for maintaining the momentum of advance, would act like a binding brake throughout the whole of *Compass.*

In the event, these were minor considerations: the men and the *matériel* sufficed. Moreover, Wavell and O'Connor between them had lifted their pocket army with the 'X quality' of inspiration. 'The army's affection for O'Connor,' wrote Correlli Barnett, (and the same could have been said of Wavell), 'its loyalty, and its confidence in him were genuine and profound. O'Connor had achieved this ascendancy with-out any of the advantages of what television calls "person-ality". O'Connor's expositions of his plans were modest and tentative. His plans spoke for him.'

But however tentative his expositions (which really means that he did not lay down the law like Montgomery with what the Germans call *quarterdeck Stimmung*) there was nothing vague about the way that O'Connor – and Wavell – agreed on the actual plan for *Compass*. The initial scheme called for a direct frontal assault on the Nibeiwa and Tummar positions in the centre of the Italian line. Since this involved a long approach-march by moonlight and a complicated final assault on fixed defences, *Training Exercise No. 1* was held on 26 November. During this shadow-play arrangements for the march were tested, and replicas of the Italian positions were attacked on conventional lines. None but a handful of senior officers knew the reason. Nothing was put on paper about this or *Training Exercise No. 2,* the real *Compass* that soon followed. But Wavell's deceivers used the first exercise well, whispering that it was a precautionary insurance against an Italian advance. 'Back in the Delta it was not difficult to put about stories that routine reliefs were taking place in the desert and that the British forces were being weakened, and would be weakened still further, to provide reinforcements for Greece.'[2] The exercise itself, however, raised grave doubts.

As they reviewed its results O'Connor, Wilson and their senior staff officers realized that a direct standard-pattern attack on a wide front by the infantry of 4 Indian Division entailed unacceptable delays. After that long advance by night the artillery would need some three hours to register and engage Nibeiwa's perimeter defences. All surprise would be lost: in a hundred minutes the deception scheme orchestrated over so many weeks would be dissipated. There was only one way. Reconnaissance disclosed the tracks of vehicles running into the camp at a point on the further or western side. If the Matildas could rush this gap, which was presumably free from mines, surprise could be achieved before breakfast. Tanks first, then the infantry, on the enemy's side of his camp: and this meant pushing the assault troops by night through the desert to a point west of Nibeiwa, so that they would be on their start-lines before dawn. Military convention was being thrown to the winds – and when the plan was put forward Wavell accepted it without hesitation.

The imaginative daring of O'Connor in proposing and of Wavell endorsing this unorthodox venture has often and rightly been praised. What is not always brought out with sufficient clarity is the extent to which the long chain of successes during the following weeks depended on it. Had caution prevailed, anticlimax might have followed. *Compass* provides a classic example of the domino effect: as the British rolled westwards first Sidi Barrani, then Bardia, then Tobruk and then Benghazi fell, each because its predecessor had collapsed and because the shock-wave of despair affected the Italians more powerfully as defeat succeeded defeat. Without the shock the dominoes might well have remained upright – and the wave began at Nibeiwa.

Moreover, every stage in his advance revealed to O'Connor the fact that the Italian gunners were the most steadfast and soldierly element in Graziani's army. So it was at the beginning, and then at Bardia, and at Tobruk. The memoir he wrote as a prisoner recalls his impressions. The artillery, at least, was prepared to fight it out. And such was Rommel's view: contemptuous in the main of his ally's military capacity, he always preserved a strong regard for the gunners. If we then envisage a conventional assault on Nibeiwa – a pounding by the weak British artillery, an advance by the Indian division over the mines and wires, a follow-up by the Matildas – it seems not impossible that the Italians, with time allowed them to shake off surprise and alert their gunners, might have put up a vigorous and even effective defence, as they did more than once in similar circumstances during the campaign. We have to ask, in fact, how things might have been if through caution at the top the first phase of *Compass* had failed or – no less disastrous – proved indecisive.

Caution was not Wavell's creed. Nevertheless, there is something ambivalent about his declarations of intent as D-Day, 9 December, drew near. On 28 November he gave his final instructions to Wilson:

> I know that you have in mind and are planning the fullest possible exploitation of any initial success of *Compass* operation. You and all Commanders in the Western Desert may rest assured that the

boldest action, whatever its results, will have the support not only
of myself but of the CIGS and of the War Cabinet at home. . . . I
am not entertaining extravagant hopes of this operation, but I do
wish to make certain that if a big opportunity occurs we are
prepared morally, mentally and administratively to use it to the
fullest.

Though the message did not precisely name any distant objectives, it is impossible not to feel that at the last minute Wavell
was increasing the scope and extending the horizon of
*Compass*. Exploitation, the boldest action, a big opportunity:
these are the words of a committed mind.

And yet (under pressure from Churchill to disclose the date of
his attack, which he steadfastly refused to do) on 6 December
Wavell signalled to Dill: 'Feel undue hopes are being placed on
this operation which was designed as raid only. We are greatly
outnumbered on ground and in air, have to move over seventy-
five miles of desert and attack enemy who has fortified himself
for three months. Please do not encourage optimism.' Dill
concealed this pallid statement, but Churchill sniffed it out and
was apoplectic. On the 7th he minuted to the CIGS: 'If, with the
situation as it is, General Wavell is only playing small, and is not
hurling on his whole available force with furious energy, he will
have failed to rise to the height of circumstances.' Of course
Wavell knew what he was doing. He later noted that 'I always
meant to go as far as possible and exploit any success to the full,
but I was a little apprehensive that Winston might urge me to do
too much, as limitations of supply and transport never made
any great appeal to him.' In fact it was an ill-advised and perhaps
indefensible signal for a Commander-in-Chief to send to his
military and political superiors in London just before a major
offensive. It was misleading, and it was meant to be. Dill must
have felt despair when he received it and realized how far a
mutual and corroding suspicion now separated two men whom
he held in honour and respect.

Still, the day came. On the 7th, as Churchill was writing
about Wavell 'playing small', he and his family went imper-
turbably to the races and that evening gave a large dinner
party: all a cover for the initial approach-march of the Desert
Force. And then at 04.45 on the 9th the forward squadron of

Matildas crashed into Nibeiwa, the infantry followed fast, the Italian commander General Maletti was killed and within hours the camp had surrendered. It only took three days to roll up the whole Italian line from Sofafi to Sidi Barrani: by the evening of the 11th Wavell's direction and O'Connor's dash had earned their reward – 38,300 prisoners for a loss of 624 killed, wounded and missing. Admittedly the captives were Italian. Nevertheless, it was the first British victory in the field since the outbreak of war.

But now the bomb-shell burst. A week before *Compass* began, on the 2nd, Wavell held a conference in Cairo with General Platt from the Sudan and General Alan Cunningham from Kenya. He then shared with them a secret to which nobody but General Wilson was privy – nobody in London, not even O'Connor: he intended very shortly to switch 4 Indian Division from the Western Desert Force to the East African front. This was 'the most unwelcome piece of news' that O'Connor received on the morning of the 11th just as he was setting off to visit the division's commander, General Beresford-Peirse, 'an extrovert, plain-spoken, orthodox soldier who chain-smoked Indian cheroots, which he kept in a kind of reticule'.[3]

Both Wavell and O'Connor later set down in private their thoughts about this dramatic event. Wavell's plan was to replace 4 Indian as soon as possible with the still unblooded 6 Australian Division, now assembling in Egypt. But O'Connor wrote in his prison-memoir about the Indians' departure:

> I had received no warning of this whatsoever and consequently had made no plans to meet such a contingency. Its withdrawal at this juncture would produce a difficult situation. It left the 16th British Brigade alone [i.e., as the only spare infantry brigade for assaults on fixed defences: 7 Armoured Division remained as a mobile formation] and no Field Artillery in the Force as all those Regiments were included in the withdrawal orders.

The Australians, O'Connor recalled, could not appear immediately and anyway had only two artillery regiments, equipped with guns from the First World War. A more urgent factor was their lack of transport. The Indians had a full complement and 'this windfall', O'Connor noted, 'would no longer be available' – neither for the hectic business of building up supplies for a further advance, nor for the irritating but unavoidable task of feeding, watering and removing the embarrassing thousands of prisoners. Yet he was burning to continue the chase.

At the end of the war O'Connor sent Wavell a copy of his memoir, on which the Viceroy commented in a letter from Simla on 27 June 1945. About this specific point he observed:

> I am not quite sure whether you ever realised the necessity for the withdrawal of the 4th Division immediately after Sidi Barrani. It was a matter of shipping; a convoy had come into Suez, and I could use some of the returning ships to carry part of the Division to Port Sudan, the only means by which I could get the Division complete in the Sudan by the time I had fixed as the latest favourable date for attacking the Italians. I could not hold up the ships, and if I lost the opportunity I did not think I could have attacked from the Sudan that winter. The people at home were, incidentally, rather nervous about the Sudan. . . . My decision was a difficult one, but I am sure it was right.[4]

Churchill, who could be objective when he chose, summarized the consequences of the switch in generous terms. 'The immediate course of events both on the North African shore and in Abyssinia proved how very justly the Commander-in-Chief had measured the values and circumstances of the situation.' He spoke of 'a wise and daring decision'.

As one follows the widely separated careers of the Indian Division and the Western Desert Force one recognizes the validity of Churchill's praise. Yet one doubt remains. The Prime Minister himself seems to have felt no rancour, this time, about Wavell's secrecy: he had victories for solace. But it requires very little imagination to sense the turbulent feelings of shock and disappointment with which O'Connor received the news of his loss. His total loyalty and his grasp of strategic values stood the strain, and the record shows that during the coming weeks his panache was undiminished. Yet perhaps no other British general in the course of the war was exposed to so brutal a test – not even Alexander when he learned that some of his finest divisions must leave Italy for Normandy and southern France, thus emasculating his armies. Wavell rarely acted without brooding forethought. He knew that he could ask anything of O'Connor and his subordinate obeyed. Still, it is curious that he failed to trust a man so trustworthy: even more curious that he did not spur him on by warning him in advance that he must take Sidi Barrani 'on the run' because he would shortly lose half his strength.

Conveyed down the Red Sea and the Nile Valley, 4 Indian Division began to re-assemble on the northern rim of the East African theatre early in the New Year. The situation there was virtually stalemate. Within the enemy-held territories of Eritrea, Ethiopia and the Somalilands the Duke of Aosta, a man with more breeding than military fibre, disposed of a huge army – some 250,000 men: but it was a miscellaneous mob, containing Italian units of sterling quality but many of low grade, while the bulk consisted of native troops whose skills were as uncertain as their ultimate loyalties. Aosta's stance was dignified but defensive. His frontiers sprawled for many hundreds of miles. Beyond them Wavell had by now grouped substantial forces (too many, Churchill considered): but half, in fact, was far to the south in Kenya, under General Cunningham, while the rest gathered under Platt in the Sudan, a potential threat to Eritrea and the northern flank of Ethiopia. Immense distances, the terrible terrain, lack of transport and the shortage of water amid the harsh mountains and wastelands all impeded Wavell and his generals in their efforts to make effective combinations and, by a unified strategy, to slice the Italian empire into pieces. Yet this, in the end, is what happened.

Nor, in retrospect, is such a conclusion surprising, for the campaign has been described as 'the perfect (if rather minia-ture) example of the cryptographers' war'. Cryptanalysis cannot move mountains, produce water-points in the wilder-ness, or overcome any of the material difficulties which now faced Wavell and his generals: but it is an immense alleviation to know just where your enemy is, in what strength, with what condition of morale. To an exceptional degree cryptan-alysis provided this information, particularly during the second and critical half of the campaign. According to the Intelligence History:

Early in January the revelations that the Italians were withdrawing from Kassala enabled the British advance to begin nearly three weeks earlier than planned, on 19 January instead of 8 February. From then until the end of the campaign the Cs-in-C in Cairo were able to read the enemy's plans and appreciations in his own words as soon as he issued them; indeed, they sometimes received the decrypts while the Italian W/T operators were still asking for the signals to be checked and repeated. The flood of intelligence was not confined to any sector or level of command, but it was general throughout the whole area of operations and throughout the whole of the enemy's chain of command from the Viceroy himself down to the smallest garrison detachment. It extended from the reading of the Viceroy's daily situation report for the Italian government down to the reading of detailed instructions for the evacuation of Italian wives and families, and included by the way such material as the Air Force Command's regular previews of the operations it had planned for the coming week, its reports on the progressive disintegration of its resources and the orders and appreciations issued by the Italian Army Commander in connection with his successive withdrawals during the one important engagement, the battle of Keren.

Intelligence of this quality was unprecedented. The revelation, in 1979, of its existence means that all previous accounts of the East African campaign are, in the deepest sense, fictions, and that a detailed new version must be awaited which describes in the fullest manner the character of this intelligence and the precise day-by-day effect of its application in the field. This is a small-scale, but nevertheless a beautiful, example of how the increasingly available evidence of the cryptanalysts' achievements has thrown historians of the Second World War into turmoil.

In East Africa the final result was so cataclysmic that all the operations leading up to it seem pre-ordained. But Wavell was careful not to call his hand too high – nor, of course, could he reveal his secret sources. In his Despatch on the campaign he referred to

a pincer movement on the largest scale, through Eritrea and Somaliland, converging on Amba Alagi [where Aosta made his last stand] combined with a direct thrust through Western

Abyssinia by the patriot forces. It looks Teutonic in conception and execution; but this result was not foreseen in the original plan. . . . It was in fact an improvisation after the British fashion of war rather than a set piece in the German manner.

Montgomery would have thought little of that observation!

Wavell was too self-deprecatory. He certainly evolved the concept of 'a pincer movement on the largest scale': indeed, since Platt and Cunningham were separated by so many hundreds of miles there was no other realistic course. But the many difficulties – particularly of transport, water and supplies – made initiative essential from the start, and it is in this respect that Wavell and his generals so notably revealed the quality on which Marshal de Saxe laid most stress, 'a talent for sudden and appropriate improvisation'.

There was another difficulty: Churchill. Whenever his attention turned to East Africa a fusillade followed of minatory and often contradictory signals. The weight of his variable pressure on the Chiefs of Staff also meant that during the period of the campaign Wavell was never really working to a clear and explicit directive from London. His problems are pin-pointed in the Official History:

> The main operation in East Africa had therefore succeeded beyond all expectations, and had ended just in time. This was largely due to the steadiness of purpose of General Wavell and Air Chief Marshal Longmore, who had to achieve a workable and appropriate balance of forces while doing their best to comply with a rapid succession of instructions and suggestions, such as to part with forces from Kenya, to capture Kismayu quickly, to capture Eritrea quickly, to deter the Japanese by 'liquidating Italian East Africa', to treat as a 'first duty' the air defence of Malta, to be prepared to send ten squadrons to Turkey, to regard the capture of Rhodes as 'of first importance', and to 'let their first thoughts be for Greece'.

So unexpected but timely a success was due not merely to Wavell's broad supervisory control of the campaign, but also to specific factors for which his foresight and good judgement were primarily responsible. It was he alone who risked the transfer of 4 Indian Division which, with its companion 5 Indian Division, was to play a decisive part in the only desperate battle of the campaign, the fifty-three days of struggle for the heights of Keren whose capture presented Platt with Eritrea and broke the Italians' nerve. It was Wavell who, when 5 Indian Division was switched from Iraq to the Middle East, ordered it to Sudan.* The rising of patriot irregulars who captured ground and eroded Italian confidence within Ethiopia was envisaged, supported and officered by Wavell:

> As far back as September 1939, he had, on the advice of his Intelligence Staff, sent for a certain D. A. Sandford, a former gunner officer who, after service in the Sudan, had settled in Ethiopia, farming and acting as occasional adviser to the Emperor, and who was at that time treasurer of Guildford Cathedral. . . . He at once began to plan the raising of a revolt inside the country.[5]

It was Wavell who accepted the offer of Orde Wingate, whose unorthodox talents he had noted in Palestine, and set him to work with Sandford in fermenting revolt. Later he described the first meeting, on a mountain air-strip in the Abyssinian wilderness, of this odd couple. 'Few people looked more like a fiery leader of partisans than Wingate, few looked less like one than Sandford – solid, bespectacled, benevolent – who was in his way as bold and active as Wingate.' Yet in spite of friction, insubordination and misunderstanding, these two gave the main impulse to that tide which swept Haile Selassie back to his emperor's throne in Addis Ababa.

Without the aid of conventional forces the Ethiopian patriots would, of course, have been as impotent as the resistance movements in Europe. It was the converging pressure of Platt and Cunningham (as well as the psychological effect of O'Connor's victories in *Compass*, to which we must shortly return) that at last destroyed the Italians' imperial dream – what Count Ciano had called 'the chance of five thousand years' – and caused the Duke of Aosta to surrender as Viceroy on 19 May 1941. After Keren fell there was nothing, in fact, left to fight for but castles in the air – the phantom possibility of an ultimate German triumph and, somehow, an Italian renaissance. The Viceroy preferred to march out of Amba Alagi with

---

* 'To General Wavell belongs the credit for allotting to the Eritrean front the two divisions most likely to adapt themselves to the conditions and best able to work in double harness.' *The Mediterranean and the Middle East,* vol. 1, p.440.

full military courtesies and a Guard of Honour.

But this, the moment to pick up the continuing story of *Compass,* is also the moment to ask whether on the highest level of strategy Wavell's commitment to East Africa was worth while. There is, indeed, a connection between the two themes.

Churchill's own attitudes about East Africa were so weathercock in variety that both Wavell and the historian may be excused for being uncertain about what he really wanted. Now he argues that the Italians should be left to rot, now he is demanding an *attaque brusquée* which will finish the job clinically and release troops for the Mediterranean fronts. In December the ruling idea in Wavell's own mind, according to his Despatch, 'was that the formation of the patriot movement in Abyssinia offered with the resources available the best prospect of making the Italian position impossible and eventually reconquering the country. I did not intend a large scale invasion . . . .' Yet the transfer of 4 Indian Division in mid December (along with some tanks and extra guns) was a considerable shift in that direction. Gradually, under pressure from home and from his own expanding sense of the possible, the idea of a two-pronged invasion developed – and fed on its own successes.

Yet in spite of the completeness of Wavell's victory its value is open to question. Churchill's instincts were not always wrong, and Wavell's first thoughts might have been the best. Suppose Aosta and his vast garrison had in fact been allowed to wither, with all their arteries severed and the abscess of a patriot resistance sapping their strength? The most sinister threat might have been to Britain's line of communications through the Red Sea, but Italian aircraft and warships along the East African shores were so unadventurous and ineffective that this was a trivial issue. There was a propaganda gain, certainly, in the destruction of a fascist fief and the restoration of a charismatic Emperor. But strategy is more concerned with brute fact than with newspaper headlines. We have to ask whether admirable units like the two Indian divisions could have been better employed in the Western Desert – whether the 100,000 shells fired in the final stage of the Keren battle (and carried in 1000 trucks) were spent to the best purpose. Some answers to these questions may be found in the evolution of *Compass* from the point at which, to O'Connor's dismay, his Indian Division was transported suddenly from Sidi Barrani to another commander and a remote campaign. And the answers may be given quickly, for analysis of the subsequent evolution of *Compass* suggests that the effect of 4 Indian Division's switch was at the worst marginal.

By 16 December – less than a week after the fall of Sidi Barrani – General Mackay, commanding 6 Australian Division, reported forward to O'Connor who had already sized him up in Palestine. Though only one brigade of the division was immediately available – the arrival of the other two being delayed by shortage of transport – under O'Connor's tutelage Mackay swiftly and stoutly tackled the problem of capturing with a few thousand British and Australian infantry and a handful of 'I' tanks the next objective, Bardia, whose harbour defences and strong perimeter contained, it was reckoned, over 20,000 men. (Had Marshal Graziani had his way the garrison would have already evaporated, for in mid December he proposed to Mussolini a withdrawal to the 'fortress' of Tobruk. But the Duce replied with the dictator's inevitable 'Stand Fast', and in fact the true figures for the force in Bardia now facing O'Connor were enormous: 45,000 men and 400 guns.) On New Year's day, 1941, the Western Desert Force was re-christened 13 Corps. Before dawn on 3 January this new formation began the assault which was to produce its first victory, for by the early afternoon of the 5th Bardia's defences were shattered. This lightning defeat cost the Italians another 40,000 men, 400 guns, 130 tanks and (for O'Connor the most valuable of all) some 700 trucks. Since the start of *Compass* no less than eight enemy divisions had already been eliminated – in less than a month.

O'Connor was now directly responsible to Wavell, for at the beginning of the year the unnecessary interposition between them of General Wilson (as commander of British Troops in Egypt or BTE) had been removed. They were thinking in unison and far ahead, though Wavell, with so many other preoccupations, was necessarily more tentative than his ardent commander in the field. On 5 January Wavell informed his Chief of Staff, Arthur Smith, that he would 'like the Joint Planning Staff to prepare as a matter of urgency a paper on the subject of an advance from Tobruk to Benghazi:. . .', but O'Connor recalled in his prison-memoir that when he paid a brief visit to Cairo after the capture of Bardia Wavell 'discussed with me the possibility of a *raid*\* on Benghazi but would have liked it to have been on a permanent basis rather than a *raid*. However, I was delighted to think that there was a possibility of an attempt of some sort.' It was, in fact, O'Connor's dynamism, foresight and generalship that kept the advance flowing: but his flair for the quick-moving battle of exploitation, unequalled by any British general in the Second World War, would never have flowered with such dramatic effect had he not been conscious throughout, to a point that became almost instinctive, of a sense of harmony between himself and his Commander-in-Chief.

Even before the attack on Bardia, he had given to 7 Armoured Division a code-word on receipt of which it would instantly speed westwards to the investment of Tobruk, and even before Bardia had surrendered the division was on its way. With extraordinary determination the Australians were next ferried forward, and in what can only be described as a 'crash action', on 21 and 22 January, Tobruk's invaluable harbour with its distillation plant and 10,000 tons of stored water was secured along with another 25,000 prisoners, 208 guns and 87 tanks – at a cost of a mere 400 casualties in the whole of 13 Corps. O'Connor had now obtained the forward administrative base which was vital to the maintenance of his advance.

And he would indeed race onwards – though not to the Tripoli of his dreams. But the unexpectedly rapid seizure of Bardia and Tobruk, and the immense haul of prisoners, booty and undamaged facilities, show with sufficient clarity that the removal of 4 Indian Division can only have delayed O'Connor by a factor, at most, of a few weeks. There was only enough transport to maintain – with considerable difficulty – one infantry division forward as well as the armour vital for pur-

* Author's italics.

suit, so that even had he kept 4 Indian he would not have been
able to employ the Australians. And though at Bardia the
latter, in their first major action, were not entirely at home, in
the assault on Tobruk their merciless self-assurance and
Mackay's efficient conduct of the battle could hardly have
been surpassed, or perhaps equalled, by the more experienced
Indians. So that when to these considerations is added the
transforming impact of 4 Indian Division on the East African
campaign, Wavell's judgement – at a time when all was uncertain and strategic calculations had to be based as much on
hunch as on arithmetic – survives a critical scrutiny. Even if it
is true that the destruction of Mussolini's East African empire
was irrelevant, nobody has convincingly demonstrated that
retention of the Indian division would have carried O'Connor
with significantly greater speed to Benghazi and beyond.

Indeed, in a sense the whole argument is irrelevant. Despite
further brilliant successes, *Compass* was in fact doomed, and in
relation to the thunderclap that was about to burst over the
Balkans Aosta's surrender at Amba Alagi seems a trivial re-
compense. For throughout that victorious winter there was a
cancer in the side of Wavell's command, insidiously and at last
fatally draining its strength. The cancer was Greece, and the
growing German threat to the Balkans.

At the battle-front O'Connor suffered most directly from
the pain of this seepage. Looking back from his prison-camp in
Italy he recalled his frustration at being 'constantly embarrassed by the assistance we were required to furnish to Greece'.

> I fully realise that this assistance was arranged by political agree-
> ment and had to be given, and am only stating the difficulties it
> caused to the Western Desert Campaign. Not only were the
> resources ear-marked for Greece in the GHQ pool not available,
> but units were withdrawn from 13 Corps in the middle of opera-
> tions. These were mainly transport and labour units, and some
> AA guns. Engineers also were put under orders to move. This
> move though subsequently cancelled nevertheless prevented their
> employment for a considerable period. Worst of all, RAF units
> continued to move to Greece or Crete, and we again were the
> losers. Captured war material also in the shape of guns, ammuni-
> tion, AA weapons and transport vehicles were urgently required

by the Greeks; so we lost not only much transport which could have been converted for our own use, but also for a considerable period the transport required to carry or draw this vast quantity of material to Alexandria.

Nevertheless, Wavell alone bore the full brunt of the Balkan distraction. He was responsible for the whole Middle Eastern theatre, from Tripolitania to the Tigris and from the northern shores of the Mediterranean to the wild lands of Ethiopia. Even as *Compass* gathered momentum his mind was diverted from relatively easy victories over Italians to the grim, and almost certainly hopeless, task of foiling Hitler in what was now his obvious determination to subdue south-eastern Europe. It was on 13 December 1940 that the Führer issued his directive for operation *Marita*, a drive through Bulgaria into Macedonia and possibly the whole mainland of Greece. At his headquarters in Vienna Field Marshal List now set in train the plans, already well advanced, for a southward thrust by four armoured and fourteen other divisions. Wherever he looked within the vast regions under his command Wavell could see no force capable of taking the shock, and the decisive day of 13 December committed him to one of the most desperate of juggling-acts. We know now that there could be no effective resolution of his dilemma. One of his favourite quotations was General Wolfe's dictum, 'war is an option of difficulties', and the chief question posed by Wavell's handling of an impossible situation is whether, of all the options, his choice was possibly the best.

Among the myths surrounding Wavell's name perhaps the most delusive is the *canard* that he was reluctantly hounded into Greece by an obsessed and obdurate Prime Minister. But though a critical posterity has selected Churchill as scapegoat in respect of many British disasters during the Second World War, for once the facts are indisputable: if responsibility for the tragic expedition to Greece is to be correctly assigned, then Wavell's name must be entered on the charge-sheet. There was much justification for Churchill's bitter outburst to Lord Boothby in 1948: 'They say now that I went to Greece for the wrong reasons. How do they know?' Evidence that has emerged during three subsequent decades demonstrates conclusively that if Churchill was indeed wrong, he was not without companion. If the political decision was taken by the Prime Minister (and endorsed by the Cabinet and the Chiefs of Staff) it was based on and supported by the unquestioning authority of his Commander-in-Chief.

The tap-roots of the disaster ran deep – to Good Friday 1939, when Mussolini invaded Albania and Chamberlain, with the strange bravado that seized him that spring, joined France in a guarantee to Greece and Rumania of armed support in the event of Axis aggression. Here was a political fact whose military consequences could not be honourably evaded – and Wavell's spirit was that of Mowbray in Shakespeare's *King Richard the Second*:

> Mine honour is my life; both grow in one.
> Take honour from me, and my life is done.

During the winter of 1940–41 the menace of operation *Marita* made those consequences stark and plain.

There is an angry assessment of Wavell at this time in Sir Francis de Guingand's *Generals at War* – of which it must be said that though Sir Francis was later able to see things in the large as Montgomery's Chief of Staff, he was only moved from Haifa Staff College to the post of G1 on the Middle East Joint Planning Staff in December 1940. Though he observed much of the Greek imbroglio at first hand, and though he makes many shrewd and just points in criticism of Wavell, his assessment has an intemperate quality which seems excessive in relation to the level of his position and the brevity of his experience. After the war Wavell happened to run into de Guingand at a dinner in Johannesburg. He just tapped him on the chest and remarked, 'There was more in the Greek business than you knew about.' One thing Wavell knew is what Sir Francis overlooked in his repeated proposition that the British kept missing good opportunities to extricate themselves *with honour* from their Greek commitment. A promise made freely in the spring of 1939 still stood, unqualified, in the spring of 1941. The British could certainly have reneged – but with honour? This the watching world understood – perhaps particularly the Americans. So did Wavell. A frank examination of his actions and attitudes during the Balkan crisis, as will be seen in the next chapter, discloses a fallibility of judgement. Yet behind everything there was this beckoning ghost – the promise of 1939. By operation *Marita,* in fact, Hitler effectively called the bluff of the British. How good, now, was their good faith?

These are intangible matters. In any case, on the main issue Wavell was consistently pragmatic: as he thought, realistic. Just before he left England to take up his appointment as Commander-in-Chief in Cairo, he set out for the CIGS on 31 July 1939 the strategy he intended to adopt in the event of war. 'Whether Italy is openly hostile or nominally neutral,' he wrote, 'our only possible counter to the German intention to bring SE Europe under her power is by domination of the Mediterranean at least as complete as in the Great War as early as possible.' Throughout 1940 and early 1941 these twin concepts – the danger of German aggression in the Balkans and the overriding need to maintain command of the Mediterranean – never left his mind, whatever his preoccupations in the Western Desert or in East Africa. This was his fundamental policy: and he continued to defend it until shortly before his death when, in an article for *Army Quarterly* of March 1950, he affirmed:

> I am still sure that my instinct, to fight as far forward as possible in defence of the Middle East, was correct. We did not know then that the Germans would attack Russia. I believed that they were more likely to concentrate on the Middle East, and that we must gain time; we could do this best by fighting well forward.

He was only repeating what he had written to O'Connor in 1945, when from India he commented on the text of the latter's prison-memoir.

> The story of the genesis of the Greek expedition is a very interesting one, which has not yet been told. It was not undertaken because the advance to Tripoli was deemed impossible; but *because of our obligations to our Greek allies,* and also because from the strategical point of view it was judged of the greater importance to maintain a foothold in Europe . . .*[7]

---

* Author's italics.

There is no hint of reluctance here: and it must be remembered that Wavell was writing, in private, to an old friend whom he deeply respected and for whose misfortunes as a prisoner of war he certainly felt a responsibility. He was telling the truth, and in so doing he set down the two principal bases on which his thinking about Greece was founded – a sense of obligation, and a strict calculation of military necessity. No one can censure the first. If he proved to be arguably wrong over the second, well, that was his case.

The crunch of the first pressure on his small resources came even before *Compass* was launched. As early as November 1940 a Cabinet directive started a movement to airfields near Athens of several bomber and fighter squadrons from the Desert Air Force, together with their necessary equipment and ground crews, and a *leitmotiv* for a long *marche funèbre* was announced when Eden, leaving Egypt two days later, signalled to London that 'he and Wavell and Longmore agreed that although the plan involved additional risks in the Western Desert, these must be faced "in view of political commitments to aid Greece" '. By mid November the Army had also dispatched from North Africa over 2000 men and 400 vehicles (from forty different units) to provide engineers, signallers, supply facilities and anti-aircraft defence. But the skies steadily darkened over the Balkans. On 10 January, therefore, the Chiefs of Staff peremptorily instructed Middle East Command that 'His Majesty's Government have decided that it is essential to afford the Greeks the maximum possible assistance with the object of ensuring that they resist German demands by force.' Moreover, their signal specifically authorized the further dispatch, up to prescribed limits, of tanks (both infantry and cruiser), anti-tank and anti-aircraft equipment, two medium regiments of artillery and more RAF squadrons. Though Wavell replied immediately with a blunt warning about the effect of such moves on *Compass* Churchill informed him on the same day, the 10th, that 'nothing must hamper capture of Tobruk but thereafter all operations in Libya are subordinated to aiding Greece'.

Wavell made no demur. On the 13th – even before Tobruk had fallen – he found himself in Athens conferring with the

King of Greece, his Prime Minister, Metaxas, and the Com-mander-in-Chief General Papagos. It seemed as though the future of *Compass* might now be decided in sight of the Acropolis and the bay of Salamis where, so many centuries ago, the Greeks had repelled an earlier invader.

Yet events in war are sometimes decided by a joker in the pack. Churchill on the 10th had informed Wavell that 'we expect and require prompt and active compliance with our decisions and for which we bear full responsibility', and during the Athens conference Wavell pressed home the British offer of aid with absolute loyalty. He knew that if the offer was accepted his position in North Africa would be dangerously weakened, yet he showed no doubt or reluctance in presenting his case to the Greeks who, it might have been supposed, would have welcomed the overtures of a great ally. On the contrary: the cards fell otherwise. Reversing the doctrine *'timeo Danaos et dona ferentes'* – 'I fear the Greeks even when they come with gifts' – Metaxas refused the British offer, outright. Shrewdly noting that the military gifts in Wavell's hands were too few to be significant and that there was no conceivable hope of that major expeditionary force which alone could turn the scales in the Greeks' favour, he decided that a mere British gesture would be worse than nothing. It was more likely to provide the Germans with a specious *casus belli* than to stiffen effectively the Greeks' defences.

Such a response was not irrational: it was the regular reac-tion of weak countries desperately afraid of provoking aggres-sion. In 1939 and 1940 the Belgians passionately persisted in refusing all overtures from Britain and France. The hard-headed Turks, certain that they would never receive adequate aid, consistently rejected all attempts to make them enter the war and thus precipitate a German invasion. So Wavell, accepting Metaxas's rebuff, returned to Cairo and on 18 January sent a careful signal to the CIGS in which, having faithfully argued in Athens the brief from his masters in London, he now pointed to its weakness: the half-measures proposed by the British would probably be useless. Prophe-tically he warned that 'we shall almost inevitably be compelled to send further troops in haste or shall become involved in retreat or defeat'. He therefore reported: 'My conclusion is that we should accept Greek refusal but should make all necessary reconnaissances and preparations of Salonika front without giving any promises to send troops at future date.' The next day he sent another signal: 'Against present opposition I am prepared to continue advance towards Benghazi with present air protection . . . but effect of appearance of German aircraft in Libya remains to be seen.' The Chiefs of Staff concurred.

Thus *Compass* again came into focus although, as O'Connor's memoir recalled, the swelling tumour in the Balkans had already begun to sap his strength. It had also seriously distracted the attention of a Commander-in-Chief who, while directing two widely separated campaigns in Africa, was forced to spend time and energy uselessly elsewhere. Moreover, there was a sting in the tail of Wavell's last communication; for in operation *Mittelmeer* Hitler, around the turn of the year, had moved from Norway *Fliegerkorps* X, complete with all its ancillary equipment, so that by mid January no less than 186 *Luftwaffe* bombers and fighters were established and in action from airfields in Sicily and elsewhere. Their essential function was to deny to the British the Mediterranean seaways:* the beginning, as Churchill said, of 'evil developments' for which the temporary elimination of the aircraft carrier *Illustrious,* during the third week of January, was but a token. But the full impact of *Fliegerkorps* X, and the final stages of the Greek tragedy, belong logically and chronologically to the next chapter. The limelight is now directly on *Compass,* since Metaxas, by his refusal of aid, had for the time being provided Wavell and O'Connor with a certain freedom of manoeuvre.

For O'Connor, unlike the Greeks, a little was enough. Before the fall of Tobruk, as before Bardia, he had alerted 7 Armoured Division to be ready again for the chase, and on 24 January Wavell (having received a signal from Churchill on the previous day which began 'I again send you my most heartfelt congratu-

---

* A substantial detachment, however, was soon operating from Italian airfields in North Africa: a potential new threat for the desert army. The stage by stage arrival of *Fliegerkorps* X in the Mediterranean theatre – on bases stretching from Rhodes through Sicily and Sardinia to Cyrenaica – was tracked by Bletchley with remarkable accuracy. By 26 January GCCS had established the presence of eighty bombers and dive-bombers at the Benina base outside Benghazi.

lations on the third of the brilliant victories which have in a
little more than six weeks transformed the situation in the
Middle East, and have sensibly affected the course of the
whole war'), was now able to signal himself to the CIGS – that
his armour had already surrounded the garrison at Mechili,
100 miles west of Tobruk, and that his forward elements had
pressed to within 20 miles of Derna.

A map instantly reveals the tactical significance of these
advances. Derna lies by the sea, just beyond the point where
the coastline and the coastal route, the Via Balbia, have swung
north in a great loop around the jutting *massif* of the Jebel
Achdar, or Green Mountain. Its defences thus commanded
that single metalled road which, after arching around the Jebel,
runs due south again in conformity with the coastline until it
begins another, but this time westward, curve. Following
thereafter the beach of the Gulf of Sirte, and then keeping
roughly to the shoreline, it reaches at last the famous port of
Tripoli whose capture now seemed to O'Connor not only
desirable but even, if the luck held, just possibly within his
reach. And should he prefer to take an inland route (cutting
somehow across the base of the Green Mountain) the track-
centre of Mechili, amid the wasteland south of the Jebel,
offered its options. There would be many complications – not
least those of supply, of tiring tanks, and of terrain (for both
the broken hill country and the surface inland were formidable
obstacles) – but with single-minded intensity O'Connor now
knew where he meant to go.

For Wavell however everything was, as usual, complicated:
no single course or target presented itself in shining simplicity.
There was a current mandate from London to seize Benghazi,
certainly. The arrival of *Fliegerkorps* X had spurred the interest
of the Chiefs of Staff in what could become a strong air and
naval base. But the *Luftwaffe's* presence had a radiating effect.
It looked as though the Dodecanese, Alexandria, the sea-lines
to Greece and Turkey and even the Canal itself might be
threatened.* On 21 January, therefore, Wavell was told by the
Government that he must be prepared to capture the eastern

---

* By the end of January the *Luftwaffe* was indeed disrupting the Canal traffic by
mining.

islands, particularly Rhodes – that will-o'-the-wisp which throughout the Mediterranean war danced before the strategists' eyes, inviting and unattainable. To get Rhodes Wavell was ordered, once again, to use his own resources and even the reinforcements – in the shape of Commandos in their specially adapted transports – which were due to arrive in the Middle East early in March. So to the problem of *Compass,* East Africa and Greece was added that of mounting amphibious operations with few ships, inadequate air cover and a scratch assault force: moreover, a staff trained in the complexities of such manoeuvres did not exist in Cairo – or in London, for that matter, in early 1941. Wavell's performance at this time must always be judged in the light of these many and incompatible demands made – through the necessities of the day – on his own resilience and inventiveness and the paucity of his means. And then there was Turkey.

For Churchill (with Gallipoli surely in his subconscious) the entry of Turkey on the side of the Allies was one of the great strategic prizes that haunted his imagination throughout the hard first half of the war – and was never grasped. The menace of *Marita* drew him into the dream of a Balkan alliance, stretching from Yugoslavia to Turkey, with which the countries of that theatre would unite with Britain to form a seamless front against the Nazi aggressor. It was a delusive obsession, well illustrated – though out of chronological context – by the message sent by Churchill to the acting Prime Minister of Australia, Mr Fadden, immediately after the military *coup d'état* in Yugoslavia which on 27 March unseated the pro-Fascist Regent Prince Paul.

> When a month ago we decided upon sending an army to Greece it looked rather like a blank military adventure dictated by *noblesse oblige.* Thursday's events in Belgrade show the far-reaching effects of this and other measures we have taken on the whole Balkan situation. German plans have been upset, and *we may cherish renewed hopes of forming a Balkan front with Turkey, comprising about seventy Allied Divisions from the four powers concerned.**

At the Foreign Office Eden shared and perhaps nourished the fantasy. This dream was politically naïve, and based on wildly

* Author's italics.

exaggerated estimates of the quality and capacity of the troops and equipment such an alliance, even if it could be soldered together, would be able to command. Still, the dream existed and there was desperation behind it, since the now universal fear of German intentions was founded not on guesswork, but on accurate and indisputable intelligence.

This lattice-work of manifold threats from the enemy and self-contradictory demands from London, whose shape changed almost daily, forming a criss-cross pattern in Wavell's mind, must be seen in its entirety if one is to appreciate the immense and exhausting pressures to which he was exposed. Nor can one fully comprehend, without such an appreciation, the robust acceptance of risk with which Wavell now endorsed, unhesitatingly, O'Connor's brilliant but perilous plan which produced for *Compass* the final, decisive *coup*.

O'Connor himself was under great strain. In the desert 'command from the front' is always taxing, and O'Connor had driven himself mercilessly. He had also been quite unnecessarily disturbed by interventions on the part of General Wilson and his chief staff officer, Brigadier Galloway. In mid January, while still technically under Wilson as the Commander of British Troops in Egypt, he wrote to Galloway that he had asked Wavell to visit him. 'If he finds he is able to do so, I propose to ask him to relieve me of my command. . . .' And now, at the end of January, Wilson as Military Governor (designate) of Cyrenaica was again trying to get into the act, giving O'Connor instructions which conflicted directly with his own ideas, and O'Connor again exploded. Of course all was papered over, for the understanding between Wavell and O'Connor was complete.'

Yet it was grotesque for a commander like O'Connor, so ardent in action but so gentle in spirit, to have been distracted by petty annoyances involving another general of lesser quality at a time when he himself was advancing from one striking victory to another. Wavell created the situation, and Wavell must bear the responsibility. One of the functions of high command (in which Montgomery, for example, was meticulous) is to establish quite clearly, before an operation begins, the channels and relationships between subordinate generals and their chief.

Wavell allowed this to become blurred in *Compass*. One reason may be that as he started with 'a raid' in mind, and as the operation thereafter developed on an *ad hoc* basis, he never troubled to clarify the command structure: he was in tune with O'Connor, thought Wilson sound enough, and assumed that all was well. Alternatively, he had so much to do that he forgot. But then, as so often during these confused months, one has to ask why his Chief of Staff, Arthur Smith, did not act constructively by noticing that things were awry and drawing the matter to Wavell's attention. A Guards officer loyal to his core, a Christian profound in faith and practice, Arthur Smith perhaps lacked both the vision and the cutting edge which Wavell so needed in his right-hand man.

Suddenly all this was beside the point. By 1 February sufficient evidence had accumulated for O'Connor to feel certain that the Italians were about to abandon not simply Benghazi, but the whole of Cyrenaica. Air reconnaissance revealed masses of transport moving southwards from the port and down the coastal road towards the Gulf of Sirte. Any hope of intercepting this attractive prey depended on immediate action: depended, moreover, on O'Connor's ability to pass a cut-off force at speed over the appallingly rough going at the base of the Jebel Achdar. He was awaiting replacements and reinforcements for his battered tanks and trucks, but there was no time to wait. He decided to act. By chance Dorman-Smith of Wavell's staff had come forward to prepare a report on the unfolding of the offensive since Sidi Barrani. John Connell in his biography gives an evocative description of what followed.

> Early next morning, at O'Connor's urgent request, Dorman-Smith flew to Cairo to see the Commander-in-Chief and get his authority for a rapid advance to intercept the Italian retreat. Wavell saw him that same evening. As Dorman-Smith told the story, all expression drained from Wavell's countenance. To Marshal the pencils on his desk in a parody of parade-ground drill was his manner of doodling. He took them up in handfuls; they formed fours, they formed threes; they were ranked in close order and in open order. From time to time, when Dorman-Smith paused for breath, he observed, 'Yes, Eric, I see.'
>
> At the end he looked up. 'Tell Dick he can go on,' he said, 'and wish him luck from me. He has done well.'

O'Connor had indeed done well, for he had lifted Wavell off the hook. Late on the 29th the CIGS in London had signalled: 'Please tell me urgently date when you hope to capture Benghazi. Information will be kept strictly secret but is required in connection with assistance it may be necessary to give Turkey.' Wavell replied at midday on the 30th with his usual caution '. . . As rough forecast we may capture Benghazi *about the end of February, but this may be optimistic.*'* He added that he hoped to give a more accurate estimate 'next week when we know O'Connor's new plan'. Well, now it was next day: the new plan was daring beyond London's wildest dreams, and he had told O'Connor to get on with it – accepting as a calculated risk the vile going in the Bad Lands which O'Connor's spearheads, weak in equipment and laughably inferior in numbers, would have to negotiate. He had weighed it all up, and placed his trust in his commander on the spot. The scene in the Cairo office on that February evening was one of the most refined examples of Wavell's military judgement.

The result was a minor epic which it would be a pleasure to describe in the glowing colours it deserves, were it not that so many have previously attempted the task. More inhibiting is the knowledge that within a few weeks of the dramatic conclusion of *Compass* everything gained by O'Connor's skill and the courage of his troops would be dissipated by incapacity, error, and an intolerable force of circumstance. Put briefly, therefore, 7 Armoured Division survived the cruel cross-country journey, cut the coast road, stopped the Italian retreat and, desperately out-numbered, broke the enemy's nerve. It was the end of an army. During the whole of *Compass* no less than ten Italian divisions were eliminated, and their surrender produced 130,000 prisoners, 845 guns and some 400 tanks. O'Connor had indeed done well.

All students of military history, except O'Connor himself, would readily agree. But during his imprisonment in Italy, and throughout the post-war decades, the bright quality of his triumph at Beda Fomm had been tarnished for him by the feeling that, if only he had then exercised his initiative power-

* Author's italics.

fully enough, he might have carried the *Compass* operation onward and captured Tripoli. Wavell, who knew the realities, tried to persuade O'Connor after the war that Tripoli was beyond reach. Field Marshal Lord Harding, who during *Compass* was O'Connor's indefatigable chief staff officer, also came to see in retrospect that the hope was vain.[8]

The simple military realities were in themselves adverse. The reinforced garrison of Tripoli was larger than was thought at the time. O'Connor's tanks and transport were war-weary. Even if the shattered morale of the Italians had allowed them to surrender the port, neither the Navy nor the RAF could have protected the convoys necessary to maintain a British force so far to the west – particularly in view of the omnipresent and devastating aircraft of *Fliegerkorps* X. There was not enough spare transport in good condition to sustain a force in Tripoli by the long landward route. So that though O'Connor might have reached Tripoli it is impossible to see how – without one of those miracles which were in short supply in 1941 – he could have survived.

There was, in any case, a *force majeure*. O'Connor went so far as to send Dorman-Smith back to Cairo again to present to Wavell the case for advancing to Tripoli, but when his messenger arrived the point of no return had already been passed. Wavell himself, on the 10th, had sensibly signalled to the CIGS that a small force expeditiously handled might be able to capture Tripoli, though he pointed out that he had not thought the project through and that the naval and air commanders-in-chief might oppose it. The gesture was vain, for on the 12th, the day on which Dorman-Smith reached Cairo, there also arrived a long *Diktat* addressed to Wavell by Churchill himself. The third paragraph stated:

> We should have been content with making a safe flank for Egypt at Tobruk, and we told you that thereafter Greece and/or Turkey must have priority, but that if you could get Benghazi easily and without prejudice to European calls so much the better. We are delighted that you have got this prize three weeks ahead of expectation, but this does not alter, indeed it rather confirms, our previous directive, namely, that your major effort must now be to aid Greece and/or Turkey. This rules out any serious effort against

Tripoli, although minor demonstrations thitherwards would be a useful feint. You should therefore make yourself secure in Benghazi and concentrate all available forces in the Delta in preparation for movement to Europe.

There could be no further argument. A new phase of the war in the Mediterranean was in fact beginning. It would have two dominant themes. The first, as Churchill forecast, was Greece. The second was announced even as the Prime Minister's signal was being studied in Cairo. On 12 February it was not O'Connor who arrived in Tripoli, but Rommel and the leading elements of the Afrika Korps.

# 4

# The Hounds of Spring

When the hounds of spring are on winter's traces,
The mother of months in meadow or plain
Fills the shadows and windy places
With lisp of leaves and ripple of rain. . . .
SWINBURNE, *Atalanta in Calydon*

When Swinburne's *Atalanta* was first published, undergraduates of Oxford could be heard chanting in the High
Street the words of its famous chorus. But this was a paean in
celebration of rebirth and renewal, of promise and of hope. In
1941 spring for Wavell was an augury of disaster: the loss of his
gains in North Africa, the collapse of British authority in the
Mediterranean and, finally, his own displacement. For him the
hounds of spring brought nothing to sing about.

Immediate pressure on Cairo to supply aid to Greece was
relieved, as has been seen, by the refusal of the President of the
Council, General Metaxas, to have anything to do with the
trivial reinforcements offered to him. That pressure was now
renewed. Its strength – leading to the despatch of an expeditionary force, and all that followed – may be said to have
stemmed from two events. On 29 January the recalcitrant
Metaxas died: his successor Koryzis, a man of weaker and
more pliable metal,* had stiffened himself sufficiently by 8
February to confirm that Greece would resist German aggres-
sion *à outrance,* that British help would be requested when the
Germans crossed into Bulgaria, and that it would be opportune
to consider whether the scale of British assistance would in fact
be enough to hold the Germans and encourage Yugoslavia and
Turkey to join the common cause. The British Military Mission
in Athens passed on this overture to Wavell, who quickly
signalled to London his estimate of what could be spared.

* His response to the German invasion was suicide.

The second event was a message to Wavell from Churchill, on 12 February, informing him that Eden and Dill, the CIGS, were coming to Cairo 'to give the very best chance of concerting all possible measures, both diplomatic and military, against the Germans in the Balkans'. In fact Eden as Foreign Secretary received virtually plenipotentiary powers to achieve what his personal brief from the Cabinet described as 'the sending of speedy succour to Greece against attack by Germany'. In retrospect it may be doubted whether this was the ideal mission for a man consumed by vanity, who believed that war was the conduct of Foreign Office policy by other means. It was these two developments, however, that redressed the stage for a Greek tragedy.

By now there was a more definite appreciation in Athens, in London and in Cairo of the gathering German menace. Through rumours and reports from many sources the Greeks formed their own picture. In London the intelligence was cast-iron. Regular deciphering at Bletchley of *Luftwaffe* signals disclosed a steady transfer of enemy strength from the West to the Balkan region. The Joint Intelligence Committee on 28 January affirmed that 4000 German Air Force and 1500 anti-aircraft personnel had already entered Bulgaria to establish bases, as well as signals and airfield units, while 400 aircraft were due for transfer there. Army intelligence was less sure, since the Army Enigma was more difficult to read.* But fears already well-based were sustained by a large over-estimate on the part of Military Intelligence in London, which reckoned that by 13 February the German build-up in Rumania would reach twenty-three divisions   the correct figure being nine! In the circumstances, however, it was an error on the right side, and these indications had been supported earlier in the month by a timely cryptographic *coup*. The Enigma cipher for German rail traffic in the Balkans was suddenly broken, and so, the Intelligence History records, 'As early as 6 and 7 February a massive movement by rail of GAF ammunition, fuel and other stores to destinations in southwest Bulgaria, on the axis of advance through the Rupel

* *Luftwaffe* traffic, however, was now, as ever, an abundant source of information about Army matters.

Pass to Salonika, was identified from the Enigma traffic.'[1] This was an arrow pointing to Greece.

Apart from the new climate of opinion in Athens, it was decrypts like these, combined with evidence from Secret Service and diplomatic sources, that led Churchill and the Defence Committee on 11 February to order Wavell (in the message quoted at the end of the last chapter) to forget Tripoli and give priority to preparations for assisting Greece. It was on this decisive day, also, that Eden and Dill were dispatched to the Middle East. But the question is, how much was Wavell himself in the picture?

He had not lacked warnings. As early as 10 January the Chiefs of Staff had advised him that a German drive from Bulgaria to Salonika might soon be expected, with three divisions and three or four more as a follow-up, plus some 200 dive-bombers. Wavell had then replied that he trusted the Chiefs of Staff would 'consider most urgently whether enemy's move is not bluff ' – an attempt, in fact, to disperse the British forces now so far forward in North Africa. This sceptical mood persisted in Cairo certainly until mid February: the too-frequent response of commanders and staffs who, while involved in a campaign, are inclined to discount intelligence which might lead to diversions from what, in their eyes, is the main front. Nevertheless, by 19 February Wavell had a clear view. On that day he wrote an appreciation for his chief intelligence officer, Brigadier Shearer (headed with his favourite quotation from General Wolfe: 'War is an option of difficulties') in which he argued that to let Germany over-run Greece 'would lose the British almost as much prestige as a military defeat' and ended: 'To sum up, we have a difficult choice, but I think we are more likely to be playing the enemy's game by remaining inactive than by taking action in the Balkans. Provided that conversations with the Greeks show that there is a good chance of establishing a front against the Germans with our assistance, I think we should take it.'[2]

Significantly, Wavell composed his appreciation *before* the arrival of Eden and Dill, whose flying boat had been held up all along the route, so that they did not touch down on the Nile in Cairo until late on the night of the 19th. It was his own conclusion, reached on the basis of intelligence locally available plus whatever had been fed out from London. If he had known all that was known in Whitehall, it seems certain that his mind would have cleared earlier. But we now realize that the service of Ultra intelligence to Cairo in early 1941 was of a most rickety character. Compared with the smoothly-running systems enjoyed, say, by Montgomery and Alexander at a later stage the provision and handling of Ultra for Wavell was more rudimentary.

Until mid March 1941 the War Office and the Air Ministry generally supplied the Middle East with a digest of what Bletchley extracted from the German and Italian signals. There was no arrangement, such as existed later, for the direct transmission from Bletchley to the Commanders-in-Chief in Egypt of *all* relevant Ultra material. An obsessive concern for security prevailed. Even after 13 March, when an embryonic system was introduced, the material from Bletchley was paraphrased before transmission to Cairo and even the Director of the Combined Bureau Middle East, who was responsible for distributing the intelligence to a very restricted group, was not told until May that its origin was the Enigma traffic. Nor was it until August, well after Wavell's departure, that a Special Liaison Unit was activated in Cairo to receive Ultra direct from Bletchley and to look after distribution and security, as would later become the normal practice.

Thus Wavell in February can have had only a general idea of the wealth of information accumulating in London about the German build-up. Nevertheless, by the 19th he had already settled in his heart for going to Greece. The detailed scenario which Eden and Dill could present from their special knowledge must therefore have had a tremendously confirmatory effect. Certainly from this point onward it is difficult to identify any qualms or hesitation on Wavell's part. Nor, as has already been indicated, did he betray any in retrospect. The most telling evidence of his undeviating faith is contained in a letter which he wrote to Liddell Hart on 13 May 1948, a private and confidential communication to an old, respected friend:[3]

It was not, I believe, nearly such a desperate military undertaking as events made it appear, and I am quite sure that from the political and psychological point of view we were right to undertake it. And I believe that on the whole it may have had a favourable effect on the war. I have written frankly to you, but only for your private eye.

In England Dill had felt many reservations, but in the atmosphere of Cairo and Athens these seem to have dissolved,* at least to the point of his accepting the necessity of an expedition even though his forebodings remained. Eden's performance throughout can only be compared with that of a self-important *maestro* seeking to wave a magic wand over the scene and produce political combinations which would resound to his credit. Wavell was committed, in essence, before the other two arrived, and his convictions were strengthened by their presence. It was perhaps not to be expected, therefore, that the anxious Cabinet at home would receive from such a group the objective advice on which to form a judgement: nor did it. The process from now on became one of carrying Britain, Australia and New Zealand into Greece on false pretences.

Indeed, for those who still believe that Churchill 'forced' Wavell into Greece it is worth while to compare the attitudes in Whitehall and in Cairo on 20 February, the day when the trio first assembled for discussion. In Cabinet Churchill spoke with magnanimity, saying that if the Greeks stood up to the Germans Britain must give the fullest help. But if the Germans offered attractive peace terms, the Greeks *could not be blamed for accepting and indeed their acceptance must not be viewed too tragically:*† Britain would have done her duty. At the same time a signal was on its way from the Prime Minister to Eden saying, quite specifically: 'Do not consider yourself obligated to a Greek enterprise if in your hearts you feel it will only be another Norwegian fiasco. *If no good plan can be made please say so.*' No 'forcing' there.

Yet this message crossed with one from Eden reporting on

---

* 'Dill told the VCIGS that he had gone to the Middle East with the firm idea that forces sent to Greece would inevitably be lost, and that instead Turkey should be supported; but after hearing the Commanders-in-Chief on the spot he was satisfied that the only hope of saving the Balkans from being devoured piecemeal was to go to Greece with all the forces that could be spared as soon as it could be done.' Charles Cruickshank, *Greece 1940–41*, p. 107. The PRO reference is PREM 3 206/3, f.173.

† Author's italics.

the day's conference with Dill, Wavell, Cunningham and Longmore which stated, in effect, that a plan had already been made! It described arrangements for guarding the desert flank in Cyrenaica, specified the divisions and brigades which Wavell could produce for Greece, and noted without undue alarm the problems of shipping and administration. 'My own conclusions,' Eden reported, 'which General Dill and Commanders-in-Chief share, is that in the immediate future assistance to the Greeks, who are fighting and threatened, must have first call on resources.' In a further signal next day he repeated '. . . though campaign is a daring venture, we are not without hope that it might succeed to the extent of halting the Germans before they overrun all Greece'.

It is essential to grasp the tone of these exchanges. They coloured all subsequent considerations. A scrutiny of relevant Cabinet papers makes it clear that right up to the launching of the expedition Churchill and his advisers, though driven by a sense of duty and indeed of practical necessity towards helping Greece, were nevertheless haunted by unresolved doubts and reservations. Yet always one finds them drawing comfort from a feeling that 'the men on the spot' say all will be well: that the offer to admit that no good plan is possible has not been taken up. Moreover, one of Churchill's prerequisites for a Greek expedition was an assurance that in the western desert the flank would remain secure. After Eden's first report that security was never doubted. Wavell had underwritten it. It never entered further into the debate. In his memoirs Churchill's right-hand man, General Ismay, observed of the Chiefs of Staff at this time that 'they took it for granted that the security of the desert flank of Egypt was receiving first priority, and that the despatch of help to Greece would in no way prejudice that security. If they had had any doubt on that score, it is pretty certain that they would have advised against the enterprise.' Yet all of these assumptions, both spoken and unspoken, both about Greece and about Africa, would shortly be blown to pieces. And they were assumptions based, to a large degree, on Wavell's military judgement.

The scene is about to shift to Athens, where on 22 February Eden and the service commanders arrived for a secret conference in the royal palace at Tatoi. Before departing, however, Wavell had taken another step towards commitment by writing, on the 21st, to General Wilson and informing him that he was to command the Greek expedition under consideration. Can Wavell really have believed what he wrote? 'You . . . with your tactical and strategical knowledge and the prestige of your recent successes are undoubtedly the man for the job and it will greatly relieve my mind to know that you are there. . . .' What was really wanted, it seems, was a good front. Private information from the man who had truly been achieving recent successes, Sir Richard O'Connor, suggests that he was the first choice for command, but was set aside on the grounds that (brilliant fighting soldier though he was) his quiet style and short stature would impress the Greeks less than the towering bulk of Jumbo Wilson.

At Tatoi a basis for discussion was laid (and perhaps some Greek blackmail introduced) by a formal statement on the part of Koryzis which announced that Greece would fight to the end at the side of Britain, and would resist a German invasion – if necessary, alone.* Had the British team felt any overwhelming doubt, on military grounds, about moving into Greece this noble declaration would have caused grave discomfort, for in the minds of all of them the moral obligation to support Greece was a prime factor and the statement, whether so intended or not, was an implicit appeal to the British sense of honour. If he had felt compelled to present a professional case for not sending an expeditionary force Wavell, in particular, would have been torn by a conflict of obligations. However, since there were no such doubts the rest of the meeting was concerned with practicalities.

The central question was, where to stand and fight? *At the time*† General Papagos, the Greek commander, appeared to

---

* King George insisted that this declaration should be made privately by Koryzis to Eden before the conference opened, so that the British Government would realize that the Greek decision to fight had been made *before* it was known whether Britain would send help. Still, whether intentionally or unintentionally, the element of moral blackmail existed.

† The British official record (in F9 371/33145) of the final plenary session at Tatoi on 22 February 1941 registers a firm mutual assent on this vital point. Papagos in his *Battle of Greece* is evasive. The official Greek record of the Tatoi conference has vanished.

accept the force of military logic, which dictated that the exposed port of Salonika and the Macedonian hinterland were untenable against German divisions pouring through the Rupel Pass from Bulgaria and *Luftwaffe* bombers working from established bases. So a general agreement was reached, as it seemed, to concentrate further south on the so-called Aliakmon Line – a purely topographical expression – which ran for seventy miles north-west from the Olympus range to the Yugoslav frontier: high wild country split only by four passes or valleys one of which, that of the river Aliakmon, gave the Line its name. It might be made into a defensible position *if* the British got there in time and *if*, as was agreed, Papagos pulled back his divisions from Macedonia.

Wavell, as his biographer recalled, took notes during the conference, 'in pencil on sheets of palace writing paper stamped with the Greek crown'.

Line to be held [he wrote] depends largely on Yugoslav attitude. If Germans attack, offensive operations in Albania must stop. We must therefore establish a line behind which Albanian front can withdraw. If YS do not play, Aliakmon is only possible line and all troops in E Macedonia must be withdrawn to it.

Eden in his memoirs stated that 'I emphasized that it was important that we and the Greeks should take our decisions independently of the attitude of Turkey and Yugoslavia', but this was a pipe-dream, since a German thrust through Yugoslavia would gravely threaten the northern flank of the Aliakmon Line. Thus the contingency of 'the Yugoslav attitude' could not simply be waved away, and circumstances drove Eden into a move which – as will be seen – had an unfortunate after-effect: he offered to send a staff officer to Belgrade to feel out the ground.

Nevertheless, in his report to the Prime Minister of 24 February Eden confirmed that agreement had been reached with the Greek Government on all points, and added, 'We are all convinced that we have chosen the right course, and as the eleventh hour has already struck felt sure that you would not wish us to delay for detailed reference home.' It was not the fault of Wavell, but of the plenipotentiary Foreign Secretary, that what in effect happened at Tatoi was a committal of

Australian and New Zealand units to a desperate venture without detailed reference to *their* home governments. (Dominion troops bulked large in the proposed expeditionary force.) This was a *gaffe* which it would take all Churchill's rhetoric and not a few white lies to overcome: in performing this distasteful task, he was constantly misled by the current of optimism flowing from his advisers in the Middle East.

The Prime Minister and the Chiefs of Staff endorsed the Tatoi agreement with the signal 'while being under no illusions, we all send you the order "Full steam ahead!".' But in fact they were deluded. The agreement rested on a series of presuppositions most of which proved to be false. Even though in due course the Dominion governments, after much heart-searching, authorized the use of their troops, the expeditionary force was never able to occupy and fortify the Aliakmon Line as Wavell envisaged. The Greeks, as will be seen, never fell back from Macedonia.* The only result of Eden's approach to the Yugoslavs was a shrouded message, on the 27th, conveyed to him by the Yugoslav Ambassador in Ankara, that in the circumstances Belgrade could not 'adopt a definite attitude'.

As for the Turks, to whose capital Eden and Dill had now repaired, they represented the greatest presupposition of all. It was certainly hoped by Churchill and his Foreign Secretary that commitment to Greece would bring them nearer to or even into the war. (While Eden was in Ankara Churchill wrote to Smuts, on the 28th, 'We have taken a grave and hazardous decision to sustain the Greeks and try and make a Balkan Front.') Such, anyway, was the object of Eden's visit which proved, predictably, abortive. In an article on 'The British Expedition to Greece, 1941,' published in the *Army Quarterly* in 1950, Wavell wrote:

The Turks entirely approved of our decision to support Greece

* There was a genuine problem of local morale, but this should have been ventilated and taken into account at Tatoi. A week previously the commander of the Eastern Macedonian army had written to Papagos: 'The Greek army and people are convinced as a result of propaganda, films etc., that this line is strongly fortified . . . its capture by the enemy without serious resistance would have a disastrous effect on the morale of both the army and the public'.

but would not agree to commit themselves in action. I suppose they were wise from their point of view and possibly also from ours in the long run. They were, in fact, in no state to undertake an offensive war, and were in some apprehension that they themselves might be attacked.

Even at the time, Wavell knew that this must be so. If his long experience as Commander-in-Chief Middle East had not disclosed to him the realities of Turkish self-interest (for there had been many earlier comings and goings between Cairo and Ankara) he now had first-hand evidence. There was a British Mission actually working in Turkcy as a 'liaison staff' at the time of the Greek negotiations. Its members were unlikely to be fooled. General Sir James Marshall–Cornwall, at its head, was a qualified Turkish interpreter who after 1918 had spent two years as the British member of the Thracian Boundary Commission. The air member, Air Vice-Marshal Elmhirst, had served as Air Attaché in Ankara from 1937 to 1939. The staff officer was Wavell's former ADC, Bernard Fergusson. The autobiographies of Marshall–Cornwall (unpublished) and of Fergusson (published as *The Trumpet in the Hall*) make plain that the mission had no illusions about Turkish reluctance to become belligerent. Fergusson, who before Eden's visit to Ankara had attended all Marshall–Cornwall's discussions with the Turkish Commander-in-Chief, summed up the Mission's view: 'We all knew that the Turks were sensibly refusing to be bounced off the fence on which they were sitting.' (Sir Thomas Elmhirst has confirmed this to the author.) And Marshall–Cornwall, in his private memoir, registers that his first return from Ankara to Cairo occurred on 19 February, the day that Eden and Dill arrived, and that he had 'a long talk to Wavell'.

It must therefore be assumed that when Wavell advocated at Tatoi an expedition to Greece he did so on a strict assessment of the possibilities of an Anglo–Greek defence *within Greece itself*. He clearly looked for little from Yugoslavia and, on the evidence just quoted, it is barely conceivable that he expected the Turks would act like Blücher at the coming Waterloo. (At a meeting in the Embassy in Cairo on 15 March, when his troops were already committed in Greece, Wavell turned down a proposal from Eden for a second visit to Ankara. 'I believe,' he said, 'that Turkey has so little offensive power that she would be a liability, not an asset, if she entered the war at this stage. And even if the Turks were to come in, we have nothing to spare for them.'[4]

But there were liabilities closer at hand. On 2 March Eden and Dill, returning to Athens, were staggered to discover that in spite of the Tatoi conference Papagos had issued no orders for withdrawing troops from Macedonia – or from Albania, for that matter. Yet on the previous day Bulgaria had joined the Axis, and on the 2nd the German 12th Army moved south across the Bulgarian frontier. The threat was now unmistakable, but the Greeks were already weaker by a self-inflicted wound. A series of hectic discussions during the night between Eden, Dill, Koryzis and Papagos produced more heat than light. Papagos, who advanced argument after desperate argument for holding his troops in Macedonia and even thrusting British troops so far forward, was to maintain later that the Tatoi agreement had depended on establishing the attitude of Yugoslavia and Turkey – thus profiting from the convenient escape clause which Eden's proposal to send a staff officer to Belgrade had provided. But in his biography John Connell noted that 'Wavell held, until his death, that this was certainly not the British understanding. The evidence of his own notes at the time . . . sustain this contention.'

In any event, there was a crisis. After two more days of intense debate a military agreement was finally reached, signed by Dill and Papagos, whereby the British would occupy the Aliakmon Line as soon as possible while the Greeks, though retaining three divisions forward in Macedonia, would assemble in the Line their main force in the east.* This was a fatal compromise. Still, a full report was sent by Eden and Dill to Churchill on the 5th, which they summed up by saying 'our military advisers did not consider it by any means a hopeless proposition to check and hold the German

---

* The reaction of the King, who disapproved of Papagos's tergiversations, was withering. According to the British record, 'His Majesty the King said that General Papagos, *now that he had decided to face the Germans,* would do it with the same determination whatever the troops available and whatever plan was adopted.'

advance on this line [the Aliakmon], which is naturally strong, with few approaches.' The chief military adviser was, of course, Wavell.

There are two relevant comments on this compact. First, it was made entirely, and voluntarily, by 'the men on the spot', against the background of the permissive message Churchill sent to Eden on his arrival in Athens: 'I should like you so to handle matters in Greece that if upon final consideration of all the factors . . . you feel that there is not even a reasonable hope, you should still retain power to liberate Greeks from any bargain and at the same time liberate ourselves.' Instead, the bargain had been re-affirmed: and in sealing it with the promise of an expeditionary force including Australian and New Zealand troops Eden for a second time – and this time with firm commitment – had acted without the proper authority of the Dominion Governments.

'A marked change,' Churchill not surprisingly wrote, 'now came over our views in London.' The worst fears of the Chiefs of Staff had been realized and because of Greek intransigence, they reckoned, 'the hazards of the enterprise have considerably increased'. Churchill forwarded their detailed and pessimistic appreciation to Eden next day, the 6th, repeating that 'we must liberate Greeks from feeling bound to reject a German ultimatum' and observing: 'We do not see any reason for expecting success, except that of course we attach great weight to opinions of Dill and Wavell.'

The critical significance of those opinions for the War Cabinet became plain within twenty-four hours. During the 6th a meeting was convened in Cairo to review *Lustre* (as the Greek expedition was code-named) in the light of London's reactions. Sir Thomas Elmhirst was present. He recalled:

About the decision to start. I was at the meeting in Wavell's office in Cairo (I was called in by Eden as an expert on Balkan air forces: I had just been to Ankara and Athens with him). At the meeting was Wavell, definitely presiding in his chair behind his desk, the rest of us, Arthur Smith, Dill, Eden and his Private Secretary (Bob Dixon), Longmore (or Tedder or both), the Admiral, A. B. Cunningham, and myself. When all had had their say Eden said to Wavell, 'It is a soldier's business, it is for you to say.' Wavell's

reply was, 'War is an option of difficulties. We go.' I walked away
from the meeting with Dill (we had been to Athens and Ankara
together). His gloomy remark was, 'I am afraid there will be a lot
of bloody noses this spring in The Aegean.'[5]

During the evening Eden reported this considered verdict to
Churchill:

> Chief of Imperial General Staff and I, in consultation with the
> three Commanders-in-Chief, have this afternoon re-examined
> the question. We are unanimously agreed that, despite the heavy
> commitments and grave risks which are undoubtedly involved,
> especially in view of our limited naval and air resources, the right
> decision was taken in Athens.

It is fair to say that by this signal the hands of the Government
in London were tied. Churchill in his memoirs honourably
declared that 'I take full responsibility for the eventual decision, because I am sure I could have stopped it all if I had been
convinced.'

But Eden's signal produced precisely the opposite conviction in the minds of both the Prime Minister and the Chiefs of
Staff. In a rapidly developing situation, with German forces on
the move, how in fact could they resist what Churchill called
the 'steadfastly expressed opinion of Commanders-in-Chief
on the spot'? On the 7th, therefore, he advised Eden that the
Cabinet, accepting full responsibility, authorized him 'to proceed with the operation'.

Churchill was now, in fact, in a false and delicate position.
Early in the day he had sent a signal to Eden warning him that
the Dominion governments would have to be persuaded that
'Dill, Wavell, and other Commanders-in-Chief are convinced
that there is a reasonable fighting chance' and adding 'in your
stresses, so far, you have given us few facts or reasons on their
authority which can be presented to these Dominions as justifying the operation on any grounds but *noblesse oblige*. A
precise military appreciation is indispensable.'

Such an appreciation never reached London. The Cabinet
bought operation *Lustre,* it might be said, 'sight unseen' on the
basis of broad but not fully itemized conclusions from 'the
men on the spot'. Apart from the grave fact that *Lustre* was
permitted to be launched, Churchill himself was trapped

unwittingly into prevarication and misrepresentation. For example, a dominant theme throughout the whole debate over Greece was the question of American public opinion if Britain failed in her obligations. On 10 March Churchill proudly reported to Roosevelt that 'we are sending the greater part of the Army of the Nile to Greece' and stated specifically that Wavell and Dill 'believe we have a good fighting chance'. He did not then realize that the decision he was communicating to the President had been formed on the wrong advice. Again, during the Cabinet meeting on the 7th which authorized *Lustre,* the Australian Prime Minister, Robert Menzies, was present. Menzies, a world away from his own seat of government, had a lonely responsibility for a decision involving Australian troops. He expressed serious and well-founded doubts. Churchill silenced him by saying that a full military appreciation supporting the conclusions they had already received was on its way. Yet that appreciation never arrived.

From the beginning to the end of the *Lustre* story Wavell's name re-appears like a *leitmotiv.* It was indeed proper that the main factor affecting the Cabinet's decision should have been the judgement of a Commander-in-Chief with such a long experience in the Middle East Theatre and with the recent achievements in Africa to his credit. But can that judgement be upheld?

There are those who maintain that *Lustre* should never have been mounted and that Greece, in effect, should have been left to her fate. At moments even Churchill, as he anxiously revolved the pros and cons, drifted in that direction. One must have a point of view, so it must be stated unequivocally that both honour and expediency summoned Britain to Greece in 1941. The appeal of honour was felt by all those responsibly concerned with decision. From the point of view of expediency, it must simply be asserted that Britain's status in the Middle East, already so vulnerable, could hardly have been preserved if the Germans had been allowed to sweep down to the Parthenon and the Peloponnese unopposed, while a revulsion in American public opinion would have encouraged Roosevelt's Chiefs of Staff, already highly dubious about the value of Britain's involvement in the Mediterranean Theatre, to recommend a reduction in the flow to the Middle East of armaments which they so acutely needed themselves. This did not happen: but one must ask in retrospect how the restoration of the British position, up to Alamein and beyond, could conceivably have been attained without that constant flood of American equipment and supplies. Wavell was right in telling Liddell Hart that 'from the political and psychological point of view' *Lustre* was justifiable.

But from the military? Hindsight follows a clear beam, indicating that the only defensible basis for *Lustre* would have been a Cabinet decision, founded on accurate information from the Commanders-in-Chief in Cairo, that the expedition must be indeed despatched, but as an obligatory sacrifice, since no hope of success in the field could be entertained. Because Wavell offered hope Churchill and his colleagues, misled themselves, both seduced the Dominion governments and presented Roosevelt with the wrong picture. Yet the only terms on which *Lustre* could be properly undertaken were as a calculated act of duty and despair, not because of even the most minimal expectation of military success.

Wavell was not denied the option of bringing this home to the Cabinet. As has been seen, Churchill consistently gave Eden and his service colleagues the opportunity of saying that no good plan could be made. Even at the last, a military appreciation was requested – but not forwarded. Yet Wavell would have always been within his rights as a Commander-in-Chief in a theatre of war if he had signalled to London that on military grounds *Lustre* looked hopeless, but that as there might well be overriding political grounds for the expedition he awaited instructions.* There is a precise analogy. When Eisenhower faced the alternative of making for Berlin or driving eastwards for Leipzig, he preferred Leipzig, reporting to the Combined Chiefs of Staff that a move towards Berlin would be militarily unsound. Nevertheless he added:

* 'The main point is that *you* should make it quite clear what risks are involved if a course of action is forced upon you which, from the military point of view, is undesirable. You may even find it necessary, in the extreme case, to dissociate yourself from the consequences.' Dill to Auchinleck, on his taking over from Wavell, 26 June 1941.

I am the first to admit that war is waged in pursuance of political aims, and if the Combined Chiefs of Staff should decide that the Allied effort to take Berlin outweighs purely military considerations in this theatre, I would cheerfully readjust my plans and my thinking so as to carry out such an operation.[6]

That was a model use of a Commander-in-Chief's prerogative which Wavell never appears to have considered. On the contrary, the documentary evidence that he accepted the military viability of *Lustre* is irrefutable.

In fact both Wavell's unchanging view about *Lustre* and, more importantly, his awareness of the rights and duties of a Commander-in-Chief in the field may be demonstrated by a single short quotation. During his ABDA Command in Java in 1942 the question arose as to whether the Australian forces returning from the Middle East should be diverted to his theatre. He wrote to London in terms which allow no doubt.

Immediate problem is destination of Australian Corps. If there seemed good chance of establishing corps in island and fighting Japanese on favourable terms I should unhesitatingly recommend risks should be taken as I did in matter of aid to Greece years ago. *I then thought that we had good fighting chance of checking German invasion and in spite results still consider risk was justifiable. In present instance I must recommend that I consider risk unjustifiable from tactical and strategical point of view. I fully recognise political considerations involved.*★

As one reads those simple sentences the myth that Churchill forced Wavell into Greece against his will dissolves. But why did he not send a similar signal about *Lustre?*

Since Wavell was not a lightweight, but a mature commander with an exceptional width of experience in operations, and since his optimistic assessment of *Lustre's* possibilities was not a snap judgement, but one reached gradually and then persistently maintained, it is reasonable to put hindsight on one side and to consider factors which were or should have been evident *at the time,* and which ought to have persuaded him that – at least militarily – *Lustre* was a forlorn hope. Some might say that there is no point in pursuing the matter: the British had a duty to go to Greece, anyway, and Wavell merely supplied the wrong reason for their arrival. But War Cabinets

★ Author's italics.

should not finally authorize for the wrong reason an expedition about whose outcome they and their Chiefs of Staff have been consistently dubious; yet Wavell's stance was unquestionably a main influence in driving Churchill and his men to undertake in good faith an enterprise which, if undertaken at all, should have been endorsed by a clear-sighted Cabinet in full possession of the actual, the attainable and the utterly discouraging facts. So it is fair to ask, what were those facts and why did Wavell disregard or discount them?

1 The pivot of *Lustre* was the exposed flank in the Western Desert. As early as January, Churchill laid down that the security of this flank was a pre-condition for expeditionary aid to Greece. He and the Chiefs of Staff were thereafter lulled by Wavell into assuming that the flank was firm. And yet, as the next chapter discloses in detail, within a brief space Rommel and the Afrika Korps proved that this 'firm' flank was no more than a house of cards. Without pre-empting the next chapter it is possible to be summary – for the relevant facts were certainly not invisible at the time – and to say that Wavell's misjudgment in respect of his ability to maintain a secure flank in the desert was disastrous.

2 It was obvious at Tatoi that Papagos, if not his King, was fearful of taking any step that might provide the Germans with a *casus belli* and precipitate an invasion. This was, of course, the attitude of an ostrich. But often, in the history of war, commanders have had to deal with allies who wanted to ignore unwelcome truths in the hope that they might miraculously disappear. Even though Wavell's conference notes suggest that the Greek promise to withdraw from Macedonia to the Aliakmon Line seemed credible, it was an essential condition, on which even the remotest possibility for *Lustre* depended. Why was the agreement not treated more sceptically? Why was the promised withdrawal not monitored? The Tatoi date is 22 February. Why was it not until 2 March, when Eden and Dill arrived in Athens, that they discovered the truth and summoned Wavell post-haste from Cairo? The answer is simple.

Throughout the whole proceedings, from the early

negotiations to the actual arrival of the *Lustre* contingents, the British treated the Greeks with kid gloves. This was partly a consequence of Churchill's re-iterated warning that undue pressure must not be applied, that the Greeks must be free to make terms with Hitler, and so on. It was almost certainly a consequence, too, of Eden's plenipotentiary role. The atmosphere within which everything was conducted was more that of the Foreign Office than of the War Office: political and diplomatic considerations were paramount, the mirage of 'a Balkan front' danced invitingly, and thus though hostilities were so near – and could be seen to be so near – a ruthless concentration on military necessities was subordinated to preserving 'good relations'. This delicacy may well be compared with the merciless German pressure, first diplomatic and then military, on the Balkan states.

One fact was nevertheless established. On 24 February Miles Reid of the GHQ Liaison Regiment was allowed by the Greek General Staff, who had previously resisted such intrusions, to carry out in plain clothes a reconnaissance of the Macedonian front. He reported back to Dill and Arthur Smith in Athens that once the Rupel Pass entry from Bulgaria was forced, the remaining territory north-east of the Aliakmon Line could not be defended – and that the Greeks, anyway, had prepared no defence.[7] Thus Wavell had every ground for ensuring from the start that a withdrawal so critical for *Lustre* was faithfully executed. Still more had he justification, once it was known that the withdrawal had not occurred, for advising that on military grounds no hope for the expedition could be offered. In neither case did he act.

3  This disregard for the obvious is characteristic of the vein of amateurishness and *dolce far niente* which runs through the whole *Lustre* story. When General Wilson arrived in Athens he was kept in purdah for weeks, lurking in the British Legation under the name of Mr Watt: the theory being that Greece's present neutrality must not be damaged. Yet in that city of sharp eyes and quick tongues his unmistakable bulk had often appeared in press photographs of the African campaign, and baggage marked Sir H. Maitland Wilson was to be seen in the Legation.[8] Meanwhile the advance elements

of W Force, as the *Lustre* expedition was named, were arriving – leaderless. Wilson's chief staff officer, Brigadier Galloway, was still in temporary charge of Crete. So when the Australians' commander, General Blamey, reported for orders, a relatively lowly Major (though a future Major-General) called David Belchem – the GSO2 or Operations Staff Officer on Wilson's headquarters – had to sit up half the night concocting for him the directive which common practice required that he should receive.[9] To apply a familiar expression, this is not the way to run an army.

When Belchem himself disembarked at the port of Athens, Piraeus, he noticed two German officers on the quay, in uniform, busily taking notes. And indeed it was the case that since no state of war yet existed the German Embassy, well staffed, continued in action – and continued to monitor and report to Berlin on the arrival of W Force. The accuracy of this reporting was actually known in London by 15 March, when Bletchley deciphered an estimate sent to Berlin by the German Military Attaché in Athens. Including deductions from the *Luftwaffe* reconnaissance flights, the Attaché reckoned W Force at 50,000 to 60,000 (the true figure being 58,000) and the RAF presence at 70 aircraft (the true figure being 80). As the fact of these reconnaissances, whether dockside or airborne, was common knowledge, it is difficult to explain why Wavell, against Churchill's wishes, insisted that no announcement should be made about the landing of British forces in Greece. An earlier inhabitant of Athens, the comic dramatist Aristophanes, invented a good name for such a state of affairs. He called it Cloud-cuckooland.

4  Thanks to Ultra and other sources a great deal was known about the German build-up, yet intelligence about the Greeks themselves, whether in terms of military capability, or of administrative resources, or of the effect of their terrain on communications, was singularly limited. How was it, for example, that only on 6 March, with W Force already in transit, did Wilson learn from Papagos that merely two trains a day would be available for his command by 8 March, that they could be increased to six per day by 15

March, but that then there would be no more coal: nor, as the Greeks needed them all, would there be any ambulance trains for the British? Undoubtedly the Greeks resented the size of the Military Mission sent out from England under Major-General Heywood, and for this and other obvious reasons, including a fear of provoking Hitler, they were uncooperative. But undoubtedly, too, the Mission itself was neither sparkling nor sufficiently energetic.

This intelligence vacuum was another recognizable fact which Wavell simply tolerated. The contrast between the meticulous preparation for *Compass* and that for *Lustre* is striking. When the troops of W Force arrived in Greece they entered *terra incognita*. If we compare the preliminary arrangements for *Lustre* with those of the German command the contrast is even more painful. Its carefully thought-out *Marita* plan was executed phase by phase, smoothly and efficiently: even when Hitler made his impromptu decision to eliminate Yugoslavia, the German staff-work was so sound that an annihilating assault was organized virtually overnight. For many years Wavell had advocated and exploited the benefits of good reconnaissance and good intelligence. This paucity of information about the actual military capacity of his new ally and the terrain over which his troops would have to fight must have been evident to his acute mind. Why, as a commander sending his men into action, did he not press insistently for the essential intelligence that Wilson and W Force required? Why, moreover, did he not advise London that the military feasibility of *Lustre* was gravely impaired by this lack of information and by the Greeks' inhibitions? Churchill and the Chiefs of Staff would have understood. They had been there before. In 1940 the refusal of the French to co-operate or to supply information about their own capability or intentions had been a fatal impediment for another British expeditionary force.

5 The intervention of powerful German armoured divisions was expected and the phased build-up of the *Luftwaffe* in the Balkans was known. On the British side, Longmore made it only too plain that the RAF in Greece would be lamentably weak. Just one armoured brigade was sent to Greece, its

tanks already feeble: indeed, during the fighting more British tanks became casualties from mechanical faults than from enemy action. These were not veiled mysteries: they were palpable facts. How did Wavell persuade himself that this scratch and impoverished force could make a stand against Germans whose ability, weapon-strength and *Blitzkrieg* assurance had been demonstrated in Poland, in Norway and in France? How, with few aircraft and frail tanks and a miscellany of troops whose only real strength was in their spirit, did he find it possible to offer to his Government the delusive hope of military success?

He had too much to do: an answer that cannot be an excuse, though it must serve as an explanation. If a commander fails within his own terms of reference he must expect criticism, and *Lustre* failed though Wavell claimed that it was feasible. Yet even if we accept that the Tatoi agreement produced 'a good plan' – which is a large assumption – and even if we can believe that the Aliakmon Line could have been held by a combined Anglo–Greek garrison, it is hard to understand how – in the light of all he knew – Wavell could continue to advocate *Lustre* as militarily viable once it was discovered that Papagos was not withdrawing from Macedonia. Excuses are not in order.

Yet charity should not be silenced. Though this chapter has concentrated, for clarity, on the Greek affair it would be wrong to forget that throughout these vital weeks Wavell was also preoccupied with the campaign in East Africa and, still more, with the imminent collapse of his desert flank in Cyrenaica. He was also under continual pressure from London to mount an assault on the Dodecanese – particularly on Rhodes – an operation for which he rightly believed he lacked resources: but the pressure was there.

In such a situation an oppressed theatre commander depends to a great degree on the quality – and the quantity – of his staff. During the spring of 1941 the size of the staff in Cairo was not commensurate with its responsibilities. It also had too much to do, and a group which admittedly worked wonders over the planning and logistical support for *Compass* and East Africa might reasonably claim overwork as an explanation if it is held to have been at fault over *Lustre*. But the question of quality cannot be ignored. If Wavell's team be compared with those of Montgomery at all times, or of Alexander in Italy, there is a distinctive difference.

Tedder's war memoirs, *With Prejudice,* fully justify their title, and it was probably with pique that he wrote in his diary for 18 April the entry which he quotes:

> Wavell, I think, is a fine man, but the rest?!!! They swing daily from easy optimism to desperate defeatism and vice versa. It is really tragic that Wavell has not got a really solid right-hand man who can relieve him of some of the burden. He has got a terrific load, and he is damn badly served.

Tedder had a wasp's sting, yet there was some cause for his venom. Many an observer considered that during Wavell's command – and indeed after Auchinleck took over – Cairo was too noticeably the realm of 'the decent chap'. Whilst it is true that in those early days of the war Wavell could not expect good men from home, and had only a limited choice in the Middle East, a suspicion nevertheless lingers that he himself was too permissive: not ruthless enough in his selection, and not stern enough at sacking. These characteristics will certainly become visible in the next chapter.

And another plea in mitigation may be made. Wavell never shirked the burden of responsibility for *Lustre,* but it should be recalled that all the main messages of encouragement from the Middle East to London stated that not simply Wavell but all the Commanders-in-Chief supported the expedition. Yet it is indubitable that Longmore had the gravest doubts: his paralysing shortage of aircraft alone made the proposition not 'a good plan' from the RAF's point of view. And though Cunningham in *A Sailor's Odyssey* declared that 'I was tolerably certain that the Navy could get all the forces that could be collected to Greece in comparative safety,' he also added that during the decisive meeting in Cairo on 6 March 'I gave it as my opinion that though politically we were correct, I had grave uncertainty of its military expediency. Dill himself had doubts, and said to me after the meeting, "Well, we've taken

the decision. I'm not at all sure it's the right one".' It is true that
A. B. Cunningham, the dashing destroyer captain of the First
World War, entertained great scorn of all the King's enemies
and believed implicitly in the superiority of the Royal Navy.
His creed was 'attack' and it was his aggressive spirit that kept
the battered Mediterranean fleet in action. But many of his
staff lacked faith in *Lustre* and on his own admission he was not
convinced that it was 'on'. Was it a traditional and stultifying
protocol that prevented the commanders of the Navy and Air
Force from voicing their inmost fears and ensuring that they
were brought to the attention of their superiors in London?
Wavell's own misjudgement was merely accentuated by this
acquiescence on the part of his colleagues.

The same, too, may be said of the Dominion leaders. After
Papagos's refusal to withdraw his division from Macedonia
became known, they were informed.

> Neither Blamey nor Freyberg dissembled when the fresh news
> was broken to them in Cairo: both were downcast and made no
> secret of it. Wavell told Freyberg, but Freyberg did not consider
> he had been consulted in any real sense; he said later he had merely
> been instructed "to get ready and go".

Blamey went further. On 7 March he handed to one of his
officers 'a sheet of paper on which he had drafted a message
giving his opinion that the expedition to Greece was fore-
doomed and setting out his reasons for thinking so'.[10] Yet
neither Freyberg nor Blamey spoke out forthrightly, either to
Wavell or to their governments: they were inhibited by the
belief that those governments already knew the full facts and
had agreed to the expedition. But the Australian and New
Zealand Governments were being misled, unwittingly, by
Churchill. Thus Wavell's failure to set before the Cabinet the
need to make a political choice, since military success was
impossible, in the end placed his Dominion generals beside his
naval and RAF colleagues as supporters of a plan in which
none of them believed. It was a vicious circle. The unreserved
professional comment which was necessary if Wavell was to
face reality was denied him.

So far the facts are well documented. The effect of a

commander's personality on his decision-making can rarely be presented as a fact: the material is too nebulous, the issue is riddled with subjectivity. However, in maintaining that *Lustre* was militarily feasible Wavell accepted the concept of fighting the enemy as far forward as possible, and he undertook an operation which, at best, was risky. For all his withdrawn and monosyllabic manner, his lucid intelligence, his deep attachment to order and tradition, it has been seen that romantic tides raced powerfully beneath the classical exterior, and that the ideas of risk-taking and 'forward engagement' were dominant elements in his military philosophy. James Thurber's dictum in *Fables for our Time* would have been relished by Wavell: 'You might as well fall flat on your face as lean too far backwards.' To attempt to prove that such considerations – perhaps such yearnings – influenced his decision about *Lustre* would be shallow and anyway impossible. Nevertheless, to suggest that they should not be ruled *hors concours* is perhaps to be permitted.

Unfortunately, in *Lustre's* case the principle of fighting forward did not allow Wavell to seize an initiative which, in truth, had been in Hitler's hands ever since he decided on operation *Marita*. From the moment when the expeditionary force began to disembark during the early days of March events were out of the hands of the Commanders-in-Chief. The *coup* in Belgrade, the switch of German troops into Yugoslavia, the pell-mell invasion of Greece itself turned the whole theatre into a maelstrom where the only cry could be *sauve qui peut*. In war both success and failure tend to be incremental. It was symbolic of British weakness and the enemy's strength that on the day the Germans marched, 6 April, a *Luftwaffe* raid hit an ammunition ship in Athens' harbour of Piraeus, *Lustre's* main channel for entry or retreat. The explosion virtually removed the port from the British lines of communication. As Wavell himself admitted in his Despatch, 'while the whole expedition was something in the nature of a gamble, the dice was loaded against it from the first'.

The greater proportion of the *Lustre* force, about 58,000, was successfully evacuated against all reasonable expectation and thanks to the Navy. But the way that Wavell's responsibilities interlocked – the way, too, that his judgement could be blurred by confusing directions from London – is very well illustrated by the orders sent to him on 18 April (when the decision to evacuate was already hardening). The Chiefs of Staff informed him of a ruling by Churchill that victory in Libya had priority over evacuation from Greece and that 'Crete will at first only be a receptacle of whatever can get there from Greece. Its fuller defence must be organized later.' Two German generals, Rommel and Student, would soon put these propositions to the test.

# 5

# Things Fall Apart

Things fall apart; the centre cannot hold
W. B. YEATS, *The Second Coming*

As Eden and Dill were ordered to Cairo on 12 February, General Erwin Rommel arrived in Tripoli with the first elements of his Afrika Korps. Exactly two months sufficed for him to invest Tobruk, take Bardia on the run and establish a foothold on the Egyptian frontier. 'So there we were,' Wavell wrote in retrospect, 'by the middle of April back to much the same position as in December before I started the offensive . . . .' Such was the strength of the desert flank on which Churchill and the Chiefs of Staff had been persuaded that they could confidently rely.

The Germans did not descend on Africa like a bolt from the blue. All Wavell's strategic reflections since the summer of 1940 had allowed quite specifically for this contingency – a calculation, indeed, which no alert commander could have avoided. In London, moreover, as early as August 1940 the bold decision to send precious tanks to the Middle East was based on a War Office appreciation that Germany was 'prepared to bolster up an Italian attack on Egypt while the outcome of the Battle of Britain was still undecided'. Yet when the time came it was only reluctantly that either Wavell or Whitehall was able to believe in a predictable happening. Wavell, it is true, was daily preoccupied by the knowledge that Germans in far greater strength were about to erupt from the Balkans. The intelligence staffs in London, for their part, were seriously distracted by rumours that Hitler intended to break into Tunisia.

This critical moment in the Mediterranean is curiously

analogous to the eve of the Ardennes offensive. Senior Allied intelligence officers subsequently agreed that, had they not closed their minds and dismissed a German assault as impossible in late 1944, there was abundant evidence to warn that one was not merely possible but actually imminent. So now from many sources (diplomatic, prisoner interrogation, Secret Service, Ultra), signs accumulated of German troop movements southwards through Italy; of great shipping concentrations at Naples; of practice embarkations in Sicily. Then there were those units of *Luftflotte* X already working from African airfields. Yet even a Bletchley decrypt of a signal dated 9 February 1941, which ordered special air cover for a Naples/Tripoli convoy, and indications of increased transport flights a few days later from Italy to Libya failed to carry conviction. It was not until 17 February, when Rommel was already moving eastwards from Tripoli, that Middle East Intelligence reached a solemn conclusion: Hitler was aiming to reach Egypt from Tripolitania rather than through Turkey. And only on 24 February were doubts finally dispelled in London and Cairo, after a clash of armoured cars occurred at Agheila and history, selecting the appropriate man, chose Lieutenant E. T. Williams – later to be distinguished as Montgomery's chief intelligence officer – to identify a German presence on the British front.

It was not, apparently, until 3 March that Ultra disgorged the name of Rommel as commander of these new arrivals,[1] but a certainty had already emerged that there was a substantial number of Germans – perhaps a brigade group – out there in the sands. Sometimes it is suggested that this extra factor should have prevented – even at the last minute – an expedition to Greece. To make this claim is to misinterpret the contemporary climate of opinion and to apply a hindsight derived from Rommel's subsequent operations. During those vital days of the first week in March the German threat in Africa was discounted, both in London and in Cairo. Compared with the imminent explosion in the Balkans and the commitment to the Greek government, any menace in Libya seemed minor. Moreover, had not Churchill and the Chiefs of Staff Wavell's assurance – soon to be reiterated – about that desert flank? So

*Lustre* went ahead inevitably. Yet the image in Wavell's eyes, as he looked towards his troops in the west, was little more than a mirage. ('Mirage: an optical illusion, common in hot countries and especially in sandy deserts.')

With that patient honesty which characterized his signals and despatches Wavell himself laid the facts on the table for the Prime Minister at the time, and students later, to dissect at their will. Rommel had already begun to reach out beyond the Gulf of Sirte and past Agheila, thus creating alarm in London, when Wavell on 23 March confessed to Churchill:

> I have to admit to having taken considerable risk in Cyrenaica after capture of Benghazi; in order to provide maximum support for Greece. My estimate at that time was that Italians in Tripolitania could be disregarded and that Germans were unlikely to accept risk of sending large bodies of armoured troops to Africa in view of inefficiency of Italian Navy. I therefore made arrangements to leave only small armoured force and one partly trained Australian division in Cyrenaica.

But while there is always something noble and winning about Wavell's honourable but not infrequent admissions of error and miscalculation, the dissecting critic is entitled to examine their validity.

Of all the assumptions underlying the statement quoted the only sound one was that the Italian army in North Africa, *per se,* could be disregarded. As to the Italian Navy, the record shows that in February and March 1941 no less than 220,000 tons of Axis shipping sailed from Italy to Libya, of which only 20,000 tons were intercepted. Apart from one or two damaging sinkings, the build-up of the Afrika Korps in fact continued (if somewhat spasmodically) till its planned level was reached. It might have been wiser, therefore, if Wavell had concentrated his thoughts less on the inefficiency of the Italian Navy and dwelt more pessimistically on the need of the Mediterranean Fleet to escort the Greek convoy-traffic, on the universal shortage of aircraft cruisers, destroyers and sub-marines, and on the crippling by the *Luftwaffe* of Malta as a base for strikes against Axis surface craft. So long as a ship could move and steer, in the spring of 1941 there was no great risk of interruption by the British during the passage from Naples to

North Africa.

But Wavell's phrase about a 'small armoured force and one partly trained Australian division' was a more serious understatement of the realities. It is not a matter of the weaknesses disclosed when Rommel struck, but rather of what Wavell should have known from the start and should have brought to London's attention. To begin with, once the move to Greece began there was no senior officer at the desert front with experience or competence. O'Connor, exhausted, was back in Egypt with John Combe, Wilson was in Greece, Galloway was first in Crete and then in Greece: only John Harding remained. In place of Wilson at Cyrenaica Command Wavell brought Philip Neame VC from Palestine, staff-trained, *un bon général ordinaire,* but a stranger among the sands and a tyro at high command. The armour suffered too from a Wavell appointment. 2 Armoured Division, fresh from England, had been led since 1940 by a true tank veteran, Justice Tilly, who unfortunately died suddenly at Bardia while the division was still training. Now it had become the 'small armoured force' at the front in Cyrenaica, under General Gambier-Parry whose agreeable personality and marked success as the recent head of the Mission in Greece was not balanced by the least acquaintance with desert warfare. No professional German commander-in-chief would have tolerated such a dearth of experience among his senior subordinates. As the campaign expanded and Rommel's own generals were killed, wounded or captured, it is noticeable how often the Germans rushed in *battle-hardened* replacements – not infrequently from the Russian front.

And the troops themselves were a travesty. One brigade of 2 Armoured Division and much of its Support Group went to Greece. The remaining brigade contained a regiment of ancient cruiser tanks, a regiment (under strength) of virtually useless light tanks, and a third which, for lack of anything else, was equipped with those famous death-traps, the Italian M 13 medium tanks about whose maintenance or tactical handling the crews' knowledge was minimal. The divisional armoured car regiment had just converted from horses! John Combe, the brilliant and veteran commander of 11 Hussars who made

Beda Fomm possible, later wrote for O'Connor a note on his successors so contemptuous that it is best left unquoted.[2] As for that 'partly trained' Australian Division, this was the admirable 9th under Morshead: but two of its own brigades had been sent to Greece and replaced by formations backward in training and dangerously short of weapons and, above all, transport. 'Division' was a misnomer for a body which was neither an organic whole nor an effective fighting machine. To crown all, Neame's Cyrenaica Command was organized as a static area headquarters, lacking the proper staff, transport and radio facilities necessary for controlling a quick-moving armoured conflict.

Wavell may be excused – though he condemned himself – for failing to inspect personally the terrain south of Benghazi, over which the coming battle would be fought. That, at least, was the responsibility of the local commanders rather than of the Commander-in-Chief. But can anything excuse his assurances about the security of his flank, in the light of the deficiencies described above which should all have been obvious at the time? It is not surprising that when he did at last visit the front, in mid March, he returned, as he put it, 'anxious and depressed', alarmed that of the fifty-two cruiser tanks on strength half were in workshops and the other half regularly breaking down: appalled, too, at the unwarlike arrangement at Gambier-Parry's headquarters. That Wavell was an outstanding personality and in his day an outstanding commander is a truth which must be asserted and reasserted: but lack of awareness and then resigned tolerance of such a state of affairs is difficult to explain. Had Montomery or Slim made such a visit it is certain that, whatever the consequences, Neame or Gambier-Parry would have been out on his ear. In a few weeks Rommel's handling of his unsatisfactory General Streich would provide a ruthless example.

Neame's force was evidently not comparable with the highly-trained and highly-motivated divisions which destroyed the Italians in *Compass*. Still, Wavell could at least argue with some reason that this tatterdemalion collection was secure enough so long as only Italians lay to the west, since after their thrashing another forward move was improbable.

But the known arrival of German units raised very different considerations. On 28 February Bletchley broke the latest version of the Mediterranean *Luftwaffe* cipher (known as Light Blue) and continued to read it currently. Thus in early March the scale of Luftwaffe and Afrika Korps elements in Tripolitania, their bases, Rommel's presence and indications of gathering reinforcements were soon established.*

Naturally the Chiefs of Staff were concerned at these manifestations and asked, in effect, whether the desert flank was really firm. Wavell's reply of 2 March was categorical, nor does it seem to have been questioned: not surprisingly, since Whitehall assumed that Neame commanded a competent force, and since Wavell's arguments were based on logistical factors comprehensible to any trained staff officer – including the German High Command who, for similar reasons, neither expected nor desired Rommel to advance. Any staff college in the world would have accepted these two paragraphs in Wavell's signal.

2   Tripoli to Agheila is 471 miles and to Benghazi 646 miles. There is only one road, and water is inadequate over 419 miles of the distance; these factors, together with lack of transport, limit the present enemy threat. He can probably maintain up to one infantry division and armoured brigade along the coast road in about three weeks, and possibly at the same time employ a second armoured brigade, if he has one available, across the desert via Hon and Marada against our flank.

3   He may test us at Agheila by offensive patrolling, and if he finds us weak push on to Agedabia in order to move up his advanced landing grounds. I do not think that with this force he will attempt to recover Benghazi.[3]

Brigadier Shearer concocted for Wavell a brilliantly perceptive appreciation written from the viewpoint of the German Commander in Africa, as of 5 March, which estimated that 'unless the British substantially reinforced their present forces in Libya' he 'could successfully undertake the reoccupation of Cyrenaica', but the scenario was rejected.[4] Logistics and some obscure sense that German generals followed the same guide-

---

* The first units of Afrika Korps came, of course, from 5 Light Division. The second major formation, 15 Panzer Division, was notified by Bletchley to Cairo on 2 April as moving south into Sicily for embarkation.

lines as British convinced Wavell that no significant attack would come till May. He was not now so complacent about his flank, and it was, indeed, soon afterwards that he went up to the desert and discovered the appalling truth which he should have sensed earlier. Neame's tactical dispositions, he wrote, 'were just crazy'. But there was little left for him to do except to purge the command – which he failed to do. Shakespeare in a sonnet defined his dilemma.

> I sigh the lack of many a thing I sought,
> And with old woes now wail my dear time's waste.

However wrong Wavell may have been in allowing himself and his government to believe that he had set up a western wall and not a paper-thin façade, no reasonable critic can blame him for being taken by surprise when Rommel raced eastwards, since the prolonged advance of the Afrika Korps was an affront to all the best staff opinions in Berlin, London and Cairo.* Moreover, though Ultra revealed in mid March that Rommel was visiting Germany, nothing further emerged to indicate that what was logistically unsound had been authorized by his masters. Actually, of course, Rommel's request to launch an offensive and to be given reinforcements over and above the promised 15 Panzer was rejected. Instead, he was told to stay in Tripolitania until mid May. It would therefore have required a sixth sense for Wavell (already overwhelmed by the problems of Greece and *Lustre*) to guess that by 4 April Rommel would be at Benghazi, by 6 April at Derna, by 10 April at Tobruk and, by the end of the month, sitting on the Egyptian frontier. Only Hitler, at this stage, understood Rommel's dynamism: 'I picked up Rommel because he knows how to *inspire* his troops, just like Dietl up in Narvik. This is absolutely essential for the commander of a force that has to fight under particularly arduous climatic conditions like North Africa or the Artic.'

By the time the Afrika Korps was threatening Benghazi Wavell had already flown again to the front. Still unhappy about Neame's battle control, he was fortified by John Harding

---

* And to the future Field Marshal Lord Harding, then Neame's chief of staff, who with all his desert experience nevertheless issued, on 30 March, an instruction that no attack by Rommel could be expected in the foreseeable future.[5]

who privately pleaded with him to recall O'Connor to take charge. Bringing Brigadier Combe with him as a trusted aide, O'Connor arrived on 3 April, to persuade Wavell that Neame should remain in command with O'Connor at his shoulder as an adviser. Later O'Connor bitterly and rightly criticized himself for this recommendation. But it should be noted that Wavell accepted it not instantly, but after several hours' thought. There is probably no serious student of military history who would support this decision: since O'Connor was the experienced senior, to have influence without executive command placed him in an intolerable position, and dual control is notoriously the worst way to run a battle. In any case Wavell's earlier visit had shattered his confidence in Neame. Now the evidence of his own eyes demonstrated that in battle Neame lacked grip, insight, poise. In a year when so many things went wrong for Wavell this episode is the most difficult to credit. Did O'Connor over-persuade him? A Commander-in-Chief's job is to resist the seduction of others and found right decisions on the rock of his own judgement.

There was a tragic consequence. By 6 April those units of the armoured division which had not been destroyed or captured were in full flight, the wastelands of the Jebel Achdar resembling a nature reserve when herds of wildebeeste and antelope stampede before some prowling beasts of prey. Benghazi was already lost, and during the night of the 6th O'Connor, Neame and Combe, travelling in one vehicle, made for Derna. O'Connor was a seasoned mariner in the desert seascape. But the car belonged to Neame, who was driving: a novice, who thought he knew best. Ignoring O'Connor's protests, at first instinctive and then confirmed by compass, that they were seriously off course, Neame persisted. German orders to hold up their hands were the depressing consequence, for by following the wrong track Neame had presented one of Rommel's reconnaissance units with the gift of two generals and the most battleworthy brigadier in the western desert. O'Connor's plans for an escape began immediately, continued during his flight to Italy, and were repeatedly – and at last successfully – put into effect during his years of imprisonment.[6] To Wavell he wrote at the end of the war, 'Please don't think I ever blamed you for my being taken.' Yet by keeping in command a man in whom he had lost confidence Wavell must certainly accept some blame for those unnecessary errors amid the dust and darkness along the route to Derna.* The victor of *Compass*, the British general most daring yet most competent in the special art of mobile warfare, O'Connor would not lead an armoured corps into action again until the campaign in Normandy. His loss was symbolic of a prevailing ineptitude.

Yet suddenly things began to fall into shape. As Neame's chief staff officer, Brigadier John Harding was increasingly concerned by the silence of the two generals. The citation for his first DSO specifically emphasized his sound judgement and initiative during these taxing days, when no one else could take the snap decision. First he moved into Tobruk and with Morshead decided that the reforming Australians must hold it. He also warned Wavell about the missing generals and asked him to come forward. Wavell reached Tobruk on the morning of the 8th, having brought with him Major General Lavarack of 7 Australian Division. John Connell caught perfectly the atmosphere after his arrival:

> On the airfield to meet him were Major-General Morshead and his GSOI, Colonel Loyd. They were dog-tired, unshaven, and conscious that they looked and smelt of the desert, of defeat and of retreat. Wavell's presence gave them back their confidence – in him and in themselves. Tobruk, he said, was to be held; he had merely come to settle the method by which this was to be done.

Behind his mask Wavell's character was varied and complicated. The risk-taker, the cavalier, the seeker after deception and surprise: these were the facets often revealed. But the situation at Tobruk in April 1941 appealed to something deep in his nature whose quality was of a different order. It was perhaps another aspect of the romantic. In any case the notion of the last ditch, of holding on to the last man and the last round, of 'no surrender' also moved him so powerfully that

---

* At least he sought to make amends, proposing that any six Italian generals should be offered in exchange for O'Connor. After prolonged deliberation the Cabinet's Defence Committee decided that 'we cannot discriminate in favour of generals'.

his generalship, at times, may even have been warped by its influence. His responsibility for the stand at Singapore and at Rangoon – as will be seen – is not straightforward. But at Tobruk his immediate grasp of what must be done and his energetic insistence on getting the right thing done was invaluable. An army in retreat: his best commanders missing: scarce equipment abandoned: a triumphant and advancing enemy: a shambles in Greece – these were considerations which might have made other generals accept their reverse and scuttle for the Egyptian frontier as was done, with perhaps no greater reason, in the summer of 1942. But Wavell, who knew his A. E. Housman, might have recalled in that Tobruk hotel where the decisions were taken:

> *The King with half the East at heel is marched from lands of morning;*
> *Their fighters drink the river up, their shafts benight the air;*
> *And he that stands will die for nought, and home there's no returning.*
> The Spartans on the sea-wet rock sat down and combed their hair.

The strategic value of Tobruk as a potential sally-port on the enemy flank was obvious to any educated soldier: blindingly obvious to Churchill. What was not clear, however, when Wavell made the decision to retain a garrison there, was whether with his small resources the huge perimeter was defensible (for during the winter O'Connor had demonstrated that it was not): and, in particular, whether the skills of the Afrika Korps in mobile operations were matched by comparable abilities in the arts of siege warfare. These matters could only be tested by trial. The success, as it turned out, of the experiment bequeathed to the British a position at Tobruk which, so long as it was occupied, continually distracted Rommel and on the eve of one great battle, *Crusader,* almost precipitated his defeat. Churchill had cause to be exceptionally fulsome when he signalled to Wavell on the 10th, 'We all cordially endorse your decision to hold Tobruk and will do all in our power to bring you aid.' Rommel looked at it differently. 'Wavell was obviously intending to maintain his hold on Tobruk and to supply it by sea, assuming, that is, that our first attacks on the fortress did not succeed. I knew that we should then find ourselves in an extremely unpleasant situation, both tactically and strategically. . . .' Of all the British commanders he fought, Rommel gave as his final conclusion that 'the only one who showed a touch of genius was Wavell'. Amid all the welter of unavoidable criticism, the flash of this accolade gleams in the memory.

And Wavell was right. Neither the first nor any other attack on Tobruk succeeded while he was Commander-in-Chief. Day after day throughout April Rommel strove to break in, using all means available – dive-bombing by Stukas, armoured jabs, infantry assaults. His papers reflect his increasing despair and a realization that in 'the position battle' his troops were not as skilled as the British and Australians. 5 Light Division lost heart, and Rommel wrote a text-book appreciation of its failure: 'The division's command had not mastered the art of concentrating its strength at one point, forcing a breakthrough, rolling up and securing the flanks on either side, and then penetrating like lightning, before the enemy had had time to react, deep into his rear.' The attacks petered out, and Wavell (with Morshead and his Australians in Tobruk) had won an important success. The Egyptian base, the Canal, the Fleet's harbour at Alexandria had been preserved – preserved, as it happened, for the rest of the war. But there was a further consequence. The German High Command, irritated by Rommel's slap-dash methods (as they seemed from the perspective of Berlin) by a supreme irony sent out General von Paulus of Stalingrad to report on the siege of Tobruk. His pessimistic assessment was deciphered at Bletchley and swiftly reached Churchill and Wavell. The after-effects, as will be seen, were not what might have been expected.

It was indeed well that the Fleet's base at Alexandria was intact, for Admiral Cunningham now faced his greatest ordeal. During the evacuation from Greece a considerable proportion of the troops – roughly 20,000 – was simply lifted to Crete instead of back to Egypt, the quicker turn-round being more economical in transport-miles and less expensive from the point of view of attack from the air. An unimpressive miscellany of 10,000 other troops already on the island completed a 'garrison' which by every military standard looked rough rather than ready. There was little artillery, field or anti-aircraft. The scurry of evacuation meant that

> thousands of men, mixed indiscriminately, and almost entirely
> without equipment, were gathered in transit areas at the foot of
> the mountains. Here were gunners without guns, drivers without
> vehicles, and signallers without apparatus for signalling; some-
> thing might yet be made of them if they could be provided with
> rifles.[7]

And now, on 28 April, Wavell received a signal from
Churchill:

> It seems clear from our information that a heavy airborne attack
> by German troops and bombers will soon be made on Crete. Let
> me know what forces you have in the island and what your plans
> are. It ought to be a fine opportunity for killing the parachute
> troops. The island must be stubbornly defended.

Something of a change, certainly, from that message sent ten
days previously: 'Crete will at first only be a receptacle of
whatever can get there from Greece.' And the island still, in
truth, looked much like a military dustbin.

Realization that Crete would be attacked from the air came
gradually, but then with terrifying certainty. Many indications during March and April, from Bletchley's decypherment
of *Luftwaffe* traffic, showed that the crack airborne *Fliegerdivision* 7 and masses of Ju 52 transport aircraft were moving
into the Balkans, but the object was uncertain – not surprisingly, since Hitler did not authorize until 25 April the attack-
plan for Crete (Operation *Merkur*) which had been put up by
the brilliant General Student, now commanding *Fliegerkorps*
XI, of which the airborne division was the central core. In spite
of Churchill's dogmatism on 28 April, the Chiefs of Staff and
Wavell still suspected that Crete might be a deception and that
the ultimate target might be Syria or Iraq: names – as would
soon be seen – of ill omen for Wavell. But daily from 1 May,
with an accumulating weight of authority, Ultra's decrypts
pointed to Crete. By 6 May the estimated date for the comple-
tion of German preparations, 17 May, had been acquired, as
well as

> the exact stage of the plan from D-Day beginning with the landing
> of paratroops by *Fliegerdivision* 7 and other units of *Fliegerkorps* XI

The Chief *(BBC Hulton Picture Library)*

Above: The *Compass* trio in the desert (1941). (Left to right) Generals O'Connor, Wavell, MacKay

Left: General Sir Richard O'Connor *(both photographs by courtesy of Sir Richard O'Connor)*

The Afrika Korps arrives at Tripoli (above) and
marches into history. German photographs, hitherto
unpublished, from the author's private collection.

The Chinese connection. Wavell with Generals Yu Ta Wei and Ho Ying Chin. On the right is Lt.Col. L. E. Wilson, a liaison officer with the Chinese. *(Courtesy of Lt. Col. Wilson's daughter Mrs Enoch Powell)*

An English rose for India's new Viceroy, Wavell, in London, August 1943 *(BBC Hulton Picture Library)*

Wavell asks for a baton. For a full account of this episode, see page 207.

GENERAL HEADQUARTERS,
MIDDLE EAST FORCE.

Private and Personal          August 20. 1942

Dear Prime Minister

I have never before asked for anything for myself, but I am going to ask you now for promotion to the rank of Field-Marshal. I have commanded very considerable armies and held very responsible positions and had at least two very successful campaigns — in Cyrenaica in the winter of 1940-41

---

PRIME MINISTER'S
PERSONAL MINUTE

SERIAL No. M. 331/2

SECRETARY OF STATE FOR WAR.

    I am strongly in favour of this, and so is the C.I.G.S.  The letter is of course strictly private, and should be returned to me without being made official use of in any way.

    It would seem right to make the appointment in the next Honours List.  Meanwhile I should like to tell General Wavell that this will be done.

                 WSC.

                 27.8.42

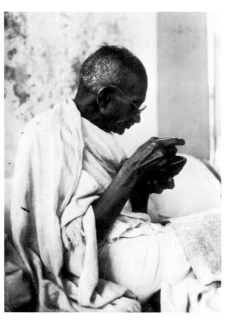

Above: Mahatma Gandhi.
Above right: Pandit Jawaharlal Nehru.
*(both BBC Hulton Picture Library)*

Right: Mr Jinnah, the Indian Muslim
leader *(Popperfoto)*

Left: Lord and Lady Wavell in the gardens
of Viceroy's House *(Popperfoto)*

Top: Wavell of the Black Watch. As Colonel of the Regiment, Wavell takes a march past of the Highland Brigade at Duisburg, West Germany, in 1948. The brigade commander, David Belchem, is standing beside the dais and third from left is Bernard Fergusson, commanding the First Battalion, the Black Watch. *(Courtesy of Major-General David Belchem)*

Above: Burial of a scholar-soldier. A bearer party from the Black Watch lowers Wavell's body into its resting place at Winchester College *(Southern Newspapers)*

in the Maleme-Khania area (the main sector) and at Heraklion and
Rethymon, and proceeding, through the transfer of dive-bombers
and fighters to Cretan bases, to the sea transport of flak units,
supplies, equipment and three mountain regiments of ground
troops.[8]

On 19 May Wavell knew from Ultra that D-Day was probably the 20th. Churchill later wrote in his memoirs, 'at no
moment in the war was our Intelligence so truly and precisely
informed'. And yet, although the quality and quantity of
Ultra's contribution during these hectic days marvellously
demonstrated the ability of Bletchley's cryptanalysts, Ultra
alone was not enough.

The Cretan disaster is a classic exemplification of Edmund
Burke's dictum that 'for evil to succeed it is enough that good
men do nothing'. When all the appropriate qualifications have
been made, the evidence now available still suggests that in
this case the good man was Wavell.

For the truth is that the strategic significance and, at the
same time, the vulnerability of Crete were not disclosed at the
last minute in some sudden revelation. Even before the fall of
France there had been an Allied understanding that if Italy
entered the War French troops from Syria would garrison the
island. And as soon as Mussolini invaded Greece Churchill
(who in his memoirs recalled that 'one salient strategic fact
leapt upon us – CRETE! The Italians must not have it. We must
get there first and at once.') signalled on 29 October 1940 to
Eden, then in Khartoum: 'We here are all convinced that an
effort should be made to establish ourselves in Crete, and that
risks should be run for this valuable prize.'

Wavell could rightly point out that, from October 1940
onwards, the London view of how Crete should be used soon
degenerated from Churchill's initial grandiose concept of 'a
second Scapa' in which Suda Bay would be developed into a
major defended base for the Fleet. As the best historian of the
campaign has written, 'Crete became first a minor garrison
area, after that a dumping ground, and at last a battlefield. It
was never "the fortress" that had been promised, never remotely a "Scapa".'[9] But no plea in mitigation on Wavell's
behalf can conceal the fact that Crete was constantly brought

to his attention, nor that between the invasion of Greece by the Italians (which underlined Crete's importance) and the invasion of the island itself in the early hours of 20 May 1941 a good six months were available for defensive preparations. Resources were obviously small in an over-taxed Command. Nevertheless, the central question remains: did Wavell, in spite of his many other preoccupations, apply to Crete that gift for sudden and appropriate improvisation which Marshal Saxe considered to be the hall-mark of a good general?

Certainly no student of military affairs can feel comfortable about the succession of officers who, during this critical half-year, came and went from the commandpost in Crete, each of them reminding one of Matthew Arnold's verdict on the poet Shelley, 'a beautiful and ineffectual angel, beating in the void his luminous wings in vain'. On 3 November, when the 'second Scapa' concept prevailed, Brigadier Tidbury was put at the head of the forces in the island. On 8 January he was replaced by Major-General Gambier-Parry, who a month later departed to command 2 Armoured Division in the desert. An anti-aircraft colonel, C. H. Mather, now held the fort until on 19 February Brigadier Galloway (General Wilson's chief of staff) arrived. But on 7 March Galloway too departed – to Greece – and Mather took over again. Then on 19 March a Brigadier Chappel grasped the strings. He too was succeeded, at the end of March, by a Marine, Major-General Weston. At the last, to fight the inevitable battle, Wavell on Dill's recommendation appointed the incomparable New Zealander, General Freyberg vc, as supreme local commander. Even if there were valid operational reasons for Gambier-Perry's departure to Africa and Galloway's to Greece, such a quick-change act of commanders at varying levels of seniority shows no recognition of the need, in Crete, for continuity of control and an extreme constructive energy if this defender's nightmare was to be made impregnable.

There was no continuity. Yet it is grotesque to treat a potential 'fortress' as if it were an hotel with a constant change of tenancy in the Executive Suite. Had Wavell grasped the significance of Crete – he who always believed in fighting forward – he would surely have put in a good man and kept him there. His failure to do so is as much an indication of his indifference as is the general tone of *non possumus* which colours all his communications with London about Crete until the very eve of the German assault. It was his blind spot, and Crete is to Wavell as Antwerp is to Montgomery, a damning error of oversight by a normally alert commander whose attention was otherwise engaged.

Yet in those last six months there was so much that could have been done. No local labour force was assembled, on the grounds that the able-bodied men had gone to fight in Greece. This is a statistical nonsense: the island's population was 400,000, and in any case did not Wavell remember the elders – and the women – of his own Highlands, active and able-bodied until death? The Germans would soon have found a labour force. And what of the 15,000 Italian prisoners of war on the island?

> There had cried aloud the need for five simple, immediate measures: the improvization of landing facilities at the southern fishing ports; the completion and improvement of the roads leading north from these ports; the construction of fighter airstrips, with camouflaged protection pens, in two or three of the mountain-locked plains where they would be remote from the nerve centres of the island's defence; the mining or destruction of airfields in the north; and, finally, the arming of the Cretans.[10]

None of these or other essential initiatives were taken. No one clamoured for the wireless sets which were disastrously deficient throughout the garrison – yet over and over again, in the final battle, at critical moments Freyberg's scattered troops were defeated piecemeal because inter-communication was impossible. We now have several accurate and minutely detailed accounts of that battle from which it is evident that the Germans' victory was not foreordained, but the by-product of mischances and miscalculations by their enemy many of which were due to inadequate preparation. That preparation could only have been achieved by a well-established local commander with a strong, clear brief. Such a directive was never issued by Wavell sufficiently far ahead. Of course his many other commitments prevented him from sending to Crete a large quantity of equipment, tanks, field and anti-aircraft guns. All this he patiently, and understandably, explained in his signals to London. But this is not the issue. Freyberg's force came within inches of defeating the German airborne troops with the meagre equipment in its hands. The question is ultimately one of attitude – of whether, once the significance of Crete was even dimly discerned, everything possible was done with the limited British and not inconsiderable local resources to make the island defensible during those long available months? To make a decent road? To reconnoitre, realize and diminish the inadequacies of the southern harbours? The men on the spot should indeed have acted, but the guiding impulse had to come from Wavell, and it might not seem unjust to say that he lost Crete in a fit of absence of mind as Montgomery, so reprehensibly, lost sight of Antwerp.*

Certainly his responsibility was grave, yet so absolute a condemnation would be excessive. In spite of his previous lethargy, the record shows that once the issue was clear he worked manfully and loyally (under almost hourly pressure from Churchill) to feed into Crete supplies and equipment from his pitifully limited stocks. A great proportion was sunk on route: but Freyberg, who might well have felt resentful, was the first to recognize Wavell's support. And in his customary way he went 'up to the front line', flying in to discuss Freyberg's problems and to ensure that he had the latest intelligence picture.

But the real truth which would make an absolute condemnation of Wavell unjust is that, in a final analysis, Crete was lost not entirely because of dereliction before the Germans landed, but also because of a simple yet fatal error in the conduct of the battle. German, British and Dominion records have subsequently revealed its course virtually from minute to minute. The turning point occurred during the first night of this ten-day conflict.

Student was in despair, shattered by the unexpected

---

* The report of the Inter-Services Committee on the fall of Crete, prepared in June 1941, elaborates these and other criticisms in scathing detail. See also Churchill's minute to the Chiefs of Staff of 14 June, beginning 'I cannot feel that there was any real grip shown by Middle East HQ upon this operation of the defence of Crete.'

casualties of the first day and the failure of his plans. Then, like a good German commander, tough in spirit and shrewd in judgement, he took stock and decided, in his own words, 'that the *Schwerpunkt* of the attack must lie at Maleme, and that the island would have to be rolled up from the west'.

Student had appreciated with one of those *coups d'oeil* which transform a battle that the only good airfield on Crete, at Maleme, was the key to the whole operation. Without it, his Junkers transports could not deliver their follow-up supplies of heavy equipment, ammunition and troops. His lightly-armed and already decimated paratroopers would be doomed. In a flash, as it seemed, Maleme was in German hands, replenishments were rolling in, and Freyberg's situation was irrecoverable. It had crumbled because for all his gallantry and tenacity Freyberg had not had a similar vision: had not grasped that whatever happened elsewhere on the island, whatever attempt might be made to land by sea, Maleme was the position of supreme priority which, if possible, must never be surrendered and, if by chance it were, must be instantly re-gained. So the defences of Maleme were inadequately organized and after the *Fliegerdivision* moved in no proper counter-attack force was available. If Wavell wasted six months in preparing for the defence of Crete, Freyberg lost it in as many hours.

For years afterwards the signal that Wavell was compelled to send to the CIGS during the afternoon of 27 May was thought to have been inevitable in the sense that Crete was doomed from the start. 'Have ordered evacuation troops from Crete as opportunity offers.' But it was not so. Resolute action in the right place at the right time must have persuaded Student, as he had already begun to believe, that the sacrifice of his *élite* division had become intolerable. And then? The triumphant signals from Churchill write themselves. Those gnawing doubts about Wavell, active before *Compass,* allayed by that victory but quickened by later events in Greece, in the desert, in Iraq, and in Syria might at least have been brought under control again in the Prime Minister's mind by a success of such striking value both militarily and politically. Instead, Wavell slid further down the slope. It has long been realized, of course, that Crete was a characteristic British 'victory within a defeat', since Student's casualties turned Hitler and the High Command against any further airborne operations. But all Churchill could see, at the time, was unmitigated disaster – for what else was there to see? Certainly he was blind to the fact that he had overloaded the Commander-in-Chief Middle East like some Arab's donkey.

One supposes that until the night of 1 June, when the final rescue convoy sailed and the last cruiser was sunk, Wavell went through the worst time of his life – worse than the hour or so during Allenby's campaign when, just before a big attack, he thought that he had forgotten to order up the ammunition: worse than the retreat through Burma or the fall of Singapore. Cunningham was getting the men away miraculously, but the rate of sinking was too high. On the island 18,000 out of 32,000 were evacuated, but in the end Crete cost the Navy three cruisers sunk and six damaged, six destroyers sunk and seven damaged, and damage to three battleships and one aircraft carrier. Each day screwed the rack of pain.

Vice-Admiral Sir Geoffrey Norman worked in Cairo at this time as a naval staff officer, reporting to Wavell regularly on Cunningham's behalf. He recalled entering Wavell's office during the last stages of the evacuation, to announce that against all possibility the Fleet would try again that night. Usually Wavell's impassivity when conferring was only qualified by a casual manipulation of the pencils on his desk. But as Norman gave the good news, he saw Wavell grasp a bunch of pencils in his hand and crush them convulsively together in a passionate reflex.[11] However, though he was prepared to order soldiers to resist to the last round, it was beyond him to insist that the Navy should fight to the last ship. At what seemed the very last, on the 31st, Wavell flew to Alexandria to see Cunningham and give him 'our decision and absolution from further effort on behalf of the Army' – to be told by 'A.B.C.' that 'the Navy had never yet failed the Army in such a situation, and was not going to do so now; he was going in again that night with everything he had which would float and could bring off troops'.

To work alongside the spirit of Nelson was an alleviation,

but nothing could remove the hurt of having to send Bernard Fergusson down to greet on his behalf the 2nd Battalion of their own beloved regiment, the Black Watch: too many of the battalion had been killed on its way back from Crete, when the *Dido* and *Orir* were bombed. Fergusson was told to say that the Commander-in-Chief was sorry he was too busy to come himself and 'hoped they would understand'. It is worth trying that on the palate as a test of true humility. And throughout the crisis Wavell, forgetting the constant spate of hortatory, interfering or irrelevant signals from Churchill, walked among his staff pointing out that however great their burdens, the Prime Minister's were greater and their duty was to ease his load.[12]

This was certainly no two-way situation. Churchill may have written in his memoirs about 'the immense emergency in the Middle East which lapped General Wavell on all sides simultaneously', but during April and May, 1941, two of the most critical months of the war in the whole Middle Eastern Theatre, he was as hard and ruthless as Hitler would have been in lashing his Commander-in-Chief onward and forcing him to stretch his resources to the limit. Throughout those eight weeks which comprised the fall of Greece and Yugoslavia, the loss of Crete and the first thunderstroke of the Afrika Korps, Wavell was also impelled, against his will, into what seemed diversionary operations in Iraq and Syria. And yet the inescapable conclusions are that in both respects Churchill was right and Wavell was wrong. The Prime Minister's methods may have been idiosyncratic and irksome, but they produced results. It is indeed a curious anomaly that by the autumn of 1941 all the territory where Wavell had thought it to be essential to 'fight forward' – the Balkans, Crete, North Africa – was either in German hands or under threat, whereas over another wide swathe about which Wavell was, at the best, cool – a spread reaching through Syria to Iraq and Iran* – the British had established an undisputed control which persisted until the war's end.

The first issue was what might be called the case of the

---

* Once he became Commander-in-Chief India, however, his attitude about Iran altered. See next chapter.

Golden Square – the name given to the junta of Colonels who, headed by the pro-German Rashid Ali, ousted the friendly Regent of Iraq at the end of March and took over the country, determined to start horse-trading with Hitler. The danger to the port of Basra, to the oil pipelines and to an alternative route to Turkey was instantly obvious in London. And what was obvious was steadily confirmed by Ultra. On 5 April, for example, Bletchley produced a report from the Italian Minister in Teheran that he and his German colleagues had agreed on Syria as the best channel for supplying arms to the Golden Square. The flow of intelligence from Ultra and elsewhere continued through April, a peak being reached at the end of the month when the Secret Service revealed that Rashid Ali had been given a week by the Iraqi Army to delete the British military presence and seal a relationship with Germany: otherwise the Army would take over from the junta.

The rest of the story is soon told. In India Auchinleck readily responded to Churchill's appeal and put a brigade into Basra. Wavell argued to the point of insubordination against providing a striking column from Palestine: the group he finally dispatched, Habforce, had only a marginal effect. Rashid's attempt to eliminate or seize the RAF base at Habbaniya was repulsed with great spirit and ingenuity by the men on the spot. In spite of inundations, Baghdad was reached and occupied on 30 May and Rashid, together with his colleagues the German and Italian Ministers and that 'turbulent priest' the Mufti of Jerusalem, fled to Iran.

This rapid collapse was not due simply to the energy of the local British commanders or to the weakness of Rashid Ali's personal position. It was a perfect example of Hitler missing the bus. The pessimistic appreciations in London were well founded. He had a viable option to use Student's air corps against Iraq, working through the Dodecanese, instead of against Crete – and he could have had the British oil nexus for the picking. This was understood by the Chiefs of Staff, who were fully informed about the build-up of *Fliegerkorps* XI in the Balkans and, as has been seen, for a time nursed the thought that the threat to Crete might be a cover for ventures further east. Then, on 9 May, Ultra revealed that an alternative had been chosen.

From the *Luftwaffe* cyphers it was learned that an airfield near Athens had been set aside for special operations and during the next few days details became known of bombers and Messerschmidt fighters being ferried through Syria to Iraq without *Luftwaffe* markings. But the effort was far too small and far too late. Indeed, Hitler's Directive no. 30 of 23 May has an uncertain sound:

> . . . I have decided to push the development of operations in the Middle East through the medium of going to the support of Iraq. Whether and in what way it may later be possible to wreck finally the English position between the Mediterranean and the Persian Gulf, in conjunction with an offensive against the Suez Canal, is still in the lap of the gods. . . .

This is not the clarion call of the Führer's Directives about operations in which he believed. He was unwilling to encourage Arab nationalism, which conflicted with Mussolini's aspirations. More cogent, perhaps, was the knowledge that he would shortly be marching into Russia.

But in London Churchill and his advisers could only be aware of the evidence, gathered from all sides and from the most authoritative source, that an area vital to the economic and strategic conduct of the war was imperilled. When by 13 May Habforce was still not on the move from Palestine and Churchill signalled to Wavell, 'Every day counts, for Germans may not be long,' he was not ranting. It was his great virtue as a war leader that when he scented danger he demanded action: and the scent was now strong. So when Wavell first reacted to the proposal that he should form a striking force by suggesting that the Iraq business should be settled by diplomatic means he must have seemed to the men in London, even to a wise old friend like General Ismay, as naïvely out of touch with reality. When he wrote to the Chiefs of Staff on 3 May, 'I have consistently warned you that no assistance could be given to Iraq from Palestine in present circumstances and have always advised that commitment in Iraq should be avoided,' one can hear that other old friend, the CIGS, murmuring in gentle reproof, 'But Archie, there already *is* both a commitment and

an enemy.' On 5 May he was still obstinately arguing for a
political settlement:

> . . . You must face facts . . . I feel it my duty to warn you in gravest
> possible terms that I consider prolongation of fighting in Iraq will
> seriously endanger defence of Palestine and Egypt. Apart from the
> weakening of strength by detachments such as above, political
> repercussions will be incalculable and may result in what I have
> spent nearly two years trying to avoid, serious internal trouble in
> our bases.

And then he at last got Habforce on the move, Rashid Ali's
balloon was pricked, and nothing but good resulted.

Except for Wavell. The decline in his position was exemplified in the Chiefs of Staff signal of 6 May which rejected his
protestations and then *ordered* him to put Habforce in train.
Ismay, who watched all these events with sadness, wrote in his
memoirs that 'this was the first occasion in the war on which
the Chiefs of Staff overruled the commander on the spot, and
took full responsibility for the consequences'. More importantly, it was on this same day that the count-down began
which led inexorably to Wavell's displacement. The Director
of Military Operations at the War Office, later Major-General
Sir John Kennedy, noted: 'On the morning of the 6th May,
when I went to see Dill, he said, "There is a serious matter to
be settled today. The Prime Minister wants to sack Wavell and
put Auchinleck into the Middle East." '[13] For the time being,
for pragmatic reasons and because there was so much happening, Churchill held his hand: but in retrospect it is evident that
the determination was there and that a count-down had, in
effect, started. Iraq, Crete, the desert – all these operations, as
has been seen, brought Wavell into disfavour: but perhaps
none more so than the developments which were simultaneously taking place in Syria.

In this year of many troubles the British would undoubtedly
have been happy to let the Vichy regime in Syria, under the
High Commissioner General Dentz, wither away on the vine
– had it not been for two considerations. First, as has been
seen, there was ample and continuing evidence from Ultra and
other intelligence that the French in Syria already actively
co-operated with the Germans. Second, there was the

persistent suspicion in Whitehall, to which sufficient attention is not always given, that the real object of the known German build-up in the Balkans was to destroy the British position in the Middle East by a drive through Turkey and the Levant. (It was late in the day before the Chiefs of Staff came to see that they were wrong in believing that Hitler was not preparing to attack Russia.)

During the first half of May impressions already formed took a darker hue. On 8 May the Joint Planners even suggested to the Chiefs of Staff that the Germans might follow an airborne with a seaborne invasion of Syria. Knowledge that Dentz was providing trains to pass German arms to Rashid Ali, and granting landing facilities to the *Luftwaffe,* intensified such fears. Wavell was therefore urged to assemble a force either to aid Dentz if he resisted a German intrusion (which was uncertain: he said he would be prepared to do so himself, but would have to obey orders from Vichy) or to counterattack if the French either submitted or collapsed. There was little warmth in Wavell's response.

Combined with his current recalcitrance over Iraq, this 'dragging of feet' was unacceptable in London where, it must be emphasized, not merely Churchill but also his main advisers now saw Syria as a flash-point. On the other hand Wavell understood far more accurately than Churchill himself that the Free French troops whom he was under great pressure to use would be received in Syria not as brothers but with bitter hostility – as was proved in the event. So his honest and plain-spoken signal to Dill of 17 May had the effect of a depth-charge:

> . . . I feel strongly that Free French without strong British support would be ineffective and likely to aggravate situation and that original action must be British, to be followed by Free French if successful. . . . Hope I shall not be landed with Syria commitment unless absolutely essential. Any force I could send now would be painfully reminiscent of Jameson Raid and might suffer similar fate. . . .

It was surely unintentional, but nothing could have been better calculated to provoke that veteran of the Boer War, Winston Churchill, than a reference in such a context to the Jameson fiasco.

So the count-down continued. On the afternoon of the 19th the Prime Minister summoned Dill and told him that he had decided to bring Auchinleck to Cairo and switch Wavell to Delhi as Commander-in-Chief India. He would enjoy, Churchill said contemptuously, 'sitting under a pagoda tree'. Anyway, he didn't want him 'hanging around in London, living in a room in his club'.[14] (And he meant this. When the switch occurred in June, Wavell, who had already warned Dill that he was tired, pleaded to be allowed home for a short leave, 'to see my son and settle some business': he had, after all, been an active Commander-in-Chief since the beginning of the war. But Churchill, with that mixture of meanness and malevolence which diminished his magnanimity, wanted no unfavourable publicity or awkward questions, and sent Wavell straight on to India.)

Again the blast-off was delayed, though time was running out. Churchill had hardly finished consigning Wavell in his mind to a seat beneath *Ficus indica*, the banyan or Pagoda Tree of India, before the Chiefs of Staff were sending him another stiff signal: '. . . there is no option but to improvise the largest force that you can manage without prejudice to security Western Desert and be prepared to move into Syria at the earliest possible date. . . .' Further debate followed, particularly about the disputed employment of the Free French. Then, on the 21st, an exasperated and almost certainly overwrought Wavell laid his own head on the block. '. . . You must trust my judgement in this matter or relieve me of my command. . . .' Even now Churchill was not ready to pick up the offer, though his mind was set. Ripeness was all: dismissal of Wavell would be a major political event, and he must watch the timing. He replied the same day, therefore, with an emollient signal in which, nevertheless, was buried a scornful comment that revealed his real feelings. 'Our view is that if Germans can pick up Syria and Iraq with petty forces, tourists and local revolts we must not shrink from running equal small-scale military risks. . . .'

Indeed, a penultimate step was taken that very evening when Dill wrote a private letter to Auchinleck – who was shortly to meet Wavell in Basra to concert plans for finishing off Iraq:

*'For your eye alone:* I would like to tell you that the PM has lost confidence in Wavell – if he ever had any. I maintain that in war you must either trust your general or sack him. That being so we *may* be faced with the withdrawal of Wavell from the Middle East – even before you get this letter. If that happens you must succeed him. . . .'[15]

In a sense it was wholly irrelevant that the Iraqui affair, blowing up amid all the other great events, should have produced in Churchill's mind an unfavourable contrast between Wavell's intransigence and an Auchinleck manifestly eager to move troops in from India: the Auk's military problems were minute at that time, compared with Wavell's, and action was easy. Still, it must be added that Auchinleck and his Viceroy, Linlithgow, founded their action on a more accurate appreciation of Iraq's strategic and economic importance than did Wavell. Linked with the controversy about Syria, such considerations inevitably coloured the Prime Minister's thoughts.

So for Wavell there was little profit in that fact that at last he cobbled together an invasion force of British and Dominion troops operating, as he had insisted, alongside the Free French: for when the advance into Syria began on 8 June nothing that London and everything that Wavell had anticipated occurred. There was no quick collapse, and the Vichy garrison reacted towards de Gaulle's battalions, their 'liberators', with the savage venom that Frenchmen – as in Algeria – are particularly apt to discharge in their domestic conflicts. There were delays before Wavell's original contingent could be reinforced, and it was not until 14 July that General Dentz signed an armistice. By that time, alas, Wavell was on his way to the pagoda tree.

Many elements contributed to the Commander-in-Chief's débâcle, but the roots of the final catalytic event can be traced to a weekend in April. On Sunday, 20 April, Churchill received from Wavell a signal (marked Stop Press) that a new German armoured division, potentially of 400 tanks, had been disembarking at Tripoli and might soon be expected in the line.* The result has often been described – with glowing

---

* Bletchley through Ultra had given warning about the coming of 15 Panzer Division but Wavell appears to have expected a less heavily equipped 'colonial' division.

pride – by Churchill himself. It was a moment in the war when the Prime Minister's gifts (not always simultaneously revealed) for sound judgement, ruthless decision, daring and authority all worked together. Fighting on two fronts – against the Home Army and a dubious Admiralty – he organized within two days the removal of some 300 tanks from domestic stocks and their despatch straight down the Mediterranean, regardless of the well-known risks. In the event only one ship was lost, and of the original load 240 reached Alexandria by 12 May. *Tiger* was the convoy's code-name and 'the *Tiger* cubs' Churchill's private name for the tanks, on which – with the intensity few could equal – he now concentrated his ardent hopes for a desert victory. This did not bode well for Wavell.

And Churchill's expectations were enhanced by Bletchley's deciphering of the von Paulus report about Rommel's situation at Tobruk. The report was transmitted to Germany on 2 May intercepted, deciphered and the text passed to Whitehall and Cairo within the next 48 hours. Its contents were naturally stimulating: von Paulus spoke of the thorough exhaustion of the Afrika Korps, its need for re-organization and reinforcement, the inadequacy of its supply system, the impossibility of attempting anything more than quick raids on the Tobruk perimeter. Even when the whole of 15 Panzer Division had assembled, no major action should be taken without careful review. Here was a classic penetration by Ultra into the enemy's mind. Unfortunately it was followed by two British defeats and Wavell's ejection.

At first Wavell was able to match Churchill's mood, signalling that as soon as he had read 'the secret message' he had ordered General Beresford-Peirse, now commanding the desert army, to bend his mind to an attack: meanwhile, 'I have already issued orders for offensive in Western Desert at earliest possible date to be prepared on assumption *Tiger* successful.' *Tiger* docked on the 12th, and operation *Brevity* was launched three days later by Wavell – in view of the Paulus report – confidently taking one of those risks congenial to him and hazarding his existing armour in the sure knowledge that a windfall had arrived at Alexandria.

The object of *Brevity* was to make a push against the

Germans in the frontier area and take the key points of Sollum harbour on the coast, Halfaya Pass which links the coastal plain and the plateau above the escarpment, and Fort Capuzzo on the plateau itself. These objectives, it is clear, were limited, and the assault force was small in scale: a strong mixed brigade, at best, but even so, split by the terrain and by separate targets. Very relevant too was the fact that Rommel was well briefed about British intentions: his tactical intercept service was working well while British signal security in the desert was still, and would long remain, puerile. So *Brevity* proved to be an anticlimax, the British taking and the Germans then recovering Sollum and Capuzzo, while the gain at Halfaya Pass also became a loss ten days later as the result of a German counter-attack.

Losses in men and armour were small, however, and Churchill appeared to be temporarily at ease, signalling on the 17th, 'Results of action seem to us satisfactory.' But even so there was a sting in the tail: 'what are your dates for bringing *Tiger* cubs into action?' A sting because from now on (remembering that it was on the 18th that Churchill disclosed to Dill his final loss of confidence in Wavell) the Prime Minister's pressure on his Commander-in-Chief to hurl the newly-arrived tanks against an apparently enfeebled Afrika Korps became continuous. And yet, as is now evident, neither Churchill nor Wavell understood – or perhaps ever understood, either of them – the true significance of what had happened during *Brevity*.

Students of the North African campaign have come to see that by emphasizing the vulnerability of his frontier positions *Brevity* led Rommel to develop a new defensive device whose effectiveness was fundamental in the desert war. After the recovery of Halfaya Pass, he noted in his *Papers*,

> In constructing our position at Halfaya and on Hill 208 [a protuberance on the plateau] great skill was shown in building in batteries of 88mm guns for anti-tank work, so that with the barrels horizontal there was practically nothing seen above ground. I had great hopes of the effectiveness of this arrangement.

These hopes were realized, for the dug-in 88mm anti-aircraft gun, with its high muzzle velocity, immediately became Rommel's most devastating weapon against British armour, destroying hundreds of tanks up to the battle of Alamein and beyond.* Moreover, it gave him a tactical freedom almost never enjoyed by his enemy, since he no longer needed to fritter away his own armour by using tanks to kill tanks. At the beginning of June 1941 this sinister innovation had not been detected by Wavell's front-line commanders or by his intelligence service, yet its implications were serious . . . indeed, disastrous . . . both for the *Tiger* cubs and for the man who, loyal but disenchanted, informed Dill on 28 May that he was preparing an offensive, though the earliest possible date was 7 June, and 'I think it right to inform you that the measure of success which will attend this operation is in my opinion doubtful.' All he got back from Churchill, next day, was, 'Everything must now be centred upon destroying the German forces in the Western Desert . . . it is time to fight a decisive battle in Libya and go on day after day facing all necessary losses until you have beaten the life out of General Rommel's army.' Dill bravely pointed out that in view of Wavell's many commitments this 'fight to the death' directive was ill-judged, but Churchill remained impenitent.

So *Bruiser* – or *Battleaxe* as it was soon re-named – became a reality as Wavell issued to Beresford-Peirse his formal instructions. In essence the object was the same as in *Brevity,* using two weak divisions instead of two weak brigades: to break through on to the top of the escarpment and to exploit forwards – ideally to the relief of Tobruk. But how could Wavell believe in it? The mechanical deficiencies of the *Tiger* tanks were deplorable. His reports to London on their sorry condition have often been quoted: what never emerges is any sense of surprise among his superiors, or any realization that a tank prepared to operate in north-west Europe requires major modifications before it can function in the desert. Yet in England the tanks had been rushed on to their ships, and there can have been little time for even the most elementary check

---

* The destruction was also due to a further tactical device which Rommel perfected later and the British never paralleled, of keeping his anti-tank guns mobile and thrusting them boldly forward into the front of the armoured battle-line.

before they disappeared into the holds. This should have been obvious to the London staffs: as should the fact that a re-equipped unit, however good, needs time to practise working in harmony with its new tanks, to test and if necessary mend or replace its communication systems, to calibrate and shoot its guns, to sort out its battle-drill. Wavell received no sympathetic understanding. Perhaps it would have been wasted anyway, since Churchill didn't want to know. It is indicative that though he was aware at the time of Wavell's detailed comments on the *Tiger* cubs' failings, in his memoirs he blandly wrote that 'on May 31st General Wavell reported the technical difficulties which he was having with the reformation of the 7th Armoured Division'. In view of what followed, this is an unpardonable obfuscation.

When *Battleaxe,* delayed until 15 June, at last got into motion nothing that occurred, apart from the soldiers' courage, reflected well on the British. Once again intercepts gave Rommel advance warning: in fact he had put his front line troops on the alert before the attack started, and during the fighting – particularly in the final phase when the British were cracking – remained *au fait.* The British armour, divided into the slow Matilda infantry tanks and the quicker cruisers, had to fight down different axes and was picked off piecemeal whereas Rommel, bringing up 5 Light Division from reserve, could unite its tanks with those of 15 Panzer for the final *coup de grâce.* His 88s dug in along the escarpment were few but deadly, a surprise whose secret was not guessed. As for his enemy, the handling of the battle was neither confident, nor competent, nor coherent.

During the closing stages Wavell flew up to the front. Tedder in *With Prejudice* recalled what happened.

On the morning of 17 June, he and Beresford-Peirse were foolish enough to go up in a Proctor and land in the forward area where 7th Armoured Division was on the move. No one quite knew where the two Generals were, and it was only thanks to much good luck and a very heavy fighter escort that Wavell escaped. That evening, when he got back to Cairo, I told him politely that this had been an act of criminal lunacy.

Tedder had every reason, of course, for being buoyant. At the beginning of the month he had been appointed Air Commander-in-Chief, Middle East, in place of Longmore whose steady reporting of – or perhaps rather harping on – his deficiencies had caused his stock to fall in the Air Ministry in London. He was expendible, and he went. Tedder had been in the Middle East long enough to know that the C-in-C had endured éven greater pressures than Longmore, though he could hardly be aware that Wavell had only recently offered to relinquish his command. Still, he might have written with more comprehension about a flight to the front which, in fact, was normal practice for Wavell and which, this time, was to enable him to be immediately on hand during an operation that seemed to have turned sour. His instinct was correct, for a withdrawal was in train before he arrived.

Ever since the Paulus report Churchill had believed that Rommel was vulnerable. Ever since the sailing of the *Tiger* convoy he was convinced that he had provided Wavell with the lethal instrument. Nothing remained of his passionate hopes but dust and ashes.* All Wavell could do was to get back to Cairo, send to Dill that moving signal which began 'I regret to report failure of *Battleaxe*', and await the next move. It lay with the Prime Minister, who on the 21st informed him that Auchinleck was to take his place and that he himself was 'incomparably the best man and most distinguished officer to fill the vacancy of Commander-in-Chief in India'.† There is, as it happens, a saying which runs 'to shake the pagoda tree', and which means 'to make a fortune rapidly in India'. But all Wavell wanted, at this moment, was a few days at home.

---

* Field Marshal Lord Harding has described to the author Wavell's distressed condition when he arrived at the front and discovered the truth. This granite man had tears in his eyes.

† 'I remember him saying that he felt like a fisherman with two lines out; on one was a lively fish, and on the other a tired fish. He thought it would be advisable to change them about.' Lieutenant-General Sir Ian Jacob, *Listener*, 25 October 1979.

# 6

# The Wind from the East

It was almost certain that he would have to bear a load of defeat
in a scene of confusion.
CHURCHILL on Wavell, *The Second World War, vol. 3.*

The Prime Minister's signal giving Wavell his *congé* was dated
21 June but did not reach Cairo until early on the 22nd – about
the same time as the first German spearheads made their thrust
into Russia. He did not arrive in India as Commander-in-
Chief until 11 July. As it happened, the United States had
imposed their fatal oil embargo on Japan the day before he was
dismissed from Africa, and now the American and Dutch
governments were on the verge of freezing all Japanese assets,
thus eliminating trade between the Emperor's domain and the
rest of the world. In the chain reaction that followed, Pearl
Harbor was only months away. The war from which Wavell
had just been transferred now seems parochial by comparison
with the imminent conflict of the hemispheres.

The auspices were poor. During his flight he touched down
at Jodhpur airfield where he discovered a squadron of Audax
machines, slow ancient craft for pre-war 'Army Co-operation', masquerading as fighters. Bernard Fergusson, who
accompanied him as Private Secretary, recalled that Wavell's
first signal from India was to Tedder. 'Have just seen India's
most up-to-date fighter squadron armed with Audaxes. Does
not this make your heart bleed?' There was not, in truth, a
single plane within his new command capable of coping with
an enemy's modern designs. And then the red carpet for the
official train at Ambala beneath the Himalayas, and the hun-
dred-odd servants and dependants like termites in the Commander-in-Chief's house at Simla. Indeed, the mere fact that
the Viceroy of India and all the gross paraphernalia of govern-

ment still moved up to the hills from Delhi during the hot season, exactly as in peacetime, offered a marked contrast for a man who, a month ago, had plunged unhesitatingly into the heart of a desperate armoured battle in the furnace of the Western Desert.

Yet in a setting which, if not sybaritic, was certainly pretentious and relaxing his mind did not soften – nor did his spirit. As for his body, the punishing strains he continued to place on it almost from the time of his arrival in India could not overcome its natural resilience. He was, it may be recalled, in his 59th year and even before 1939 he had soldiered in the Boer War, Flanders, Allenby's operations against the Turks and a time of turbulent insurrection during his own command in Palestine. Vitality is a wasting asset. He had confessed to Dill, and implicitly to Churchill, that he was already battered by another prolonged and exhausting series of campaigns before he left Cairo. Yet in the period covered by this chapter, from his arrival at Simla in July to his resumption of office as Commander-in-Chief in February 1942 (after his temporary venture into fantasy as Supreme Commander in the Pacific) he flew so far, so dangerously and so doggedly that the list merely of his longer journeys is self-explanatory: to England, to Teheran, to Tiflis, to Chungking in China, to Rangoon, to Singapore, to Java. Some visits were often repeated – for example, to Burma and to Singapore. His aircraft were rarely sound and sometimes atrocious. One caught fire in flight. One landed in the dead centre of a bombing raid. During his return from England his flying-boat sank at Gibraltar with all passengers aboard. The best was good enough for Eisenhower or Montgomery, but Wavell often had to use whatever was to hand and could possibly fly. His was a poor man's war.

So this must be said. An opportunity for relative ease might have been welcome to many generals after a nightmare period of conducting three or four campaigns simultaneously; short of men and equipment, bombarded by the Prime Minister, gradually losing zest and confidence, conscious of personal error and unjust allegations. And Wavell was a dispassionate introvert. Whatever defences he might erect in his mind, he knew that his performance since *Compass* had been less than perfect. This, too, might have led a lesser man into apathy and withdrawal. Slim faced such a situation after the retreat from Burma, and what has to be noticed is that Wavell must have traversed the very mental process which Slim defined so well in *Defeat into Victory*. The defeated commander, he wrote,

> . . . will go over in his mind the events of the campaign. 'Here,' he will think, 'I went wrong; here I took counsel of my fears when I should have been bold; there I should have waited to gather strength, not struck piecemeal; at such a moment I failed to grasp opportunity when it was presented to me.' He will remember the soldiers whom he sent into the attack that failed and who did not come back. He will recall the look in the eyes of men who trusted him. 'I have failed them,' he will say to himself, 'and failed my country!' He will see himself for what he is – a defeated general. In a dark hour he will turn in upon himself and question the very foundations of his leadership and his manhood.
>
> And then he must stop! For, if he is ever to command in battle again, he must shake off these regrets, and stamp on them, as they claw at his will and his self-confidence. He must beat off these attacks he delivers against himself, and cast out the doubts born of failure, forget them, and remember only the lessons to be learnt from defeat – they are more than from victory.

But Wavell had said it all for himself, in those lectures of 1939: 'This is the first and true function of the leader, never to think the battle or the cause lost.'

As it happens, there is clinching evidence about his mood from the man who shared his flight to the East and new responsibilities. In a letter to the December 1979 issue of the *Journal of the Royal United Services Institute* Brigadier the Lord Ballantrae (Bernard Fergusson) wrote:

> Lord Wavell's exhaustion has often been alleged, but I dispute it. If he had been exhausted he would surely have slept most of the way to India. I accompanied him on that journey in July 1941 as his Private Secretary, in a lumbering and soporific DC3, and I do not remember him closing an eye in flight at all. He had only one, anyway; and for the first leg of the flight, to Lydda, he was peering with it out of the window at Sinai and southern Palestine, the scene of his experiences with Allenby during World War I. On the second leg, to Habbaniya, as soon as we had overflown Amman, he asked me if I had anything for him to read; and I lent him the

copy of Flecker's *Hassan,* which I was reading myself. Before opening it, he quoted the whole of *Ishak's Song,* by heart, and then read it happily until we touched down.

At Habbaniya, where it was devilish hot, he insisted on being driven all around the scene of the recent fighting. At Baghdad, he was dissuaded only with difficulty from flying up to Deir-ez-Zor, which had just fallen, on the grounds that it no longer came under his command: he took me and his ADC for a swim at the Al Wiya Club instead. At Basra, which in July was even hotter than Habbaniya, he was tireless in looking round the docks and inspecting the unloading of ships where men were actually dying of heat stroke on the job. At Sharja, where the total European population at that time was Abbott, the Imperial Airways agent, he was equally keen to see what little there was to be seen; and so on for the rest of the journey, until we finally chugged up the hill from Khalka to Simla, by courtesy of the old narrow-gauge mountain railway.

Next morning, with me on his heels, he took formal possession of GHQ, India. His full vigour was at once apparent; and within forty-eight hours he had despatched proposals, which were implemented within six weeks, to the Chiefs of Staff in London for the invasion of Iran.

With the recent deaths of so many who were close to him during the weeks before his departure from Cairo – people like Arthur Smith and Freddie de Guingand – there are not many witnesses left; and Sandy Reid-Scott, the ADC on that memorable journey – whom Lord Wavell described as 'one in a million' – died of cancer many years ago. But I can testify that Wavell's mood during those eight days resembled that of Christian in *The Pilgrim's Progress* when the burden fell from his back, or that of a schoolboy released for his holidays; and that he brought a gush of fresh air into the musty corridors of Simla.

A study of his actions and attitudes confirms, in fact, that for the time being translation from Cairo to Delhi gave Wavell a second wind. On the central issues his judgement is clear. His communications with London are strong and cogent but less irritable. His activity is athletic in range and duration. His prime responsibility, as Military Member of the Executive Council and second in rank to the Viceroy himself, Lord Linlithgow, is for all the armed services of the Raj: for expanding, organizing, training, equipping: and for sending abroad units which others would normally control in action. The scope of the job was huge: but this was not battle. And yet, ironically, his first important reactions were those of a man about to be engaged by the enemy: he looked to the security of his flanks. There is no documentary evidence enabling one to trace his sequence of thought, but it is as though the collapse of his flank in the Western Desert under Rommel's first assault had made him say, 'Never again'. However that may be, Iran in the west and Burma beyond the eastern mountains became his immediate concern.

The general preoccupation with Iran in the summer of 1941 can only be understood in relation to an equally general assumption in London (shared by Hitler but not by Wavell) that Russia must inevitably, and probably rapidly, collapse. A German drive thereafter through the Caucasus and Turkey long remained a fearful prospect. Iran itself seemed less exposed to an actual invasion, but the presence there of several thousand German nationals and sympathizers (including those extruded from Iraq) would obviously present a danger in the event of a *Drang nach Osten*. The use of 'tourists' and Fifth Columns was a well-established German practice, from the Levant to the borders of Afghanistan. This spread of Nazi dry rot in Teheran and elsewhere seemed to Churchill to require pesticide. But Whitehall's preliminary evolutions struck Wavell as dilatory and even though he had only been in India less than a week he wrote to the CIGS, on 17 July, without compromise.

> The complaisant attitude it is proposed to adopt over Iran appears to me to be incomprehensible. It is essential to the defence of India that the Germans should be cleared out of Iran now repeat now. Failure to do so will lead to a repetition of events which in Iraq were only just countered in time. It is essential that we should join hands with Russia through Iran and if the present Government is not willing to facilitate this it must be made to give way to one which will. To this end the strongest possible pressure should be applied forthwith while issue of Russo-German struggle is still in doubt.

Churchill re-emphasized the point to Auchinleck two days

later. 'The Defence Committee felt that Persia* was in far greater danger of German infiltration and intrigue, and that strong action may have to be taken there. This however is in General Wavell's sphere, and his evident wish is to act which is receiving urgent and earnest attention here.' Wavell had only demanded that *somebody* should take action! During the next ten days there was much discussion about diplomatic delicacies, the possible scale of resistance, and so on, until Churchill became tetchy. 'I consider that the whole business requires exploring, concerting, and clamping together.' Yet it was not until mid August that a joint Anglo-Russian ultimatum was presented in Teheran, and rejected. Now separate columns, mainly of Indian troops, pressed into Iran and before the end of the month all was over. The oil-fields were safe and the Russian link established, whilst the Shah conveniently abdicated in favour of his son, who promised a pro-Allied government. Churchill to Wavell, 30 August, 'I am so glad the Persian adventure has prospered.' It was mainly due to the focussing effect of that early pressure from the new Commander-in-Chief that Iran, the traditional western flank of the old Raj, had been brought within the Allies' net and would remain there, memorable above all as the safe inland supply-channel for nourishing the USSR.

Meanwhile, flying via Baghdad – Cairo – Malta – Gibraltar, Wavell arrived in England on 8 September. His discussions with the Cabinet and the Chiefs of Staff naturally concerned the region which had so emphatically become his concern: aid to Russia through Iran was on the agenda, and defence of the Caucasus. But his real purpose was to testify on two other vital matters. The first was the military void within India itself: 100,000 men already overseas, but in the whole Raj not a fighter-plane fit for more than an airshow, no up-to-date tanks or armoured cars, thirty anti-aircraft guns in the whole sub-continent.† Though new divisions were forming and training,

* Churchill's meticulous and only occasionally absurd concern for the right word made him insist that Persia should be used and not Iran. He claimed that this was to avoid confusion with Iraq: but what emotive associations or oratorical possibilities were there in Iran?

† In March Auchinleck in Delhi had actually written to Wavell in Cairo asking if he could spare some captured *Italian* anti-aircraft guns (such as were then being doled out to Greeks or Turks), 'We are frightfully short of anything of the kind in this country, in fact we really have none at all.'

4000 vehicles were needed and many more thousands of British officers and military technicians. Wavell knew from his Middle East experience that since Britain in 1941 had nothing to spare it was an academic exercise to clamour about shortages. The result would inevitably be a zero response – unless there was a crisis: and the crisis was not yet. But the effort had to be made. In any case the big issue, on which he hoped for some positive movement, was that of Burma: his eastern flank.

Of all the unpardonable misconceptions in the recent history of British defence arrangements, that for the military control of Burma is the least rational. A child's eye would detect that the country's geographical (as well as its historical) affinities are with India rather than with the territories further east. Since semi-independence in 1937, however, Burma also preserved a vague independence about defence until, in November 1940, a combined headquarters was established at Singapore and Burma was put under its operational control: a disregarded outpost. Before Wavell no less than three successive Commanders-in-Chief India had argued unsuccessfully that logic and practical necessity required the defence of Burma to become India's responsibility. Now, in London in September 1941, Wavell expounded the same case at the highest level, and lost – though what had been vague before 1940, or tolerable if illogical thereafter, needed to be put on a realistic basis at a time when the Japanese had already made their move into Indo-China. But the assumptions were insuperable that Singapore was an impregnable bastion, a pivot of defence for the whole of the Far East, and that from this strong fortress Burma's defences could be effectively administered – a kind of poor-relief. Yet as Wavell pointed out, Burma was the glacis in front of India's perimeter, not Singapore's: on a secure Burma depended the protection of the great industrial and harbour complex round Calcutta: and, if the crunch came, it was from India that reinforcements for Burma must flow. All this would be demonstrated – by Japan – in the months ahead.

India's eastern flank was nevertheless withheld from Wavell's control. In his Despatch he later described the continuation of so fruitless an arrangement as 'the cardinal mistake'. The fact is that none of those in high authority in London, either then or later in the war, knew or cared about the military realities in Burma: or, indeed, about its peoples. A brief glance at subsequent developments will make this myopia evident – at least in respect of command and control. Wavell remained dissatisfied. After consultations, he carried with him the Governor of Burma and General McLeod, the GOC: though not with much conviction Air Chief Marshal Sir Robert Brooke-Popham, at the head of the combined Far East Command in Singapore. So on 11 November (and one notes how the sands are running out) Wavell with impressive support sent a special signal to London reiterating his demand for a transfer. Decision was still avoided by the Defence Committee: his signal was not even answered. Yet exactly a month later, four days after the beginning of war with Japan, Churchill and the Chiefs of Staff at last decided to place Burma's defence in India's hands. In December 1941, the Official History observes, 'The Army in Burma was unfit for war with a major military power, and the country was un-prepared to face invasion'. Too late, and almost casually, hostilities had achieved what in peace had been refused: but the belated donation of control to Delhi was like that of Deianira, who by her gift of a poisoned shirt brought death to Hercules.

Though he had got what he wanted, Wavell's instinct about its implications had already been disclosed in the private note he sent to Dill along with his formal signal of 11 November. Nothing could have foretold events more precisely than:

> The last thing I desire is an extension of my responsibility but I do feel that if Burma is attacked the C-in-C Far East will not be in a position to handle it (especially if Malaya is also being attacked) and that problem may be thrown at us in an emergency without one having been able to influence plans or arrangements previously.

There were few senior officers or officials around the Far East at this time who were thinking with relevant clarity. It is greatly to Wavell's credit that now he was released from the vice-like grip of the Middle East he was revealing again a sanity and certainty of judgement – and judgement based, in his typical way, on personal investigation.

In late September and early October he was temporarily whipped off to Teheran and Tiflis to sound out the Russians about co-operation in the Caucasus should the German *Panzers* strike so far. His ability as a Russian interpreter and his knowledge of the Russian people and their history made him a useful negotiator: indeed, Churchill told Beaverbrook that he contemplated putting Wavell in charge of 'the right hand we shall give to the Russians in and about the Caspian basin'. As to their own plans the Russians remained dumb, though generous with vodka, and the Caspian command was only a Churchillian dream. Soon after his return to India, therefore, Wavell set off on a more urgent exploration. Although his command at Delhi gave him, as yet, no operational right or responsibilities beyond the bounds of India 'the Japanese attitude,' he wrote, 'was now very threatening, and I thought I had better look at the Eastern frontier': so he flew to Burma and Malaysia. In spite of an overfull life, he knew nothing at first hand of the Far East. But he applied the soldier's maxim, 'time spent in reconnaissance is seldom wasted'.

The details of his tour are unimportant. The conclusions are terrifying. Of Malaya he wrote, 'My impressions were that the whole atmosphere in Singapore was completely unwarlike, that they did not expect a Japanese attack . . . and were very far from being keyed up to war pitch.' 'As regards Burma,' he continued, 'I was horrified by the complete lack of organisation, of military intelligence, and of planning generally to meet any Japanese attack.' All these impressions are now, of course, documented fact. It might be argued that the British habit of praising the Americans for adopting a policy of 'Germany first' rather than concentrating on the Pacific should exculpate the British themselves for giving the German war priority as compared with the Far East. There is no mileage in this proposition. What horrified Wavell at Singapore and about defence policy in Malaya was not merely lack of equipment – for him this was a normal state of affairs. His reaction was against the mentality of those supposed to be in control against complacency, against lack of initiative, against a society corrupted by well-being. Singapore was asleep in a dream of satiety, and it would not be Prince Charming who would effect the awakening.

As for Burma, its deficiencies stemmed from the same source, compounded by a faith in London – far greater than in the case of Singapore – that its safety could be assumed. Hundreds of books and reports and memoirs later recorded the truth. At the time even the cool and self-contained Wavell must have felt a sense of distaste, even though he would not admit to despair, at his first sight of the inheritance that awaited him.

It was soon bequeathed. The war against Japan was heralded for Wavell by Churchill's signal of 12 December informing him that he was now responsible for Burma and that the Iran/Iraq theatre would go to Auchinleck. But it also created a false optimism. Churchill promised him 18 Infantry Division, now in convoy around the Cape: a 'special hamper' of anti-aircraft and anti-tank guns: four fighter squadrons and (by a later offer) six squadrons of Blenheim light bombers, all from the Middle East: and the use of 17 Indian Division which he was about to despatch to Iraq.* A few days later, on the 16th, he heard from the CIGS that in response to his request two brigades of East African troops would be sent to Burma or Ceylon. His claim is therefore reasonable that at this early stage he had 'ample forces in sight for the defence of Burma', and it is important to understand his belief that these promises would be honoured. In practice, of course, the benefits were trivial. 18 Division was diverted to and lost at Singapore, two brigades of the Indian division went to Malaya, and the aircraft were also sucked away. On the 21st, however, Wavell flew down to Rangoon with a faint sense of a fighting chance, feeling behind him the flow of reinforcement and sharing with Singapore Command, and indeed with London, an impression that even now Burma had time to order her defences, since the Japanese were unlikely to invade before completing what was assumed to be the prolonged operations in Malaya – and perhaps in the Philippines.

On his way to Rangoon Wavell picked up at Calcutta

---

* So unqualified a statement is misleading. The division was merely raw material, under-trained and ill-equipped. It was due to train and equip in Iraq – for war in the desert.

Lieutenant-General Sir Henry Pownall, Gort's Chief of Staff in France, who was due to take over from Brooke-Popham. Pownall's diary for the 20th is illuminating. 'The arrangements for the defence of Burma seem sketchy, to put it mildly. . . . I can see that Wavell is pretty sore at having been landed with such a deformed child.' When Wavell signalled to the CIGS on the 22nd a long list of deficiencies it was the deformity of the administrative arrangements which he particularly stressed. And it was this consideration, plus the feeling that active operations in Burma were still not imminent, that must have persuaded him a few days later to replace the military commander in Burma, General McLeod (who was not far short of retirement) with his own chief staff officer and right hand man in India, Lieutenant-General Hutton. The future Sir Thomas Hutton was by general agreement a senior staff officer of the highest quality: exactly what was required to make sense of Burma's haphazard military organization. But distinguished service in the First World War, indicated by three wounds and two Military Crosses, had been followed by staff appointments rather than operational commands. It was a hard burden, therefore, for a man with such a background to find himself responsible in Burma – as happened when hostilities commenced – for what was in effect a War Office, a General headquarters, an operational Corps Headquarters and the huge administrative problems of a Lines of Communication Area. The event showed that Wavell chose well: he was to disagree, unjustly, with certain battle decisions, but Hutton's foresight and energy played a large part in saving the Burma Army during its long withdrawal northwards.[1]

Since Pearl Harbor had made allies of the Chinese, both the British and the Americans were anxious to bring them effectively into the war. From Rangoon, therefore, Wavell flew north to the Yangtze in the company of an American airman, General Brett, their object being a conference at Chungking with Chiang Kai-Shek and the heads of the British and US Missions, Generals Dennys and Magruder. It was typical of a hundred later discussions: China had something to give as well as to receive, but giving was an unnatural act. Lease-Lend equipment was piled up around the Rangoon docks in immense quantities, subject to theft and deterioration and impossible to clear rapidly down the slow and difficult routes through northern Burma. It was obvious – as between allies – that urgent British requirements should be met from such enviable accumulations. 'This did not interest the General-issimo at all and he referred me to the Chief of Staff,' Wavell recalled. Bitter experience would teach that what the General-issimo was not interested in, nobody else would dare to put into action. The Chief of Staff was certainly no hero. Many misunderstandings and wrangles would follow in Rangoon between the representatives of all three nations, allegations of misappropriation and so on: one American officer was sacked – as a scapegoat – and the British and American governments were drawn in. Finally, but belatedly, a compromise was reached, and quantities of Lease-Lend material at last reached the indigent British. As Wavell said of the Chungking confer-ence, 'It was very interesting to get the atmosphere'.

But the main and reverberating question was that of assis-tance by Chinese troops. Chiang had declared his readiness from the outbreak of war to commit large forces to the defence of Burma – not in altruism, but because of the port of Rangoon and the Burma road which were his life-line. But when at Chungking he offered his 5th and 6th Armies (an army roughly equalling a western division) Wavell asked only for one Chinese division, the 93rd, with another regiment in reserve over the border. There was a fine opportunity here for hurt pride, which the Chinese readily grasped. Moreover, the American observers adversely reported Wavell's 'qualified acceptance' back to Washington: a wedge thrust into the ever-opening gap between British and American attitudes towards China.

As General Magruder pointed out at the time, there was no logical connection between Wavell's attempt to draw on Chinese stocks at Rangoon to help a defenceless Burma, and his rejection of China's offer to come to Burma's aid. Why then did he refuse? He was sensitive on the point, and rather carefully elaborated his case in his Burma Despatch.

Wavell's main argument was that Chiang insisted on his troops being held together and not mixed with the British: like

Australians or New Zealanders, one might say! He also insisted on separate lines of communication for his units, and for more than one division, Wavell maintained, that was impossible. There was still that feeling, also, that adequate British reinforcements were now in the pipeline. Two comments arise. First, by the end of the Burma campaign both 5th and 6th Armies were in action – and indeed, though the retreat of Slim's Burma Army has been rightly celebrated, the figures show that more Japanese were involved on the Chinese than on the British front. Secondly, Wavell's concern about 'lines of communication' has a staff college flavour almost entirely irrelevant to the behaviour of a Chinese division, which moved more like a swarm of locusts than the Brigade of Guards.

Wavell had not had enough time in the East. He did not allow enough for 'face'. Nothing significant would have been lost by responding more graciously to Chiang's offer, particularly as Chungking was the first inter-allied conference, at which a tone of amiable accommodation should have been set. Of course, whatever troops Chiang sent into Burma would not have arrived in time, or would have arrived without ammunition, or without permission to fight. But Chiang's 'face' would have been saved, and the China-watchers in Washington would have been denied a complaint. Wavell honestly admitted, in his Despatch, that he had made a mistake. It was certainly an error, at this time of crisis, to think that 'it was desirable that a country of the British Empire should be defended by Imperial troops rather than by foreign': particularly as Chiang was being pressed – in the end successfully – to make available his group of volunteer American airmen, the AVG under Claire Chennault, whose fighters performed such wonders above Rangoon.

And yet, when they are seen in proportion, how little such misjudgements disfigure the image of a notable man of war! How small such issues seem beside the fact that within a week of his visit to Chungking Wavell had flown back to Rangoon, landed in the middle of an air raid ('when it was all over I counted seventeen bombs which had fallen within fifty yards of the trench, the nearest about a dozen yards away') and been

appointed by Churchill and Roosevelt as Supreme Commander of all Allied land and air forces in the south-west
Pacific. The latter was a less than comprehensive phrase, since
the joint agreement specified an area from Malaya (including
the Burmese front) through the Philippines down to the
northern shores of Australia. Since the forces now placed in
Wavell's hands were American, British, Dutch and Australian, the command came to be known as ABDACOM or
ABDA. (And Burma, it may be noted, had once again been
removed from India's control.)

This new post, of which Wavell was the first and only
occupant, was conceived in the White House at Washington
on Christmas Day, 1941, during *Arcadia,* earliest of the Anglo-
American summit meetings. It reminds one of the love of
Andrew Marvell, about which the poet wrote that it was

> . . . of a birth as rare
> As 'tis, for object, strange and high;
> It was begotten by Despair
> Upon Impossibility.

The prime mover was General Marshall, US Army Chief of
Staff, who said he would 'go to the limit' to achieve a Supreme
Commander. But the limit to which Roosevelt and he wished
to go was the appointment of a British officer: in fact, Wavell.
Both Churchill and his advisers opposed the proposition. Dill
wrote a private letter to Alan Brooke in London (who had just
replaced him as CIGS) describing their united front. The
reason was simple. With the Japanese flooding irresistibly to
the south and west, future disasters seemed certain and no
British Prime Minister or Chief of Staff could vote for placing
one of their most respected commanders in the position of a
'fall guy'. But Roosevelt's wishes prevailed. Two other
appointments followed which, if they had little bearing on
Wavell's ABDA experience, would become only too
meaningful as the months and years passed. The announcement of Wavell's own Supreme Command was accompanied
by a statement that Generalissimo Chiang Kai-Shek had taken
on Supreme Command of all Allied forces in the China
theatre. Later in the month, on 23 January, Major-General

Stilwell was nominated with a wide range of responsibilities as the American military representative accredited to Chiang.

The six-week period of Wavell's dauntless but futile attempt to make a reality of ABDA from the headquarters which, with Pownall as his Chief Staff Officer, he established in Java has two aspects: one could be called theoretical and the other practical. Reviewing his experiences on Java Pownall wrote of Wavell: 'Of all the raw deals he has been given, the miracles he has been asked to produce without even a golden wand to wave, this ABDA Command has been the worst instance.'[2] It was the worst because there was nothing that even an available golden wand could produce: despair and impossibility were truly its parents. So all Wavell's efforts to give the command a structure and then some teeth (faithfully recorded in Connell's biography) were purely theoretical – a story, not always edifying, of arguments with the constituent governments about protocol-priorities for their representatives: of searching helplessly for warships and aircraft capable of inflicting more than a pinprick on the Japanese: of cables from home governments expecting too much from a situation they did not comprehend.

ABDACOM was a synthetic international headquarters trying to fight a real war with paper tigers. It ended with a personal signal from Wavell to Churchill on 21 February. 'I am afraid that the defence of ABDA area has broken down and that defence of Java cannot now last long . . . I see little further usefulness for these headquarters . . . . I have failed you and President here where better men might perhaps have succeeded in altering time factor in our favour.' But this was a moment of harmony between them. Churchill knew in Washington that he was offering Wavell as a sacrifice. Nothing stirred him more than courage and dignity in the face of the odds, and Wavell won his admiration and respect by accepting a post that was really a fiction and by striving, without complaint, to make it a fact. There were no recriminations. 'I hope you realise,' the Prime Minister replied, 'how highly I and all your friends here as well as the President and Combined Staffs in Washington rate your admirable conduct of ABDA operations in the teeth of adverse fortune and overwhelming odds.' The Churchill-Wavell relationship was too flawed – there was too much in the past on which the old man could brood – for such a halcyon mood to persist: but it was genuine.

Yet all was not theoretical in the vast area marked down by the Japanese as their Great East Asian Co-prosperity Sphere. For a commander with British affiliations one practical fact dominated the scene: first Malaya and Singapore itself, then Burma and the approaches to India came under attack. In spite of his broad but vague responsibilities at the headquarters of ABDA, Wavell found time and energy to intervene personally and persistently in the planning and conduct of the relevant defences. Probably no commander throughout the war worked with such constructive dynamism over so large an area. All these regions lay within the ABDA sphere, and as Supreme Commander he was entitled to become involved – indeed, without Singapore ABDA would have even less substance or meaning.* But had he not been diverted to his profitless task in Java Wavell would have had more freedom to tackle the enemy at the gate.

He first took the measure of the war situation in Malaya when, early in January, he paused for a few days on his journey to the Dutch East Indies and the embryo of ABDA. There was no comfort. 3 Indian Corps had now been in constant retreat down the peninsula for several weeks, regularly outflanked and outfought by troops who, unlike themselves, had an elevated morale and great battle-skill. Wavell knew Sir Lewis Heath, commanding the Corps, from the old days at Keren when Heath had 5 Indian Division. They could talk man to man. Wavell's impressions were condensed in a signal to the Chiefs of Staff on 8 January.

. . . These divisions have now been fighting for over a month without rest and retreating continuously under most trying conditions. Retreat does not bring out best qualities of Indian troops and men are utterly weary and completely bewildered by Japanese rapid encircling tactics, by enemy air bombing (though this has been luckily intermittent) and by lack of our own air support. Divisional and brigade Commanders I saw were calm but very tired . . .

* Wavell did not actually take up *operational* command of ABDA until 15 January, but his status and authority were unquestioned.

The stormed heights of Keren and the fall of Sidi Barrani, the days when men of the Indian Divisions were ardent, competent and triumphant now seemed like a fading image cast by a worn out bioscope. But the Supreme Commander had to get on his way. Still, he found time not only to brief the Chiefs of Staff on the plan he had approved for defending the peninsula, but also, typically, to send Hutton at Rangoon a beautifully explicit summary of the jungle tactics and deceptive tricks used by the Japanese in Malaya, as well as comments on revealed weaknesses in the defence. The old intelligence officer and the applauded trainer of troops spoke together.

Though Wavell had to depart for Java he was soon back again, flying in during the early hours of the 13th and making straight for the front along with the GOC Malaya, General Percival. 'So there,' his ADC noted, 'was the most valuable general of the war heading towards the Japanese on a slippery road with a bad driver through country infested with fifth column, with the constant possibility of running into a Jap patrol which had landed down the coast miles behind our lines.'³ However, the front was reached, the situation assessed, and a prolonged thunderstorm endured. Wavell then reported to the Chiefs of Staff: 'Battle for Singapore will be a close-run thing'.

From now on Singapore meant Wavell. It was he who struggled to inject marrow into the bone of the defence, and into its irresolute commander: it was he who ordered a fight to the death and a policy of 'burnt earth', and it was Wavell who, when there was nothing left to do and London had lost hope, personally authorized capitulation. His were the signals on which Churchill and his advisers relied for information about the developing catastrophe, and it was to Wavell that Churchill despatched impassioned reminders about how 'the fortress' should be defended and then (having discovered to his misery that Singapore was not a fortress, but a naval base with guns turned seawards and a naked rear) about how to contrive the impossible. Everything failed, but Wavell emerged from the disaster untarnished and perhaps with a firmer standing in the Prime Minister's mind. Though he tried to keep resistance going to the end, in his heart Churchill recognized that the metal was not strong enough and that Wavell, on all the issues, had acted for the best. He knew that he was himself one of the guilty men, having starved the East for the sake of the West. And then there were those home truths which Wavell set down just after Singapore's surrender:

> The trouble goes a long way back: climate, the atmosphere of the country (the whole of Malaya has been asleep for at least 200 years), lack of vigour in our peace-time training, the cumbrousness of our tactics and equipment, and the real difficulty of finding an answer to the very skilful and bold tactics of the Japanese in this jungle fighting.

What Churchill did not know was that during his final visit to Singapore, just before the collapse, Wavell had to fight a secret temptation to remain and see the thing through to the end. It would have been gallant, it would have been wrong, and Churchill would have found a good phrase to commend it.

When Wavell returned on the 13th of January from the front in the adjacent State of Johore to the command centre on Singapore Island, his most pressing problem was what the Official Historians demurely called 'the efficacy of the civil administration'. Duff Cooper, who had been touring the Far East as a kind of ministerial investigator into the state of things, was now on his way home, but he had left Wavell a time-bomb in the shape of a copy of a letter, dated 12 January, addressed to the Prime Minister and the Secretary of State for the Colonies. It began:

> Before leaving Singapore I think it right to tell you that I believe that certain changes in the local administration are of the first importance. A breakdown on the civil side may well paralyze the fighting services. There exists a widespread and profound lack of confidence in the administration. I believe that the simplest solution would be to declare a state of siege and appoint a Military Governor for the duration of emergency. . . .

Churchill approved. Lord Moyne, the Colonial Secretary, did not, but he sensibly signalled to Wavell, 'I believe you are the best judge of whether in present situation change of Governor would assist you in defence of Malaya. . . .'

Some decisions in war are of perennial interest because the

results of a different decision would have been profound and far-reaching: perhaps touching future generations. In January 1942 the situation at Singapore was too far gone for any switch of Governors to have had more than a marginal effect. Yet some effect there might have been, some lives saved, some misery abated. Behind the resistance to the Japanese was always a desperate hope of gaining time. So when days matter, marginal benefits rise in value. It seems strange therefore that Wavell, who was acutely aware of the sloth, the laxity, the lack of vision which characterized Singapore's administration, did not grasp joyfully at the opportunity offered – and supported by Churchill – to introduce a Military Governor with draconian powers. Instead, after consultations he reported that the present amiable Governor, Sir Shenton Thomas, was 'a good figurehead' and should stay. In London they acquiesced. But the Russians did not put 'good figureheads' into Stalingrad or Leningrad.

The next problem was General Percival. Nobody can carp with any justice at an officer who is posted to a position for which he is not suited: the responsibility lies with his superiors or the military secretariat. The man himself does what he can, within his limits: yet when things go wrong it is he who is condemned. After Wavell left the Middle East Auchinleck brought up to command 8th Army General Alan Cunningham, whose record in East Africa was excellent but who knew nothing about the desert or armoured warfare. It was not his fault that he failed. Auchinleck then replaced Cunningham with his own chief staff officer, General Ritchie, who was equally ignorant about armour and lacked even Cunningham's experience of operational command. He too failed – because he had been thrust too high too quickly: after maturing, he served in north-west Europe as a Corps Commander without distinction but without disaster. Much the same had happened to Percival. In France in 1940 he had performed adequately on the staff of 1 Corps: but the staff was his *métier,* and it was a cruel fate that put him in charge of Singapore's defence. As Gort's Chief of Staff, Pownall had observed Percival in France. He noted in his diary for 8 January, just after he had reached ABDA headquarters in Java, that Percival was 'an uninspiring leader, and rather gloomy'. 'I hope,' Pownall added, 'it won't mean that I have to relieve Percival, *protem.*, until someone tougher than he can come from elsewhere.'⁴★ ABDA was a tender plant supported by too many Allied susceptibilities . . . the Australians and the Americans, in particular, were always on guard against any act of British self-interest: otherwise, Wavell might well have done worse than to bring up Pownall from Java and put him over Percival's head as Military Governor of Singapore with full powers. It was not on, and it was not proposed. So Percival remained as the chief military instrument in Wavell's hands.

The instrument was not enough, and it was difficult for Wavell to impose himself on events. He must have had nightmare recollections of those days in Cyrenaica when Neame lost his grip in the face of Rommel's first offensive. Back again in Java, he sent over to Singapore on the 16th a long document in which he asked to be informed about plans for withdrawing on to the island and suggested many points for consideration. He also sent over a staff officer, after whose return Wavell composed on the 19th a signal for Percival whose implications are heart-rending. It is true that Percival had declared to the Chief Engineer, Malaya, (the energetic and aggressively minded Brigadier Simson, whom Duff Cooper forced on the reluctant administration as Director General Civil Defence) that 'defences are bad for the morale of troops and civilians' – perhaps the ultimate epitaph for Singapore. That was sufficiently grotesque. But considering how far the Japanese had now advanced in Malaya, and with what efficiency they were spreading as from a bomb-burst over South-East Asia and the Pacific, it is difficult to imagine a Supreme Commander having to write in terms like these to a senior subordinate who is just about to be put under siege.

Have seen Dobbie [the staff officer] and learn that no detailed

★ Percival's personal courage was never in question. In 1914–18 he had risen from command of a platoon to command of a brigade, winning the MC and the DSO with bar. He was much admired by Dill who fostered his career and sent him to Malaya. But he was not a soldier whose qualities flowered amid the strains and the loneliness of the highest operational responsibilities.

scheme exists for withdrawal to island and defence of it if Johore is lost. Sincerely trust it will never come to this but you must have scheme prepared . . . you must think out problem of how to withdraw from mainland should withdrawal become necessary and how to prolong resistance on island.

In just over ten days, early on 31 January, the last soldier would be extricated from Johore and the causeway linking Singapore with the mainland would be blown. Wavell always made a practice of considering, unabashed, the Worst Possible Case: it was sad that Percival had not learned that lesson and planned, even if he had not yet initiated, the necessary preparations.

So in the dawn hours of the 20th Wavell flew north yet again to visit Percival and 'hold his hand'. After a conference Percival wrote out orders, with the Supreme Commander at his side, which informed his senior officers that while the intention was still to fight and hold the enemy in Johore, and that 'withdrawal into the fortress of Singapore will only take place as a last resort', nevertheless specific roads were nominated for columns retiring to the causeway, delaying positions and ambush sites must be selected in advance, and demolitions and anti-tank blocks would be organized – 'preparations for which, where not already made, must be put in hand forthwith'. In retrospect it all seems extraordinarily impromptu – particularly by comparison with the ant-like devotion to detail shown by the Japanese in their forward planning. Late that afternoon Wavell was back again in Java, getting off a warning signal to London and Washington in which he gave notice that a withdrawal was impending and tepidly affirmed that 'if all goes well, hope prolonged defence possible'.

There was stumbling at the next stage. Wavell's signal elicited from Churchill a characteristic thunderclap. 'I want to make it absolutely clear that I expect every inch of ground to be defended, every scrap of material or defences to be blown to pieces to prevent capture by the enemy, and no question of surrender to be entertained until after protracted fighting among the ruins of Singapore city.' Wavell had already set his teeth, and needed no such exhortation. Percival required some qualifications. It was not from Churchill but from the Chiefs of Staff that a personal message was sent to him on the 21st 'calling his attention to the many failures to carry out demolitions according to plan ever since the war started, and expressing their anxiety that there should be no failure in Singapore if the worst came to the worst'. But the theme which was always dominant in the Singapore story now resounded. What, Percival replied, about the effect of calculated destruction, or even visible preparations, on the swarming multi-racial population of the island? He and the governor predicted 'a land-slide in morale'.

Percival appears to have persuaded London that his own policy was acceptable – to plan demolition of installations both public and private, to prepare as unobtrusively as possible, but only to take final action if there was a danger of losing the island. But from Wavell he had less gentle treatment:

> Policy is quite clear. . . . Scorched earth policy of destroying what will assist enemy must continue, enemy will have no consideration for native population and will take what he requires from them if we leave it. This is no time for sentiment. Chinese population of Singapore know they need expect no consideration from Japanese.

In fact demolitions at the Naval Base – docks, cranes, power and fuel depots – as well as general denial of plant and machinery – were carried out surprisingly well before the surrender day. Also, as Percival justifiably observed, a last-ditch stand and an absolute policy of denial are incompatible. The more so when, as actually happened, representatives of overseas (including British) firms appealed to their own governments against the demolition of their property or even obstructed it. In an atmosphere so unreal – where decision, though essential, was difficult – someone had nevertheless to instil a sense of purpose and resolve. It was Wavell's duty to do so. If he sometimes sounded like a bully it was because nobody else was capable of behaving like one.

There is another respect in which it has been implied that at this time he was acting with the inhumanity of desperation. On 29 January the bulk of the British 18 Division arrived from a diverted convoy. In a fortnight or so the whole of the division, less its dead, was in Japanese hands. Why was it hurled so late and so uselessly into inevitable imprisonment? The decision to divert 18 Division to Singapore was in fact made by the Chiefs of Staff: Wavell's option, as Supreme Commander, would merely have been to recommend its diversion elsewhere. Still, he did not do so, and the legitimate question stands.

It has been answered eloquently and convincingly by Connell in his biography. The effect on the exhausted troops who had fought their way in retreat through Malaya, the impact on the whole delicate structure of ABDA, had it been discovered that the British were abandoning Singapore in their minds before losing it in a last battle – these would have been cogent reasons to prevent Wavell from re-routing the division, even if he had seriously considered it. To have done so would have been to admit to himself before the end had arrived that the island was doomed, and the function of a leader in such circumstances is to refuse to accept the apparently inevitable, for how else can he lead? The French command in 1940 is a classic example of giving up the ghost too soon. In recent years Wavell had been constantly compelled to consider the impossible in terms of its possibility. He believed that something could be gained by fighting to the last gasp at Singapore, so he was determined to keep the fight going with every reinforcement he could grab and every lacerating word he might be obliged to utter. It was a cruel necessity. But from one point of view it could be argued that the chaos of Singapore was fundamentally the result of neglect by peacetime governments, of the fall of France, and of Britain's subsequent concentration of troops and equipment on domestic defence and in the Middle East. From this larger point of view Wavell . . . and indeed Percival and his colleagues . . . have the appearance of sin-eaters.

The final assault on the island began on 8 February, and Wavell immediately flew back from Java, arriving during the night of the 9th at about the same time as the Japanese commander, Lieutenant-General Yamashita, crossed over the strait from Johore and took over control of the invaders. Only a few miles away: and in only a few days all would be in

Yamashita's hands. One weakness had been the defence of the crossing-points. Percival had favoured the north-east sector, Wavell the north-west, but Wavell had let him have his way – perhaps believing that one can interfere too much with the local commander fighting the battle, perhaps recalling that the command structure he had himself imposed earlier during the Malayan phase had created difficulties. Unfortunately Wavell and not Percival was right.

There was little to do but exhort, for the evidence of uncontrollable collapse was widespread. Still, exhortation continued: from Churchill to Wavell on the 10th, 'I rely on you to show no mercy to weakness in any form. With the Russians fighting as they are and the Americans so stubborn at Luzon the whole reputation of our country and our race is involved.' Wavell repeated the gist in a personal message he left with Percival before his departure. 'There must be no thought of sparing the troops or civil population. . . . Commanders and senior officers must lead their troops and if necessary die with them.'* This is what he was tempted to do himself. Instead, as he waited down at the harbour for a motor boat to ferry him out to a Catalina, he stepped out of his car on his blind side and fell several feet down from the sea wall to the rocks and their barbed wire entanglement below. The pain was great, but his aides extricated him and somehow eased him out to the flying boat. On the 11th he was back in Java, in hospital: but though the doctors wanted him on his back for a fortnight, he imperiously returned to his desk.

Neither his visit nor Churchill's words had stemmed the tide. The Japanese got the airfields, and then the water supply. As Percival reported his fading hopes Wavell continued to press him ruthlessly. But a turning-point came. In his memoirs Churchill has described how he and the CIGS realized that the utmost had been done, that further slaughter and suffering were useless, and that they must take joint responsibility for a signal allowing latitude of decision. The weight of that decision was laid on Wavell, by a personal message to him from the Prime Minister on the 14th. 'You are

---

* When circulated, this instruction not surprisingly offended commanders who were in fact leading their troops and ready to die with them.

of course sole judge of moment when no further results can be gained in Singapore and should instruct Percival accordingly. CIGS concurs.' On the 15th Wavell gave Percival the authority he so desperately required, and in mid afternoon the news came that all was over. Wavell had saved Tobruk – for the time being – but to preserve Singapore was beyond the power of himself, or of the sorely tried Percival, or perhaps of anyone else.

While Wavell was oscillating between Java and Malaya, Hutton in Burma carried on coolly and methodically. Hostilities there not unnaturally started somewhat later than further east, and though the first Japanese assault troops were ashore in Malaya by 8 December, apart from air raids and some frontier activity no major intrusion into Burma occurred until mid January. The enemy's Southern Army then secured its first foothold, and its first airfields, by capturing the mining region of Mergui, the most exposed area in that long thin tongue of land called Tenasserim which forms a sort of land bridge between Burma and Malaya. From this moment there was only rarely a pause for breath until Slim had led the last of his defeated but defiant army to India and the end of its *via dolorosa*.*

Wavell's choice of Hutton had sometimes been questioned, though never definitively. Where, in any case, was the alternative, the 'fighting soldier' whom Wavell might have overlooked? Not in India, at that time: and it is to be noted that when 'fighting soldiers' were later required for Burma Slim was transferred from Mesopotamia and Alexander from England. When Wavell appointed Hutton he thought – optimistically – that he still had time in hand, as the record shows: he thought that reinforcements were coming along and that what was immediately necessary was a man who could impose some sort of administrative sanity in the Burmese backwater which inexorably, as its turn came, must become part of the

---

* Wavell, Hutton, Smyth and – during the retreat – Slim were of course all victims of the appreciation made before they assumed command that the Japanese would invade *central* Burma through the Shan States. The 1st Burma Division, located in the north to face this imaginary thrust, could never be concentrated alongside 17 Indian Division, and even Slim was unable at first to combine his meagre forces. This dispersion was critical for all four commanders.

ever-expanding battlefield. On that basis Hutton did all and more than could have been expected.

Indeed, it was Hutton who took a step which had vital consequences for the Burma Army. He knew that Rangoon must be held to the last: but he also knew that Rangoon's geographical position made it particularly vulnerable, and yet this was the only port of entry. To insure against its loss, therefore, he made a start on back-loading great quantities of stores up into the heart of Burma, around the key centre of Mandalay. Improvisation to an extreme degree was required and achieved. As a result, when Slim's divisions ultimately fought their way north they found sustenance instead of starvation. Such administrative foresight has the value of a success in battle, and may be compared with the dilettante quality of the arrangements in Singapore.

With these and many other administrative projects to drive forward Hutton was over-loaded, once hostilities commenced, for he then had to adjust part of his mind to controlling a rapidly moving battle. Wavell recognized this in his despatch:

> What was lacking was the close personal touch of the responsible commander. During the five weeks that Burma remained under ABDA Command, I was only able to pay hurried visits; and owing to faulty signals communications messages and reports from Burma sometimes took several days to reach me in Java. It was during these five weeks that the fate of Burma was decided.

But while this is true, it is also the case that his ideas about what ought to be done were understood and applied by Hutton. Their failure (as in the case of Malaya) were due to the quality of the enemy and the inadequacy of the defence – whether from lack of training, or equipment, or numbers, or morale. Wavell's physical presence could have done little to prevent what happened.

There are, however, those who maintain that Wavell *caused* what happened. The case may best be considered geographically. A map will show that any force emerging northwards from the throat of the Tenasserim passage-way, and making for Rangoon, must first obtain a crossing over the great Salween river which reaches the sea at Moulmein, and then

get over the main obstacle of the river Sittang to the west of
which lies the critical communications centre of Pegu and its
connections with Rangoon. On 20 January, the day he realized
that there would have to be a withdrawal into Singapore,
Wavell received official and personal signals from Hutton
indicating that pressure around Moulmein was growing, that
he had no reserves and that up to four divisions were needed as
reinforcements. The Governor of Burma signalled in a similar
vein.

Both he and Hutton were, of course, justified in expressing
an extreme anxiety, for no reserves existed and the reality was
well put by Connell: 'From the first week in December, the
Japanese could, in cold fact, have moved against southern
Burma whenever they wanted, and could have advanced as far
as they liked.' But Wavell replied, on the 22nd, like a magist-
rate addressing a delinquent, 'Cannot understand why with
troops at your disposal you should be unable to hold Moulmein and trust you will do so. Nature of country and resources
must limit Japanese effort.' Two days later he borrowed a
Flying Fortress and made a 2000 mile dash to spend a few
hours at Rangoon. He confirmed and Hutton agreed that the
Moulmein/Salween line must be held, although, as he warned
the Chiefs of Staff next day, the Burmese and Indian units at
the front were nervous and unskilled. Still, 'fight forward' was
the cry. Nevertheless, Moulmein was evacuated on the
morning of the 31st. The first of Rangoon's outworks had
gone.* Should it have been held?

Wavell's second return to Burma from Java was caused not
so much by geographical as by geo-political considerations.
Chiang Kai-Shek was at his most mercurial. A message from
the Military Attaché in Chungking reported the Generalissimo's fear that both Singapore and Rangoon would be lost
(a shrewd prediction) and that therefore the Chinese, antici-
pating increased activity against them in the future when their

---

* At the time Major-General James Lunt was Staff Captain of 2 Burma Infantry
Brigade. He noted in his diary for 2 February: 'The road to Sittang still in a very
rudimentary state. God help us if we have to withdraw along it. Why, oh why, didn't
we start building strategic roads two years ago? The dread cry of our administration in
the Far East – "Too late! too late!".'

supply routes had been cut, were now preserving their strength by ceasing to fight the Japanese except when it was unavoidable: the classic Chinese system of self-preservation by calculated non-resistance. Wavell replied robustly, pointing out that this passivity had allowed the Japanese to withdraw six divisions from China, for use in Malaya and Burma. 'You can assure them that whatever the odds we shall go on fighting Japanese to the end. . . . Americans and ourselves may begin slowly and badly but we shall never let go.' As a follow-up, Wavell seized the opportunity presented by a message from Hutton on 2 February, suggesting a meeting with Chiang who was to fly from Chungking to Calcutta. The Chinese dimension was steadily increasing and Wavell was well aware of pressure from London, stimulated by Washington, for keeping China sweet: apart from the commonsense need to maintain touch with an almost intangible but hardly negligible ally. He arrived at Rangoon from Java about dawn on the 3rd.

The Generalissimo was not there. So uncertain were communications in those days that he did not even know that Wavell was on his way, and he had flown straight to Calcutta. The episode illustrates the extraordinary difficulty of conducting 'war at the top' when senior commanders are commuting over vast distances without even being able to exchange messages. Next morning, therefore, Wavell went forward with Hutton to the headquarters of 17 Indian Division which was still maintaining a vulnerable front to the west of the Salween river. To speak of 'a division' is to misuse language. The formation which Major-General Smyth VC took over in India during December (equipped though not yet trained for desert warfare) was immediately and surgically reduced by the transfer of two of its three brigades to Singapore. By mid January Smyth was in south Burma, the mainstay against the Japanese, with his own original brigade, 16 Indian Infantry Brigade, brought down from Mandalay (feeble in strength and wholly untrained), and 46 Brigade which had just arrived from India and was desperately short of experienced men. With this conglomeration Smyth was now responsible for a line running some 150 miles northwards from the sea, and his coastal flank was dangerously exposed. It is understandable that as the commander on the spot he should have advocated pulling back to the line of the Bilin river, a less substantial waterway much closer to the vital Sittang, where he hoped to establish an effective defence. This Hutton had resisted and at the meeting on the 6th Wavell's declared policy was exactly the opposite of Smyth's. The Japanese were not supermen. Offence is the best defence. He therefore required operations to recover what had been lost in Tenasserim, and two days later Smyth produced an appreciation in which he said that his immediate object was to prevent the Japanese from making any further advance and then resume the offensive.

Whether or not these directives and decisions were correct will be considered later. For the moment it may be noticed that Wavell's visit to the front had an incidental consequence which, along with Hutton's back-loading of supplies, meant as much as anything to the Burma army from the fall of Rangoon to the last phase of the retreat. As he looked over the countryside which Smyth's division was defending Wavell was struck by the firm dry rice-paddies, and it occurred to him that they would make good going for tanks. Then he recalled that 7 Armoured Brigade was in convoy from the Middle towards the Far East. But tanks would be useless in Singapore and wasted in Java. He quickly arranged for the brigade to be diverted to Rangoon, where it went virtually from shipboard into action. Throughout the retreat its tanks were the work-horses, the communication centres, the mobile gun platforms. Slim, who knew best, has generously testified to the unique contribution of this small, tireless, professional unit:[5] but the flash of inspiration had been Wavell's.

The Japanese, however, were not to be restrained either by the Supreme Commander's exhortations or by 17 Division. Back again at what seemed the world's end, in Java, Wavell was now sharing almost hourly the last agonies of Singapore; still vainly endeavouring to give ABDA some teeth; joining unsuccessfully with Churchill and Roosevelt in an attempt to persuade the Australian government to allow 7 Australian Division, now nearing Ceylon, to be landed at Rangoon instead of returning home; and defending Hutton from the improper criticisms sent to Churchill by the Viceroy of India: 'Our troops are not fighting with proper spirit. I have not the least doubt that this is in great part due to lack of drive and inspiration from the top.' The fact is that a careful study of operations in south Burma certainly reveals cases of confusion, of inefficiency and even of craven behaviour, but it also reveals many an instance of bravery, initiative and stoical endurance in a force which, as has been seen, was nothing better than a patchwork quilt before the battle began. The Viceroy in remote Delhi might have done better if he had refrained from accusing the troops of his Raj or their leadership,* and considered whether their lack of equipment and of training – which sent men into action ignorant of a grenade, and officers who had never fired a pistol – was not 'in great part due to lack of drive and inspiration from the top' within the responsible governments of India and Britain. There was one excellent by-product from this unsavoury exchange. Churchill offered General Alexander, from Southern Command in England, to take charge of operations in Burma. Wavell welcomed the news and Hutton must surely have sighed with relief.

Yet all this was academic, and in the clouds. The crude and mundane facts are that even if the Australians had been allowed to disembark at Rangoon they would have been swallowed up – like 18 Division at Singapore – in an inevitable catastrophe, thus embittering Commonwealth relations still further; that Alexander, the hero of retreats, arrived too late to prevent one: and, above all, that in just over a fortnight after Wavell's second flight to Burma 17 Division, bustled and confused by devious encirclement, and air attacks, and dust, and heat, and thirst, and an absolute inability to form a coherent front, had withdrawn not only to the Sittang line but to the far western side of the river, blowing the vital bridge in the early hours of

---

* General Lunt, who was closer to the action than Lord Linlithgow, wrote to Sir John Smyth on 28 November 1979: 'I always remember you visiting our brigade mess two or three days after wc had got away from Moulmein. . . "a soldier's general," I wrote in my diary. Many years later when I too became a commander I tried consciously to model myself on you.' Wavell's subsequent treatment of Smyth, as of Hutton, has an uncharacteristically intolerant quality which contrasts disturbingly with the long-retained impression of a young front-line officer.

the 23rd. Everyone engaged immediately appreciated that Pegu, and hence Rangoon, were no longer tenable. There was an unforgettable silence, of awe and anguish.

Responsibility for the events at the Sittang bridge, which was blown in circumstances of great uncertanty, leaving about two-thirds of the division (many of them non-swimmers) on the enemy side of a broad and fast-flowing river is an issue about which debate has not yet ceased: a specific issue not relevant here. Except in one respect: Sir John Smyth has pointed a finger at Wavell, the implication being that his policy in south Burma up to the time of the Sittang disaster had been ruinous.[6] The narrative must therefore curve backwards to an earlier point in the story, and repeat the question which was then by-passed. Did Wavell *cause* what happened?

In a direct but not pejorative sense the answer must be, yes. But the reasons are what matter. And Smyth reduced them to a point of significance when he wrote,

> I quite understood General Wavell's reasoning with regard to this forward defence. It was comforting for Winston Churchill and the Chiefs of Staff in London, for Generalissimo Chiang Kai-Shek, for the Viceroy of India and for the Governor of Burma, to see each morning the red line on the map depicting the position of the 17th Division as far in front of Rangoon as possible: but this was a political defence plan, not a military one.

If such were Wavell's reasons then the picture presented in this book of his customary line of thought, when taking command decisions, has been consistently inaccurate and fallacious. At the heart of all his operations – even, erroneously, in the case of Greece – there was a military purpose based on a fine calculation of the possibilities: he was not, by nature, a 'political' commander.

What Wavell sought in south Burma was not some cosmetic political symbol, but time. It was a military fact that Rangoon was the only port through which the convoys of equipment and reinforcements believed to be on the way could discharge. The stocks of Lease-Lend material had to be cleared north to China. The route to China and China itself had to be kept in being – this was not just a political matter, *pace* the Americans, but increasingly a military necessity. Wavell had been tardy to recognize the need for Chinese troops, but this was daily becoming self-evident. Past lethargy had prevented the building of a road between Burma and India, so that if Rangoon fell the Burma army was trapped: it was a military consideration of great weight to prevent or postpone such a calamity. Then there were the oil stocks and fields, at Syriam near Rangoon and further inland: military stores of great value to both sides.

Wavell's reasons for 'fighting forward' for as long as possible at each bound – in Tenasserim, at the Salween, at the Bilin, and at the Sittang – included most if not all of these issues, and it was certainly because of them that Hutton supported him loyally in demanding 'no retreat' until retreat was inevitable. Both sought, above all, to keep open a port of entry at Rangoon for the relief for which they, metaphorically, scanned the horizon every morning. They needed space – sufficient space between the Japanese and the crucial Pegu-Rangoon link. Only time could preserve that space. And so it was that harshly and insensitively, as it seemed from the earliest days of the Japanese invasion, orders went out to stand fast, not to yield, to fight to the death. If Wavell had been Smyth, in command of a division, he too would have looked at the realities on his own immediate front and proposed withdrawals or readjustments. But if Smyth had been Wavell, with a larger view, he too would surely have found himself aware that he could not surrender an inch. Wavell is not the only commander who has had to buy time with the bodies of his own men.

His agitated signals suggest, and others have made the point, that his retention of 17 Division so far forward derived from a contempt for the Japanese.* He had beaten Italians with such ease and now, they say, he assumed that he was only dealing with their eastern equivalents and that if the admittedly scratch lot of troops up forward kept their nerve they should be able to hold their ground. But this is to overlook the

---

* It is, however, important to note that in early 1942 such an attitude was prevalent, not least among the troops at the front. It was fostered by gravely inaccurate intelligence estimates of Japanese capability.

lessons about Japanese battle-drills which Wavell had quickly assimilated in Malaya and had been at pains to communicate to both Hutton and Percival. It ignores his militarily sophisticated mind which was not prone, in such matters, to contempt without evidence. And while he was endeavouring, mainly from his distant command post in Java, to direct the battle in Burma he was also, as has been seen, discovering the true qualities of the Japanese in the most practical manner possible – on the perimeter of Singapore. One can do no more than estimate, and suggest that Wavell was merely doing what hundreds of commanders have done in the past when the enemy is dominant and their troops are losing heart, which is to spread the word that their own troops are splendid and the enemy vastly overrated. They whistle to keep up the courage of themselves and their men. When Rommel's image was dominant in the desert Auchinleck actually issued a special instruction to his subordinates telling them to deflate it. Wavell could only gain time by trying to make his men believe that they could hold on to space.

By the 27th Wavell was back in Delhi, taking over as Commander-in-Chief from General Hartley who had been occupying his desk. Now he could look to his left flank, Burma, without distraction, for ABDA had dissolved into thin air. On the 21st he had informed Churchill 'that the defence of ABDA area has broken down and that defence of Java cannot now last longer'. With permission, he wound up the command. Yet though this great segment of the Far East had been lost or abandoned, he still believed passionately or perhaps stubbornly in the possibility of retaining Rangoon. To this task, in familiar Delhi, he bent his mind. And if there are times, now, when his actions seem peremptory and his accent irritated, one has to recall the effect on that mind of a long period of stress still not ended, of the thousands of flying miles, the critical conferences, the mere physical battering of a body no longer young – culminating in the fall of Singapore, whose undermining effect was greater because he scorned the doctors and returned to duty. Wavell in Delhi was a tired man in a hurry.

Something unusually frenetic and short-tempered was

creeping into his signals even before he left Java. The series of directives and complaints that he hurled at Hutton on the 21st seem immoderate:

> Why on earth should resistance at Sittang River collapse? Are you not still successfully holding Bilin River? . . . What is the matter that these pessimistic reports are given? . . . There seems on surface no reason whatever practically to abandon fight for Rangoon and continue retrograde movement . . . . If at all possible Sittang River must be crossed and counter-offensive be made east of river . . .

Hutton was not a schoolboy to be taught elementary arithmetic but Wavell's trusted Chief of Staff, and what the Supreme Commander was writing was moonshine. But copies of the letters went to London and were approved by the Chiefs of Staff. No doubt it fortified them – without justice to Hutton – in their admirable decision to send out Alexander.

Yet the speed of collapse on the Burmese front, which he had not been prepared to credit or accept, was evident in papers lying on Wavell's desk in Delhi. The most striking was a breathless communication to the Viceroy from the Governor of Burma, which began, 'This is the last message I will send from Rangoon until we have recaptured it' and stated that demolitions would begin on 1 March. 'Demolitions', which meant destruction of the Syriam oil refineries, were also mentioned in signals from Hutton. Wavell flew over to Burma without delay, for a meeting at the Magwe airfields on the Irrawaddy with the Governor, Sir Reginald Dorman-Smith, together with Hutton and the RAF Commander, Air Vice-Marshal Stevenson.

His decision at the meeting, as reported to the Chiefs of Staff, was consonant with all that had gone before. He was still going to play for time, clutching at the faint but not invisible possibility that a British line might be drawn across central Burma to link up with the Chinese now moving southwards. To that end he reversed an instruction of Hutton's that 63 Infantry Brigade, *en route* from India, should be turned away (since to land it at a port about to be surrendered seemed pointless) and ordered the convoy to continue to Rangoon. Once again we see the commander with the larger picture in his mind trying to grasp any available brick with which to build a wall.

But Hutton, as a former Chief of Staff in India, knew more exactly the conditions of 63 Brigade and its probable value as a fighting unit. The state of one of its battalions, for example, is set down mercilessly in Philip Mason's history of the Indian Army, *A Matter of Honour*. The 1st/11th Sikhs had only joined the brigade two months previously. 'Hardly anyone, officer or man, had seen a three-inch or two-inch mortar, a Bren gun, an anti-tank rifle, a radio set or an armoured carrier.'[7] When they sailed for Burma there were not twenty trained men in a company. They unpacked their new weapons and practised by firing over the stern. Hutton had other considerations in mind: the blocking of the port by a profitless convoy would impede the evacuation of essential material and people. However, Wavell's ruling held: a few more days were gained, the brigade did arrive, and after a savage initiation it played its part. His strength of feeling at this time may be gauged by Hutton's recollection that at the Magwe meeting Wavell 'stormed' at him in front of the others, as though he had lost control:* the only time in their close association that Hutton had seen this occur.[8] But both generals, by now, were reaching the point where fatigue in the human metal can easily cause something to snap.

In fact Wavell was not broken. He flew south and visited Smyth at his headquarters between Pegu and Rangoon. Smyth, who had undergone a severe operation the previous year, was now in a state that required medical care,† so Wavell replaced him with Brigadier 'Punch' Cowan who continued to command 17 Indian Division in many famous actions until the end of the war. Next he flew to Lashio for two sessions with Chiang Kai-Shek, for movement of the 5th and 6th Armies into Burma (in spite of Wavell's earlier lack of concern) now

* But see footnote on page 146 for Wavell's loss of self-control on the lost field of *Battleaxe*. The dykes that held back his emotions normally stood firm. On the rare occasions when they cracked the impact of so unusual an event was greater than that of the more spontaneous outbursts of other men.

† One of the mysteries of the campaign is that Wavell seems to have been well aware from the start of Smyth's physical condition, but to have ignored it as a factor when assessing his performance in the field.

seemed vital. To the Chiefs of Staff he reported optimistically, but time would show that for the British, as for General Stilwell, a Chinese word did not necessarily imply a Chinese deed. From Lashio Wavell flew straight to Calcutta where, on the airfield at midday on 4 March, he met General Alexander and briefed him tersely on what he had to do: reporting to the CIGS, he signalled that he had 'issued instructions that Rangoon is not to be given up without battle as aggressive as our resources will permit'. But the truth was that the whole Burma campaign was about to change its theme.

When Alexander reached Rangoon on the 5th Hutton was at the front, but his staff explained the realities as explicitly as their master would have done. After going forward himself, and with Wavell's instructions in his ears, Alexander decided that in spite of what he had heard and seen he would still try to hold on. It suffices to say that, like a good soldier who has done his duty but not lost his wits, by the following evening he had accepted that Rangoon was untenable. When the withdrawal began next day, however, it was only a miracle (a Japanese inflexibility) that prevented the new Commander and a substantial part of his army being cut off and captured. A Japanese force seeking to outflank Rangoon from the west had set up a road-block, on the northward road to Prome, which effectively halted the withdrawal and which no attacks could break. To Sakurai, the Japanese commander, this block was merely a protection for his left flank until his encircling movement was complete. By mid-day on the 8th the Japanese manoeuvre was complete. The road-block was now cleared, and Alexander moved forward into history instead of into a prison-camp. Wavell knew that he had pushed the luck too far, admitting in his Despatch that his order to hold on 'eventually placed General Alexander in a difficult position and led to his forces being nearly cut off'. Still, he added resolutely, 'on balance I am satisfied that we gained by the delay'.

On balance it may be supposed that this is true. There is a conventional way of writing history which makes a sharp distinction between 'military' and 'political' matters: 'military' being concerned with guns and divisions and tactics, and 'political' being concerned with relations between states, party affairs, public opinion, events in parliaments and congresses. While this distinction is often invalid, it is never more so than in the case of alliance warfare. There were few days during the Second World War when the political climate in Washington and the tone of American public opinion were not, from the British point of view, a military factor, since on them depended allocations of weapons and shipping, postings of American divisions or aircraft, agreement about strategic planning. Often this was true of Australia (the anguished exchanges about 7 Australian Division being a good instance). In the case of China, political attitudes and military action were so interlinked as to be indistinguishable. In the spring of 1942, when Britain was at the lowest ebb, anything which to any degree decreased or stemmed the loss of confidence, in allied capitals and administrations, about the British conduct of the war was a positive military gain. Every day saved by Wavell in Malaya or Burma registered in Washington or Chungking. He was always a 'theatre' rather than a 'battle' commander, and it is those in charge of theatres of war, rather than the divisional commander at the front, who – if they are any good – come to appreciate the convergence of the 'military' and the 'political'. Wavell understood. The protection of British property and lives, the defence of strategically valuable positions, all this was a matter of course. But if his policy and performance during the early months of the Japanese war are to be criticized it is at the highest military/political level that they deserve to be assessed.

Athens. Singapore. Rangoon. Few British commanders have been associated with the loss of more great cities. But in the spring of 1942 there were excellent reasons for Wavell to ask whether Delhi might not make a fourth.

# 7

# Shaking the Pagoda Tree

Shoot Gandhi, and if that does not suffice to reduce them to
submission, shoot a dozen leading members of Congress: and if
that does not suffice, shoot 200 and so on until order is established.
You will see how quickly they will collapse as soon as you make
it clear that you mean business.

HITLER to Chamberlain, Berchtesgaden 1938

The capital of the Raj was not in danger. All the plans for
aggressive expansion prepared by the Japanese Imperial General
Headquarters in 1941 are known, and known in precise
detail. Though they ranged from Hong Kong to the Dutch
East Indies and from Siam to Singapore, they did not include
India as an objective. Indeed, Burma was itself something of
an afterthought, added because of its oil and rice and for the
protection it offered to the flank of the Southern Offensive
Zone. Even the so-called 'March on Delhi', the Japanese offensive at Imphal in 1944, was never intended by Tokyo to
achieve so delectable a result: some exploitation over the frontier, and capitalization of nationalist unrest, were perhaps the
most sanguine expectations. But, as the politicians say, we
have since been able to examine the books. In March 1942
Wavell, with less insight, envisaged a different scenario.

He made this clear to the Chiefs of Staff on the very day that
Rangoon was abandoned, 7 March, in an appreciation which
properly calculated that the Japanese would press northwards
into upper Burma, thus cutting the links with China and
making air bases available for attacks on India. Moreover, he
added, after succeeding in Burma 'he will probably attempt
attack on NE India by land, by seaborne forces and by air
attack . . . we are very thin on ground and in air'. There is an
interesting echo of these fears in the autobiography of Philip
Mason, who at the time was Secretary to the Chiefs of Staff
Committee in Delhi. Recalling the situation a few weeks later,

in April, he wrote that 'there was no reason we could see why the Japanese should not land troops in India'.[1] Indeed by 15 April (after the Japanese Fleet had made its one and only venture into the Bay of Bengal) Churchill was writing to Roosevelt about the possibility of 'invasion of Eastern India, with incalculable internal consequences to our whole war plan, including the loss of Calcutta and of all contact with the Chinese through Burma'.

For Wavell as Commander-in-Chief this was again a matter of 'backs to the wall', as it had been when so little seemed to lie between the enemy and the delta of the Nile. He was on familiar ground: habituated to 'days when Heaven was falling', and his duty to 'save the sum of things'. But by comparison with the last year's crisis in the Middle East there were two extra ingredients of great moment, each the kind of 'political' factor whose significance and effect are essentially 'military'. These were the rising tide of nationalism in India, and America's love-affair with China. The first was not fully comprehended by Wavell until he became Viceroy: the complexities of the second were beyond his understanding.

The multitudinous population of India was the sea in which the belligerent British had to swim. Yet war with Germany and Italy had been imposed on the Raj by Viceregal authority, and for the multi-million inhabitants of India was no more *their* war than was the expanding conflict with Japan: except because of loyalty. It was custom, habit and above all loyalty – to tradition, to the regiment, to individual officers – that combined with conditions and earnings beyond the scope of the ordinary peasant to knot the army together – an army which exploded from 189,000 in 1939 to 2,500,000 in 1945 and, apart from a few trivial episodes, never had the breath of a mutiny. The contempt so often cast on the British Empire may be in part rebutted by an awareness that these men in their magnificent divisions – the 4th, for example, or the 5th, the 7th, the 17th, the 19th – fought to the death in their voluntary battles, and to reject them as mere mercenaries is to degrade their spirit. Of the twenty-seven VCs awarded in Burma twenty went to the Indian Army. And throughout India there was also a greater sense of solidarity with – or, at worst, unaggressive apathy about – the Raj than was appreciated at the time in Delhi or London. Not long before Wavell's current crisis the Viceroy, Lord Linlithgow, had written to the Secretary of State, Leo Amery, that Indians had 'no natural association with the Empire, from which they are alien by race, history and religion, and for which as such neither of them [he included the Burmese, with more reason] have any natural affection'. He assessed India merely as a conquered country which had been brought into and kept within the Empire by force.[2] This, if correct, would have meant that India in 1942 was not so much a sea in which to swim as a tide-race threatening death by drowning.

Linlithgow was dealing in dangerous half-truths: the more dangerous because for Churchill they represented unqualified fact – Churchill who from the start to the finish of the war was doggedly determined to surrender no whit of Imperial power or prestige, particularly in India; Churchill who had explicitly excluded India from the self-determination clause of the Atlantic Charter. But there was another danger. For sealed minds like these, validating proof of India's unreliability was supplied by increasing pressure from the two main political groups, Gandhi's Congress Party and the Muslim League, for swift and substantial measures leading to self-government. In no important way was it – as yet – vicious or subversive. But it was genuine and it was growing.* In his succinct style Attlee summarized the force behind this pressure, observing, in a Cabinet memorandum of early February,

> The fact that we are now accepting Chinese aid in our war against the Axis powers and are necessarily driven to a belated recognition of China as an equal and of Chinese as fellow fighters for civilisation against barbarism makes the Indian ask why he, too, cannot be master in his own house.[3]

And there were other pressures – from Roosevelt, the mole

---

* Paul Scott's novels, combined as *The Raj Quartet,* contain a brilliant distillation of this mood. In one of them, *The Jewel in the Crown,* there is this relevant passage. 'What sort of White Imperial Power was it that could be chased out of Malaya and up through Burma by an army of yellow men? It was a question the Indians asked openly. The British asked it only in the unaccustomed stillness of their own hearts. And prayed for time, stability and loyalty, which are not things usually to be reaped without first being sown.'

blindly seeking to undermine British Imperialism, and in Britain itself from the Labour Party and from those who had not shut their eyes while keeping to the right. Here then was a major issue of quite a new order for a Commander-in-Chief who was not adept in the chaffering of the political market-place, but on whose desk, since he with the Viceroy repre-sented Power, the issue must certainly fall.

A key-note that might have brought harmony into all that followed had been struck early in the year by a message to Churchill from one of the least dissentient among India's elder statesmen, Sir Tej Bahadur Sapru, who declared that 'the heart of India must be touched to rouse her on a nation-wide scale to the call for service'. The answer was what came to be known as the Cripps Mission, which worked in India as a Cabinet dele-gation during late March and early April, failed to touch India's heart and ended in deadlock. Taking a position firmly at the Viceroy's side, Wavell assisted in ensuring a débâcle. Yet the military implications of this political confrontation were potentially serious, as Chiang Kai-Shek – by a combination of self-advertisement and *schadenfreude* – had spelled out in a message to Roosevelt and Churchill after a February visit to India:

> . . . if the Indian political problem is not immediately and urgently solved, the danger will be daily increasing. If the British govern-ment should wait until Japanese planes begin to bomb India and the Indian morale collapses it would already be too late . . . if the Japanese should know of the real situation and attack India, they would be virtually unopposed. If the political situation were to change for the better, this may prevent the enemy from having any ambitions to enter India.[4]

Chiang was exaggerating 'the real situation', though the dis-turbances in southern India when the Japanese Fleet penetrated the Bay of Bengal showed that the British were still far from rousing India on Sapru's 'nation-wide scale to the call for service'. How then did Cripps, recently made a Cabinet Minister, seek to meet the challenge? He carried with him a Draft Declaration, scrapped and filed by the War Cabinet after long discussion, which in effect offered to the Indian parties one vague and two definite propositions. Immediately hostilities ended, an elected body would be established whose task would be to frame a new constitution for an India to which responsible power would be transferred. Any province unwilling to accept the constitution would have the right to opt out. So far, so clear. But the offer in what became known as paragraph (e) was more obscure, stating as it did that while the British must bear full responsibility for defence so long as the war went on, 'the immediate and the effective participation' of India's principal leaders was 'invited'. Wavell powerfully supported Linlithgow in condemning the 'opt out' clause, fearing (from the army's viewpoint) its disruptive effect in the very areas which produced soldiers of quality, the Muslim-majority provinces, the Punjab, the lands of the Sikhs. But the Declaration was not to be revised. A doubt exists, in fact, whether Churchill ever intended it to have meaning and to succeed: whether it was not simply a device to hold a split Cabinet together and to produce a good propaganda effect in the United States.

Since the war was not truly 'theirs' Indian politicians – particularly the Congress men – were less concerned with offers of pie in the sky after victory than with jam today: that is, with immediate access to tangible power. It was thus around paragraph (e) that the debate revolved, with Cripps assiduously (but at a remove from the Viceroy) working on Nehru, Jinnah and the other chief protagonists. And this debate itself narrowed into profitless attempts to devise a formula whereby an Indian on the Viceroy's Council could be given responsibility for defence – *without* responsibility for defence, so far as Wavell was concerned. He dug himself in. Nothing that might erode the authority and responsibility of the Commander-in-Chief was acceptable, and of the various ingenious or naïve ideas propounded none was approved. In the end the Cripps offer was destroyed by Congress, who refused to accept the shadow of immediate participation without the substance of actual power. The future could look after itself.

There were too many occupying entrenched positions, Churchill, Linlithgow, Gandhi, and Wavell – who had not yet discerned as clearly as he did when Viceroy that India meant more than the army.* The historian Sir Reginald Coupland, who was in Delhi at the time for research into the Indian constitution, made a shrewd comment after it was all over. 'We are going to abdicate in a few years. If Wavell is sure of his own position, what does it matter if the Indian leaders are in virtual control of domestic government?'⁵ In a different climate of opinion, in a general attempt to 'touch the heart of India', with more trust and less suspicion it was not impossible that a viable Cabinet-style government might have emerged, the Viceroy still the figure-head, the Commander-in-Chief still commanding. Would Auchinleck, soaked in the Indian *ambiance*, have been more diplomatic and accommodating than Wavell? Or would he, too, have looked straight to his front?†

The essence of the confrontation was an attempt to use persuasion rather than force. The object was to tranquillize. Thus Hitler's suggestion to Chamberlain could hardly be applied, since to shoot 200 Congressmen, or even a dozen, or even just Gandhi himself would not have been à *propos*. Yet it was not long before the military consequences of this political complex made force and firearms unavoidable. The connection of cause and effect is so evident that it is worth taking a leap into the distance.

A few months later, in August and September, the Government of India was faced with what Linlithgow described to Churchill as 'the most serious rebellion since that of 1857'. Gandhi had launched civil disobedience: 'Quit India' was the cry, and what the All-India Congress Committee on 8 August activated as 'a mass struggle on non-violent lines on the widest scale', an outburst specifically related to the failure of the Cripps Mission, escalated into violence. An alert administration immediately arrested Gandhi and other Congress leaders. Widespread insurrection followed, notably in regions of military importance like Bihar and the United Provinces, an

---

* In 1945 Cripps recalled, 'Until I went and brought them together Wavell had met only Indian *soldiers* – none of the leaders. When Nehru and Wavell met the latter plainly understood little of what Nehru was driving at.'

† Such rhetorical questions are worth posing. In practice, it seems inconceivable that Auchinleck as Commander-in-Chief would have readily sacrificed any element of military authority in the threatened India of 1942, or that devious and conflicting sectarian interests could have been eased into a compromise.

insurrection which ran through the gamut of arson and sabotage to murder and the rule of King Mob. The vital railways connecting Calcutta with Delhi and Bombay, and what was literally the lifeline to the threatened frontier of Assam, were strangled.

In simple terms, this meant that Wavell and his staff had to deploy no less than fifty-seven battalions to deal with the internal enemy of which twenty-four were drawn from, and thus emasculated, the army in the field. Training, troop movements, stock-piling, the massive airfield-construction programme were all blocked or delayed. There is no evidence that the Japanese, as was thought and as would have been sensible, had stimulated this revolt. It was a frenzy born of frustration and the Mahatma's fantasies. The timing was peculiarly awkward since, as will be seen, the army was disrupted just when Wavell's offensive plans were taking shape and when he himself – during most of August – was absent at conferences in Cairo and Moscow. What is to be observed, however, is that there was no parallel with 1857: an army mainly Indian stood the strain, and no equivalent insurrection occurred throughout the war. The military implications of political factors had been fully but finally demonstrated – without a shot at Gandhi.

For the failure of the Cripps Mission and its consequences every analyst finds his own culprit – the Prime Minister, the Viceroy or, often enough, Cripps himself. Wavell was certainly an instrument, conveniently fitting into Linlithgow's hand. Yet his attitude was understandable. For nearly two years he had thought of little but action against the enemy: his decision-making, often ruthless and often desperate, had been concerned with battle. The enemy was now at the gates of India and new battles impended. No wonder that he was determined not to give away any power or prerogative that might assist him, as Commander-in-Chief, during a coming conflict which he was not even certain he could win. If some compromise should have emerged from the Cripps initiative, then there were others in London and Delhi with a wider, longer and deeper experience of Indian politics who should have drawn on their knowledge and their imagination to contrive it.

Compared with the sectarian strife of India, however, the

misconceptions, idealisms, strategic dreams, political and commercial interests which loosely combined in the American attitude towards China were a bewildering phantasmagoria. There was a long and sentimentalized Sino-American relationship, religious through missionaries, economic through traders, even military through attachments. All this had a rivetting hold on American public opinion, and therefore on a President ever-conscious of the voter. Thus when in 1942 Roosevelt and his Chiefs of Staff made a clear-cut decision to keep China in the war and Chiang in power, Wavell was presented with a politico-military situation of unusual scale.

It is doubtful whether Wavell ever comprehended fully the absolute commitment of Washington to Chungking (until disillusion soured the honeymoon later in the war) or grasped that proposals on behalf of or involving the Chinese had a symbolic aspect needing as much attention as their viability. He was certainly ignorant of the ramifications, and the narrow-mindedness, of the formidable China lobby in the USA. Churchill sought to tip him off at an earlier stage, when he wrote to Wavell in Java on 23 January about the vexed question of Chinese divisions for Burma, and added, 'I must enlighten you upon the American view. China bulks as large in the minds of many of them as Great Britain. . . . If I can epitomise in one word the lesson I learned in the USA it was China'. The meaning of that, in what the Americans called CBI or the China–Burma–India theatre, was that to them Rangoon and the recovery of Burma mattered purely as a means of opening up supplies to China by the Burma Road, and India represented a vast supply-dump and aircraft carrier from which China could be serviced over the Himalayan Hump. These were the parameters.

The Generalissimo and his magnetic wife, for their part, completely understood the American fixation and were at pains to foster it by every act of propaganda, including the nursing of their own lobby in Washington and hard work on Roosevelt himself; the well-timed protest about dishonoured promises and China's imminent collapse; unverifiable (and unfulfilled) assurances about future Chinese operations. Churchill and his colleagues were rarely taken in by this

Chinese shadow-play. But then the interests of the British Cabinet in India and Burma were of a different order: towards China itself neither sentiment nor self-interest, nor economic anticipations, nor tempting strategic concepts made any great thrust. For London the fundamental aim was to recover Singapore. Here too, then, Wavell was caught in a cross-fire.

At the centre of the beaten zone stood Lieutenant-General Joseph Stilwell. This craggy and rebarbative character was never fully appreciated by the British at the time and the integrity of his performance has subsequently been under-valued. It was a fact, however, that when in February the Americans decided to put their man into China General George Marshall, the US Army Chief of Staff, picked the best he had got – and Marshall, among his many great merits, was exceptional in the calculated accuracy of his appointments. Stilwell was already his choice to command an American army in a projected invasion of north-west Africa: Stilwell knew China and its armies intimately from years of peacetime ser-vice: so Stilwell arrived in the CBI theatre with the highest credentials which were unfortunately concealed by his open contempt for the British, his ragamuffin style and an acrid phraseology. Slim came to terms with him and Alexander endured him – but they met him at the front, in action, where he was always at his best. Wavell, who either dealt with him at a distance or in more formal meetings, perhaps never grasped the fiery inner quality of a man who was dedicated to carrying out a mission – and who would destroy himself by being too honest not to recognize and report on the squalid realities of Chiang's regime. As in the case of Churchill, one observes a loss – a loss in the effective conduct of the war, a loss at a personal level because these two minds never meshed to-gether. Amity was not increased when Wavell, for an appreci-able period, withheld his forward plans from Stilwell – fearful, no doubt, of leaks in the Chinese camp.

After arriving in India Stilwell met Wavell for the first time on 28 February in Calcutta, on his final return from Java: 'a tired depressed man pretty well beaten down', Stilwell noted.[6] Tired and depressed, indeed: but the monosyllabic Wavell could not, and perhaps never did, communicate to this *farouche* ally the extent to which it was impossible for him to be beaten down. So throughout their relationship there was a grudging suspicion in Stilwell's mind that Wavell's heart was not in the fight – or if it was, then some selfish interest of the Limeys must be involved. Meanwhile, sufficient ambiguities existed. Stilwell had been sent to China as Chief of Staff to the Generalissimo, as Commander of United States Forces in the CBI theatre and, among other more nebulous commitments, to improve American assistance to China, to improve the combat efficiency of the Chinese, and to administer Lend-Lease. From his capacious memory for English poetry Wavell might well have pulled out those lines from Goldsmith's *The Deserted Village*.

> And still they gazed, and still the wonder grew,
> That one small head could carry all he knew.

Stilwell had now to discover whether Chiang would allow this cat's cradle of assignments to function: Wavell needed to know how his responsibilities for India and Burma would be affected by them. Revelation came soon.

The Burma army in early March had fallen back about 150 miles to the north of Rangoon, with some prospect of establishing a line from their own position at Prome, on the Irrawaddy in the west, to Toungoo on the Sittang – assuming the Chinese would take post there. The command structure was now workmanlike, with Major-General Slim as a Corps Commander directing the battle, Alexander as Army Commander more widely responsible for operational control, and Wavell in Delhi as Commander-in-Chief. There was also an assumption, based on earlier negotiations, that any Chinese troops entering Burma would come under Alexander's control. Burma itself might be chaos, but compared with the early days of the invasion this chain of command was tidy and logical.

Stilwell wished to exercise an independent command over the 5th and 6th Chinese Armies, as seemed his due. (Indeed, his immediate personal priority was to conquer Rangoon and re-open a route to China. No wonder Wavell seemed to him defeatist. The conflict between British realism and American euphoria was there from the start.) When he reached Chungking on 4 March he formed the impression that freedom of his armies from Alexander's control was also the wish of Chiang, who distrusted Wavell and was unimpressed by the fall of Singapore and Rangoon. After Stilwell joined Alexander in Burma both he and Wavell were naturally disturbed, for the American had no sort of staff and too many other responsibilities. A triangular argument followed between the Generalissimo, Roosevelt and Churchill – with Roosevelt tactfully backing Chiang. Stilwell himself, having met Alexander, was now ready to serve under him or to co-ordinate the command with him. Then Alexander visited Chungking, and on 27 March Madame Chiang sent Stilwell a *billet-doux*: 'the High Command of Burma will rest in General Alexander's hands'. Such was the Chinese whirligig.

After much uncertainty, however, Wavell could say that he knew where he stood: the structure of command for the Burma campaign, with himself at the pinnacle, seemed unimpaired. But the unedifying debate had not only revealed the Generalissimo as a mercurial and incalculable ally, with Washington's back door open to him: by its apparently satisfactory conclusion it had veiled the true state of affairs, which would long persist. For Chiang not only kept Stilwell on a tight rein, issuing and altering orders imperiously so that Stilwell's genuine efforts at battle-planning were sabotaged. He also cunningly withheld from Stilwell the Kwang-Fang or seal of office, as Commander-in-Chief, which meant that any of the American's Chinese subordinates was free to disregard his orders and appeal above his head to higher authority. Stilwell was not absolute in his Chinese command, nor was it until December 1943 that he was able to write triumphantly to his wife, 'For the first time in history, a foreigner was given command of Chinese troops, with full control over all officers and no strings attached'. For Wavell this was worse than dealing with the Greeks.

In any case, he did not share Stilwell's optimism. He had presided over too many retreats. Far from recovering Rangoon, the only present hope was to extricate as much of the army from Burma as possible and until this was completed, around 20 May, there was little that Wavell himself could do. The retreat was an event inside a box. No reinforcements or supplies could be delivered over India's mountain barriers. The Japanese held the Burmese coast and dominated the air. It was fortunate for Wavell that for the first time since *Compass* he had under him a complete team, composed, from Alexander and Slim down to the divisional commanders, of men of quality who worked in harmony. They were on their own.

Both Alexander and Slim felt that loneliness. In *Defeat into Victory* Slim wrote: 'All would be conditioned by the over-riding object of the campaign. What that was we did not know. Indeed, it was never, until the last stages, clear, and I think we suffered increasingly in all our actions for this.' And Alexander wrote to Slim in 1955: 'You say we had no national directive – and you are right. I was sent out to try to save Rangoon. When it was lost, I never received any further directive – in fact I had no wireless capable of even communicating with India!'[7] As the full story of the retreat shows, fortunes changed so swiftly from day to day and even from hour to hour, and Chinese vacillation introduced such uncertainties, that it was probably wise of Delhi to leave things to the commanders on the spot rather than to issue anything as portentous as a 'national directive'.

In any case, Wavell's hand was in fact felt from time to time. On 1 April, for example, when it was evident that Prome could no longer be held, he went with Alexander to visit Slim and authorized a local withdrawal. He had already had a detailed exchange of views with Alexander about the more general principles of withdrawing from Burma as a whole and had forwarded these to the Chiefs of Staff. On 18 April, with Mandalay now endangered, he codified those principles in a letter certainly received by Alexander. This instructed Alexander (1) to maintain close touch with the Chinese and support them with part of his own force; (2) to cover the only escape-route to India, from Kalewa on the Chindwin via Tamu to Imphal; (3) to keep 'a force in being'; (4) to retain as many 'cards of re-entry' into Burma as possible; (5) to maintain contact with the Chinese and give them no ground for accusing the British of running away into India. Alexander

might well have complained that the directives he received
were too demanding rather than too few!

Contained within the first sentence of the instruction was a
curious idea which Wavell had floated and Alexander had
accepted in their earlier exchange of views. This was that if
Mandalay fell 7 Armoured Brigade and a brigade of 17 Division would retire with 5 Chinese Army via Lashio into China,
while the rest of the Burma force withdrew westwards. Circumstances fortunately obliterated this plan, which Slim
emphatically rejected and to which Alexander, surely, was
only paying lip-service. There is a point beyond which the
sacrificial becomes the absurd, and it is impossible to imagine
how Wavell thought that the utterly worn-out Armoured
Brigade would find pins or links for its tracks, or ammunition
for its armament, or replacement for its batteries, amid a
defeated Chinese army retreating through a wilderness.

This ridiculous proposition must be counted as an example
of how on occasion Wavell's sense of duty, of obedience to
orders from above – a British version of that West Point
dedication to 'the mission' which characterized so many
American commanders – blunted his instinctive realism and
blinkered his imagination. A link with the Chinese, he understood, must be maintained at all costs: therefore, at all costs, a
link with the Chinese must be maintained. Yet just at this
point, the moment when Mandalay was about to fall, another
side of Wavell's make-up as a commander – that bent for the
unorthodox in thought and action – reasserted itself.

Early in 1941 the author and traveller Peter Fleming, who
during the Battle of Britain had been charged with organizing
a system of 'stay-behind' resistance units in south-east
England to harass and sabotage a German invader, was sent
out to Cairo by SOE (Special Operations Executive) with a
group of like-minded buccaneers to raise a Garibaldi Legion
from the huge muster of Italian prisoners. Naturally there
were no volunteers and the scheme collapsed, but Wavell was
much taken by this young man of elegant mind and *je m'en
foutiste* courage who mirrored something cavalier in his own
nature. He therefore sent Fleming and his *banditti* off to
Greece to organize resistance along the German lines of

communication: instead, they spent some explosive days in carrying out demolitions behind the retreating expeditionary force. Then, when Wavell arrived in Java, he signalled to the CIGS, 'Should be glad of Peter Fleming as early as possible for appointment to my staff,' knowing that in his journeyings Fleming had travelled hard and travelled wide over the Far East. Now, in April 1942, Fleming was in Delhi.[8]

One evening, after dinner with Fleming and Fergusson, Wavell told them that he wanted to resuscitate the classic deception device which might be christened 'the Meinertzhagen ploy.' He recalled for them the story – which he had witnessed at first hand and later assessed in his studies of Allenby's campaigns – of how in October 1917 Colonel Meinertzhagen rode in front of the Turkish positions at Beersheba and, as he retired in feigned confusion, dropped a haversack containing forged papers which suggested that the imminent British offensive would be directed at Gaza, and not Beersheba. (It is reckoned that the Turks were taken in. This device of 'dropping' delusive documents was used on at least two famous occasions during the Second World War – the episode of 'The Man Who Never Was', and the planting before Rommel's army of a false 'going map' at the time of Alam Halfa, his last assault before the battle of Alamein.)

The result of Wavell's stimulus was that Fleming contrived to 'abandon' on the Japanese line of advance a car which had crashed but curiously survived, and which contained papers indicating not only that Wavell had been involved in and wounded during the retreat, but also that heavy reinforcements were arriving in India. Indeed, the cache included some 'Notes for Alexander' telling him that two armies would be available for Burma, and even hinting at a secret weapon. Verisimilitude was added – as in the case of the forged letter from the putative fiancée of The Man Who Never Was – by a missive to Wavell from his friend and private correspondent in the Cabinet Office in London, Joan Bright, laced with indiscretions about military matters.[9]

Wavell was serious. On 3 May he signalled to the CIGS:

> Have just carried out stratagem in Burma which involved loss of my despatch case containing important documents some of which

were genuine papers appropriately doctored. You will probably
get official report stating documents lost. Might help if impression of anxiety over seriousness of loss of papers in Burma were
fostered. . . .

Telegrams prefixed APW refer to loss. Please ensure that
absolute minimum persons know real truth of matter.[10]

Neither at the time, however, nor as a result of post-war
investigations and interrogation of Japanese officers, did it
ever become clear whether this Operation *Error* had achieved
its purpose. Still, it was a useful exercise. At least it indicated
that Wavell was not stale.

Indeed, with the C-in-C's endorsement Fleming quickly
followed up with a fresh idea, Operation *Purple Whales*, its
object being to establish in Tokyo three misconceptions – that
a Second Front in Europe was imminent, that the British were
going on the defensive in the Middle East, and that the Allies
were increasing their potentiality against the Japanese.
Fleming's proposition was that these notions should be em-
bedded in a fake set of minutes of the Joint Military Council,
which sat in Chungking. The thirteen-page document, concocted with the aid of the Chiefs of Staff in London, and
approved by Chiang Kai-shek, would then be sold to the
Japanese – for an appropriate sum – by a Chinese agent.
Subsequently Fleming doubted whether the text had been
designed with sufficient subtlety to convince the Japanese
intelligence staffs. In any case, there is no actual evidence that
*Purple Whales* had any more success than *Error*.

The truth is that deception is almost always a more effective
weapon in the hands of a commander on the offensive, for he
has the initiative. Fleming now became, under Wavell, the
head of the deception unit in the Far East, analogous to Dudley
Clarke at the head of 'A' Force in Cairo, but it is to be doubted
whether his efforts ever bore significant fruit until, in 1944,
Slim and the 14th Army were at last able to make the long and
arduous march back to Rangoon. Nevertheless, during that
spring of 1942 unorthodoxy was in the air and one project, at
least, achieved an astonishing result.

The details of Operation *Jaywick,* one of the most daring
enterprises of the war, have never received sufficient attention.

It started in Delhi in May 1942 when an officer of the Gordon Highlanders, Lieutenant-Colonel Ivan Lyon, walked into Bernard Fergusson's office. Lyon had already escaped from Singapore to Sumatra and, navigating a native craft, had brought a party of forty in safety to Ceylon. Now he proposed to sail a small vessel from Australia to Singapore, sink Japanese shipping in the harbour, and return to Australia. Fergusson passed the idea privately to Wavell, who seized on it and despatched Lyon with a letter of introduction to General MacArthur. The facts are simple but incredible. In the summer of 1943 Lyon and his crew, in the seventy-eight foot fishing boat *Krait,* voyaged some 5000 miles from Australia to Singapore and back (spending thirty-three days in Japanese waters), sank or damaged a considerable tonnage at anchor in Singapore Roads, and returned in triumph.* On a second venture, alas, Lyon's party was captured by the Japanese. After a period in captivity all were executed – one month before Hiroshima.[11]

These were examples of what the army calls 'positive thinking' on Wavell's part. Yet they make it more difficult to understand the workings of that complex mind, for while they were in train Wavell was also preparing for limited circulation the little pamphlet entitled 'Ruses and Stratagems of War' which was issued from his office only a few weeks later, in July. 'Possibly because of the British character which is normally simple and straightforward,' it began, 'more probably because our military training is stereotyped and unimaginative, deception does not come naturally to us.' But his way of provoking his subordinates into thinking deviously was to read them a history lesson, surveying the course of deception from the Wooden Horse outside Troy, and the feints of Belisarius – with passing reference to Gideon, Delilah and Jael the Kenite – down to 'the whistling bombs of the Nazi, the crackers and shouts of the small Japanese party which has penetrated to the rear and wishes to simulate a large force'. But there was nothing practical, nothing concrete, nothing relevant to the military situation in India in

---

* After this first venture nine participants were decorated and the other five mentioned in despatches.

1942. Wavell's generals and their staffs must have been per-
plexed and scornful: except for the quick-minded who could
catch his drift. Ironically, and with that supreme British gift
for self-parody, the pamphlet was solemnly stamped 'NOT TO
BE PUBLISHED. The information given in this document is not to
be communicated, either directly or indirectly, to the Press or
to any person not holding an official position in his Majesty's
Service.' The press, presumably, could not read Homer, the
Bible or Gibbon!

But a crippled giant under assault lashes out as best he may,
and this was Wavell's condition in the late spring of 1942. His
mental range was still wide, his horizons large: he saw what
ideally should be done, but he lacked the power to do it.
Stilwell misinterpreted his sombre manner and assumed that it
was defeatist, whereas in fact it was the result of a realistic
frustration. India may have seemed a great military reservoir
filled with many men, but as Wavell surveyed his resources
after the retreat from Burma had ended he found in his hands
little more than a toy army – Slim's shattered fragments up in
Assam, the few divisions elsewhere mainly under-trained and
ill-equipped, at least 100,000 of India's best troops overseas. At
the same time he must cope with a pressing need for internal
security and the monumental demand for manpower (both
skilled technicians and raw labour) to create in India, as he had
done once in Egypt, a country-wide base with abundant airfields, good communications, stock-piles, all the impedi-
menta and installations from which, one day, an effective
offensive might be launched.

Stilwell – and others – misread the public Wavell during this
period because they did not realize that privately he had not
altered his military philosophy: that at least, in spite of defeats
and deficiencies, his true intentions were as aggressive as they
had been during the African summer of 1940 when conventional wisdom suggested that his best course was to play a
waiting game. It is surely a sign of that indomitable quality
which only the outstanding commanders possess – something
derived from intuition and will rather than from any refined
calculation of the odds – that after the long trail of disaster
from Greece to Rangoon Wavell's single eye rarely shifted

from the distant and, it might have seemed, unattainable target of victory.

Yet this was so. The theme is established in the first sentence of that remarkable memorandum which Wavell addressed to his Chief of Staff, General Morris, on 16 April, a full month before the retreating Alexander, Slim and Stilwell were to cross the mountain barrier and find sanctuary in Imphal. 'I want the Joint Planning Staff,' he wrote, 'to begin as soon as possible consideration of an offensive to reoccupy Burma . . . on a much wider scale the Joint Planning Staff should also consider other projects for counter-offensive against Japan.' With variations the theme was developed. In June a series of exchanges with Churchill about strategic possibilities included a blunt statement from Wavell that 'we can now begin definitely to plan the recapture of Burma, *which has been in my mind ever since it became obvious that I was likely to lose it*'.* On 17 September he produced for Morris a paper entitled 'Operation Fantastical' which began

> I have a "hunch", which may be quite unjustified, that we may find Japanese opposition very much lower than we expect in Burma if we can only act with boldness and determination. . . . All this is just my private hunch but I mean to ride it for what it is worth. . . I had a similar hunch before the Sidi Barrani operations two years ago. . . . My hunch came off then and I am going to have a scenario and ideas ready for Burma, even if they appear fantastical at the moment.

It was on the very next day that he composed in his own hand the note of which the original text is reproduced in the Official History.[12] It refers to an earlier government's perplexities about an expedition to Burma:

> The Cabinet sent for the Duke of Wellington and asked his advice. He instantly replied, "Send Lord Combermere." "But we have always understood that Your Grace thought Lord Combermere a fool." "So he is and a d——d fool: but he can take Rangoon."
>
> Q = Have we a Lord Combermere?

If Stilwell was justified in giving Chiang Kai-Shek the nick-

* Author's italics.

name of Peanut, he was astray in calling Wavell 'the Weevil'. For this was the spirit which caused those around him to think of him as The Chief.

But the problem was not one simply of finding a new Lord Combermere.* The problem was how to match means with ends. And it is a hard fact that right up to the point at which Wavell became Viceroy in the summer of 1943 every prospect of achieving his ultimate aim, the extrusion of the enemy from Burma, proved to be a will-o'-the-wisp. A persistent shortage of trained troops and modern equipment, an intermittent inefficiency of commanders and staffs, shifts in the strategic requirement of Whitehall and Washington, the vagaries of the Chinese, the distraction of political disturbance and security problems within India itself all, at one time or another, diverted or thwarted Wavell as he sought to return to the offensive.

In effect, the Commander-in-Chief of the prestigious British Raj proved incapable of expelling a handful of Japanese divisions whose presence in Burma was of only marginal importance within Tokyo's master-plan. His personal responsibility for this failure must be assessed, but it is not too much to say that the true reason why an army finally returned to Rangoon under Mountbatten rather than Wavell was the brute force of circumstance. This was evident even before the evacuation of Burma was concluded. The Cripps Mission, as has been seen, distracted and wounded at a difficult moment. Then, in April, a Japanese armada arrived in the Bay of Bengal with a large superiority in warships and anti-aircraft carriers. Its attacks on Colombo and the losses sustained by Admiral Somerville's mainly obsolete Eastern Fleet set Churchill and the Chiefs of Staff astir: Ceylon's garrison must be strengthened, Madagascar occupied, and reinforcements for India reduced.

It is now obvious that the Japanese miscalculated: that the breathing-space thus allowed to the American navy (as well as its crucial insight into the Japanese naval code) made possible

---

* In retrospect the answer might appear to have been Slim. In fairness to Wavell it should be noted that at this stage Slim had not disclosed capacities for the highest command and Wavell had not experienced enough direct relationship with Slim to be able to assess the promise of his personality.

that June victory at Midway whose strategic consequences, decisive in the Pacific war, also freed Somerville and the War Cabinet from the fear of a return visit by the Japanese. But though Wavell soon grasped the implications of Midway, and though later in his despatch he freely admitted that Churchill's dispositions had been justified, at the time they were made he was vexed in mind and certainly weakened in his offensive planning. His protests to London were vehement. Their gist is in a signal sent to Churchill at the end of April: 'The War Cabinet must really make up their minds whether or not they propose to defend India and Ceylon seriously.' Looking back, he reckoned that this was 'India's most dangerous hour'. And then, hardly before there was time to realize that the menace from the sea had been over-estimated, Gandhi's 'Quit India' campaign in August sapped the strength of a still enfeebled Indian Army in ways that have already been described. Necessarily, the recovery of Burma continued to look like an 'Operation Fantastical'.

Wavell was irked by his impotence. And there was a further factor. None of the other supreme or theatre commanders was compelled to waste so much time and energy on matters which, at the best, lay on the periphery of his military sphere. The position of Commander-in-Chief India was unique. It was built into the pre-war but unchanged structure of Imperial government, so that as the leading member of the Viceroy's Council, amid an infinity of affairs both administrative and political, the C-in-C became civil and gubernatorial. Eisenhower was tossed by political tides in North Africa. Domestic issues in Italy, Yugoslavia and Greece provided Alexander with problems. Within MacArthur's great empire Australian and, later, Philippine politics created many distractions. But for Wavell the civil and the political were almost a daily diet. He endured but resented the need for long sessions with the Viceroy, the wearisome and, as it seemed, irrelevant discussions in the council and conference. He wished to wage war. Instead, he found himself doodling while others droned. His private correspondence is full of distaste amounting to despair: but this was his duty, a millstone round his neck. Lord Chandos has a relevant sentence in his memoirs. Writing about Wavell, he referred to 'the selfless and self-critical balance with which he discharged the weight of his responsibilities'.

But when he began to pick up the threads – after the retreat from Burma was over and the Japanese navy had abandoned the Bay of Bengal – and considered how the war might be taken into the enemy's camp he found that little could be sensibly proposed. For once, indeed, he had time to think. The annual monsoon, which had just failed to choke Slim's line of withdrawal, now interposed its curtain of rain and carpet of mud: the Japanese immediately went on the defensive – where, in effect, they remained until 1944. But in mid May, when Churchill began to demand an autumn offensive 'from Moulmein to Assam', it was not so much the enemy as his own shortages that prevented Wavell from offering more than a tentative push into northern Burma. The Prime Minister scornfully rejected such ideas as 'nice and useful nibbling': he asked for the coast of Arakan and Akyab island at its eastern tip, and then for Rangoon and Bangkok. Wavell therefore sent to London, in the hands of Alexander, a more ambitious outline plan for nailing down the Japanese in the north, capturing airfield sites on Arakan and then recovering Rangoon. In mid July these proposals were approved by the Chiefs of Staff on the assumption that they would be implemented during the next dry season – from October to May 1943.

Of course they were not carried out. This was the birth of that ambitious but doomed brain-child, the plan called *Anakim,* whose vicissitudes were to haunt Wavell until he relinquished his command. Even as it emerged the summer defeats in the Western Desert and a German threat to the Caucasus (which sucked troops and aircraft away from India), were followed by the Congress disturbances in August and the whole scheme was stultified *ab initio*. Yet it was characteristic of the failure to harmonize Allied strategy that while Wavell was floundering in an effort to mount even a minimal offensive Stilwell was dreaming of a large-scale onslaught.

Both Wavell and Admiral Somerville of the Eastern Fleet respected and even warmed towards Stilwell – as a person. Each called him 'the tortoise' but sensed that he was a soldier of quality. Neither, however, realized that within the general's gaunt frame a furnace raged. To train and arm the two good Chinese divisions which had escaped into India, to create from scratch another thirty out of Chiang's raggle-taggle swarms, to master-mind nothing less than a military revolution in the forces of a corrupt, apathetic and incompetent ally – such was the substance of Stilwell's reveries. It is not surprising, therefore, that when he and Wavell came together to concert their plans, in a series of meetings which started on 17 October, each received a shock. The truth is that there was a mutual incomprehension.

With great pertinacity – involving pressure on Chiang Kai-shek and many exchanges with Washington – Stilwell had achieved by October what was at least a superficial Sino-American endorsement of a plan he had personally formulated in July. This involved a pincer movement on the Japanese in north Burma by a dozen Chinese divisions from Yunnan in the east and by three British divisions from Assam in the west; the two Chinese divisions based in India were to be transferred to Ledo in the far northern mountains and then to advance down the Hukawng valley, clearing the line for a road linking the railhead at Ledo with the old Burma road and thus restoring the precious land-route into China.

The Generalissimo had added a rider so unrealistic as to suggest that he never intended to fight, though Chiang's motives were normally an unfathomable mixture: eagerness to keep his powerful allies active in his own interest, distrust of their capability, a constant desire to reinsure and, above all, a determination never to waste against the Japanese men and weapons he would need, one day, to use against his own dissident warlords and the threat of Communism in his own country. He accepted Stilwell's plan on 14 October if, and only if, a fleet of three or four battleships and six aircraft carriers were assembled to give superiority in the Bay of Bengal and even beyond, in the China Sea: and if Rangoon was to be re-captured. Three days later Stilwell joined Wavell in Delhi.

At the negotiating table Wavell's position was one of great delicacy. Stilwell's own objectives were patently unattainable:

Chiang's naval demands were a Chinese shadow-show. At the same time Wavell was already convincing himself and the Chiefs of Staff that even the British plan for *Anakim* was premature and could not be set in motion until the autumn of 1943. Nevertheless, the tri-partite alliance must not crack before it had been cemented. The tortuous discussions that continued until the end of the year may therefore be summarized in this way. The Stilwell/Chiang strategy was accepted, tactfully, as a theoretical basis for planning and preparation, Stilwell struggling for the maximum and Wavell never fully disclosing that neither he nor the War Cabinet had any intention of going beyond a minimum commitment. But the political implications were too grave for the truth to be looked in the face: the brute fact that Vinegar Joe's ambitious ideas, like *Anakim,* were half dead even before they were born. In the New Year Stilwell bitterly, though incorrectly, confided his feelings to his diary: 'The Limeys . . . will quit, the Chinese will quit, and the god-damned Americans can go ahead and fight'.

In practice the Limeys were not quitting, for it was Wavell, not Stilwell, who in early 1943 returned to the offensive, even though, as will be seen, by comparison with the grandiose concepts of the previous autumn his two efforts can only be described as 'nibbling'. Before their climax came, however, he had attended conferences in Cairo and Moscow, and become a Field Marshal.

The bearing of the first event on the second, and on the strengthening of Wavell's hand *vis-à-vis* Stilwell, has not been previously analyzed. As to the former, never before during his long period of command had Wavell been able to mingle with Churchill and the Chiefs of Staff in conditions which, however hectic the atmosphere in conference, were relatively relaxed. It was interesting, at the August meeting in Cairo, to observe Churchill injecting new life into his old desert army, as Auchinleck was replaced by Alexander and Montgomery: but it was more important for Wavell to be able to talk at ease with the CIGS, his friend Alan Brooke with whom, indeed, he kept up a private correspondence. These talks, both in Cairo and in Moscow, are often mentioned amiably in Brooke's diary. When they returned to their posts, separated by half a world, it is evident that their thoughts were in tune, and the winter of 1942–43 became for Wavell the phase of least friction between his superiors and himself. If he had not secured a political base in London, his military support at home buttressed him in dealing with Stilwell. Moreover, neither in Cairo nor Moscow (where a Second Front was the main theme) did any contentious issues arise between Churchill and Wavell, whose fluency in Russian and previous acquaintance with the capital gave him a distinct advantage. The tone of their relationship temporarily sweetened, and the timing could not have been more favourable.

For Wavell is perhaps the only Field Marshal to have received the baton at his own request. On 20 August, while still on his way back to India, he wrote a letter which began 'Dear Prime Minister, I have never before asked for anything for myself, but I am going to ask you for promotion to the rank of Field Marshal.' After listing his campaigns, the territories he had occupied and the 250,000 prisoners he had captured, and then frankly recognizing his set-backs, he pointed out that 'as I have since been entrusted with very great, possibly even larger, responsibilities I take it* that my generalship has not been held to be radically at fault'. Churchill's response to a long, an unusual and, it might be thought, a naïve application was dulcet, considering his asperity in the past. It cannot be proved, but the days he had recently spent at close quarters with Wavell may well have adjusted his vision of the man who once reminded him of a golf club's chairman.

In any case, on the 27th he simply minuted to the Secretary of State for War, 'I am strongly in favour of this, and so is the CIGS. . . .' P. J. Grigg, the carpenter's son who in 1942 took over the War Office, was a man of straight and even savage opinions. The equally opinionated Permanent Under-Secretary at the Foreign Office, Sir Alexander Cadogan, once wrote of 'P. J.' in his diary: 'One might as well argue with a stone wall.' Even Montgomery, who counted Grigg among his greatest friends, observed in his memoirs that 'he either

---

* In the original text of Wavell's letter, written in his own hand, the phrase, 'I take it' is repeated and not erased: perhaps a sign of his emotional pressure.

likes or dislikes you; you are either white or black; there are no greys or half-tones'. And Grigg, who had served in India as Financial Member on the Viceroy's Council, disliked Wavell. He therefore obstructed, replying to Churchill that no appointment to Field Marshal should be made 'until the Army has some resounding success to its credit', and 'in any event, I would not like Wavell's name to go forward to the King unless Gort's went at the same time'. But Churchill, his mind made up, was not to be defeated by a middle-grade Minister: he simply went to the King and then minuted to Grigg, 'The King seems very well disposed to the idea of making Wavell a Field Marshal in the New Year's List, and I hope the necessary Submission may be made'.

Grigg too was a fighter. 'Frankly,' he replied, 'I was very shocked that Wavell could have brought himself to ask to be made a Field Marshal. Moreover, I do not take a high view of his ability anyhow. He has, of course, any amount of brains, but I do not believe that he has any fire in his belly, or enough iron in his body.' 'Your views,' replied Churchill acidly, 'would I think astonish most people who have served under him, as well as the Chief of the Imperial General Staff.' Thus are the highest honours attained – or averted. Wavell's name appeared in the New Year's List. But he would have liked the announcement to have been made earlier. 'Life is uncertain and my military career is beginning to draw to an end,' he wrote to Churchill on 15 October in a private and personal letter. 'I confess that I should like to enjoy prestige as long as possible. Also it might help in dealing with Americans and Chinese in forthcoming negotiations in Burma. Gingerbread is always gingerbread but may I have it with the gilt on please?' It was a curious episode.[13] There is certainly something impressive about a man who, even when he is naïve, is naïve in a big way – and whose naïveté produces a baton.

Yet the baton could not produce a victory. On the contrary: before his promotion was announced on the New Year's Day of 1943 Wavell had already set in motion the first of his two offensive strokes against the Japanese, and this operation, generally known as the first Arakan campaign, ended in un-mitigated and unpardonable disaster. 'First Arakan' was the misbegotten child of a dying *Anakim*. Without an influx of fresh troops and naval reinforcements, particularly landing craft, a large amphibious enterprise was impossible: so *Anakim* faded and in mid November even a minor scheme, to seize the island of Akyab from the sea, had to be abandoned. In his desire at least to do *something* Wavell settled for the minimal option, an advance by land down the coastal strip of Arakan which, if successful, might reach the finger-end of the Mayu peninsula and a jump-off point for an assault on nearby Akyab. This meant sending his only available division, the 14th – as usual under-trained and ill-equipped – across the grain of some of the worst country in the world, a mixture of mountains, malaria and mud. By the year's end, against light opposition but in a sort of pilgrim's progress through sloughs of despond and over many a Hill Difficulty, General Lloyd and his division were reaching down to Donbaik, almost to the eastern tip of Arakan. But here the enemy, now fully alert and reinforced, dug themselves in.

The Japanese had evolved a new defensive technique as unexpected and as lethal as Rommel's employment of the 88mm gun in an anti-tank role. Heavily protected machine-gunposts, mutually supported by their cross-fire, constituted an impregnable bunker-system only to be overcome by sophisticated tactics first developed by the Australians in New Guinea and later – but not until 1944 – perfected by Slim's 14th Army. These were beyond the capability of Lloyd's virginal force which, it was said at the time, 'although impressive on paper is little better, in a large number of cases, than a rather unwilling band of raw levies'. That is too dismissive of a division which, ultimately bloated to the unmanageable scale of nine brigades, carried out hopeless frontal attack after hopeless frontal attack on bunkers where a few men with machine-guns were masters of the field.

Yet in principle the comment is fair. The 14th Division was stopped in its tracks and never recovered momentum. And now all the weaknesses, both technical and temperamental, of a great but incomplete commander were unhappily displayed. That tendency to attempt close control of the battle from too great a distance, to which Wavell had been prone in Java and during the struggle for Rangoon, was repeated as he sought to direct from Delhi a remote engagement.* And the error of overcomplicating the structure of command which had distressed O'Connor in Africa was also repeated. Wavell pulled the strings, but his intermediary was not a Corps commander in charge at the front but Lieutenant-General Irwin at his headquarters of the Eastern Army: only as the operation was guttering out was Slim inserted with his 15 Corps HQ, and rationality restored. But above all Wavell forgot the experience of his past: the folly – as demonstrated so often in the Boer War, on the Western front and in the Middle East before Allenby arrived – of thrusting troops across open country, again and again, towards an enemy comfortably ensconced in good defensive positions.

Wavell seems to have been seized by a stubborn desperation which blurred his vision and numbed his humanity. And so, throughout January and February, further brigades were fed into the mincing machine without the gain of a significant yard. At the beginning of March, when it was evident that a counter-offensive was imminent, Wavell nevertheless wrote to Irwin – on the 7th – that 'I should like to finish up this campaigning season with a real success which will show both our own troops and the Jap that we can and mean to be top dog.' As late as 3 April, when the Japanese were in the ascendant and advancing, Wavell was still instructing Irwin that 'the object of future operations was to regain the initiative and inflict a severe defeat on the enemy'. These were vain words, as empty as Weygand's exhortations to his nerveless armies during the fall of France.

Two facts summarize the futility and the waste of the first Arakan campaign. In May, when Slim's commonsense had restored the situation, the line to which he withdrew was virtually the same as that from which Lloyd had started out so many months ago. And the official history of the Army Medical Services records that

* The very qualities which fit a man for command at the highest level are liable to induce this malady from which Churchill, Hitler and Stalin all suffered. A beautiful example is that of MacArthur seeking to direct from his headquarters at Brisbane, 1500 miles away, the tactics in the desperate but small-scale operations along the Kokoda Trail in New Guinea.

The Command Psychiatrist, Eastern Command, reporting upon this period stated that no useful purpose would be served by counting psychiatric cases, for the whole of the Indian 14th Division was for practical purposes a psychiatric casualty. Afterwards, it was used only as a training division. [14]

Every serious subsequent student of the campaign agrees that Wavell deserves no admiration for refusing to break off at an early stage this marginal operation which, if successful, could only have achieved a meagre result and which, by its failure, nearly destroyed the morale it was intended to enhance. Most commanders sail into the doldrums sooner or later. This time Wavell stayed there too long.

Yet the observation made in the opening chapter, that Wavell's character and his performance were sometimes enigmatic and self-contradictory, could not be better illustrated than by the fact that during this essentially old-fashioned and unimaginative *battue* down in Arakan another event, far to the north, stimulated British morale infinitely more than even the capture of Akyab might have done, whilst its strategic consequences went beyond anything that lay within General Lloyd's compass. So great an impression and so considerable a result were caused, moreover, by what at the time seemed a breathtaking unorthodoxy of conception and execution which destroyed within a few weeks the myth that only the Japanese were lords of the jungle. And these events – the product of Orde Wingate's first Chindit penetration behind the enemy lines – were entirely due to Wavell, for it was he whose insight realized the possibilities when the venture was first proposed , and he alone who risked not only his own reputation but also the lives of his men by allowing the operation to proceed, as a calculated hazard, when the preconditions justifying it had vanished. The raid beyond the Chindwin by the columns of Wingate's 77 Brigade in March 1943 was the last irregularity by the nonconformist in Wavell whose inspiration was Stonewall Jackson. His handling of the Arakan affair, by contrast, reminds one of Haig during the most criticized phases of the Somme or of Passchendaele. 'Do I contradict myself?' wrote Walt Whitman. 'Well then, I contradict myself. I am large. I contain millions.'

It was Wavell who brought Wingate to Burma, ostensibly to take over the Bush Warfare School where the most outstanding of the Chindits' future leaders, Michael Calvert, was secretly training specialists to work with guerillas in occupied China, as SOE in England trained agents to aid the European resistance. In practice, Wavell hoped that Wingate would organize an irregular force to harass the Japanese in Burma, along the lines of his night squads in Palestine and Gideon Force in Ethiopia. The retreat put an end to such ambitions. During the summer of 1942 Wingate, still under Wavell's wing, found himself an unwelcome inhabitant of Army Headquarters at Delhi, eyed with suspicion and often hostility by the mainly conservative staff: 'A broad-shouldered, uncouth, almost simian officer,' so Fergusson described him, 'who used to drift gloomily into the office for two or three days at a time, audibly dream dreams, and drift out again . . . we used to look on this visitor as one to be bowed out, as soon as it was possible to put a term to his ramblings'.

During that drifting and dreaming, however, Wingate evolved the plan which few but Wavell thought practicable and Wavell alone could authorize. This was to insert by land-marches a considerable force behind the Japanese lines, roughly between the Chindwin and Irrawaddy rivers, where intelligence might be gained, the important north-south railway cut, any Japanese preparations for invading Assam disturbed and the feasibility of long-range penetration assessed. It would be a sheer test of survival for his scattered columns, and all would depend on a major premise: the possibility of supplying them by air.

Wavell instinctively approved of the project which, in the latter part of 1942, had much to commend it. So long as discussions with Stilwell and the Chinese kept alive the possibility of a major, three-sided offensive from Assam, from Ledo and from Yunnan, the notion of planting a disruptive force in the very heart of the Japanese communications-system in north Burma had a military *rationale*. Under Wingate's brilliant if sometimes manic inspiration, therefore, preparations moved ahead at extraordinary speed for training and equipping the miscellany, grouped as 77 Brigade, which

Wavell had placed in his hand.

By the end of January 1942 everything was ready: the brigade, ferociously trained, moved up to Imphal and was poised to march eastwards. But the great scenario had dissolved. On 16 January Chiang, using his carefully prepared escape-route, had informed Roosevelt that since the massive naval presence he had demanded in the Bay of Bengal could not be supplied his own armies could not join in a northern offensive. The allied summit meeting at Casablanca, which ended on 23 January, postponed all large-scale efforts in the CBI theatre until the next dry season. The Chindits remained, a weapon without a role.

Wavell's reaction was characteristic. On 5 February he went up to Imphal and talked to Wingate, having, – as the latter's biographer, Christopher Sykes, noted – 'made it known that he had come to cancel Wingate's expedition, but, being the man he was, he would not take a final decision before hearing the arguments on both sides. Wingate spared him no argument that he could think of. They conferred for two hours.' Balancing the certainty of large losses for no strategic gains against the sum of possible benefits, Wavell gave the order to go ahead. Like the decision taken by Slim in the summer of 1944 to launch the second Chindit expedition even though, at the critical last minute, it seemed that the Japanese might have been forewarned, this was a matter of now or never. The troops were at their peak. A delayed operation might be endangered by the arrival of the monsoon. Certainly if Wavell had cancelled or postponed the project the whole concept of long-range penetration might have been discredited or simply discarded. Both then and later there were those like Field Marshal Slim who would not have wept if this had happened.

Nevertheless, the results of that familiar first essay of the Chindits were remarkable. Few, perhaps not even Wingate, expected that the Japanese would be seriously wounded, nor were they. All, including Wavell, expected a high casualty rate. In fact, after covering distances of up to 1500 miles in four months, well over 2000 out of the original 3000 made their way back to India, but only about a third of these were to recover and be rated as fit for further active service. Wingate himself made some grave errors of judgement in the conduct of the campaign and expected, when he re-crossed the Chindwin, to be court-martialled.[15] None of this mattered. The world's press announced a new 'Clive of India'. The army in India and the public at large, perceiving for the first time that their countrymen could tackle the enemy on his own ground and survive, felt a new sense of release and anticipation. But the most important consequence had not even been imagined, either by Wingate or Wavell or anybody else. The Japanese, having observed this demonstration that the mountain chain between Burma and India was not impassable by foot-soldiers, as they had tended to assume, were encouraged to make the attempt themselves; not with a brigade, but with an army. Thus in 1943 the Chindits sowed the seeds of the disaster which, at Imphal in 1944, was the turning-point on the road back to Rangoon.

The decision that led to these agreeable results was an act of moral courage on Wavell's part. He had served as an impresario for Wingate in Palestine, in Ethiopia, and now in the Burmese drama. It counted for nothing. An indelible mark was made on Churchill's mind, so far as Wavell was concerned, not by the apparent triumph of the Chindits but by the ignominy of Arakan. And so, when Wavell was summoned by the Chiefs of Staff to London in mid April, he travelled under a shadow. As it happened, he had left his last military command.

# 8
# Quite a Respectable Position

The stone which the builders rejected is become
the head of the corner.

*Psalm 118*

Wavell became Viceroy of India by chance or perhaps by default. In the spring of 1943 Linlithgow had run his course: his long-anticipated replacement was now urgent. But as Wavell returned to England on 22 April the thought that he himself might occupy the imperial throne of the Raj was far from dominant: it was, in fact, distasteful. When he started his *Viceroy's Journal* on 24 June his first entry summarized the events leading up to his appointment and the sequence of his own thoughts. It began:

> I had seen enough of the business of the government of India by sitting on the Executive Council, discussions with the Viceroy and others, to convince me that I had no inclination or capacity for that sort of work, and I privately thanked heaven that there was no chance of my having to do it.

Heaven let him down. On 8 June Eden's Private Secretary Oliver Harvey noted in his own diary, 'PM has now decided to recommend Wavell. Thank God! But it is a funny choice.'[1] Later on an obsequious Indian, seeking to congratulate the new Viceroy, put it rather differently. 'At last, your Excellency,' he said, 'you have reached quite a respectable position.'

The story of how Linlithgow's successor finally emerged is not unlike the caucus-race so precisely described by Alice in Wonderland:

> There was no "One, two, three, and away!" but they began running when they liked, and left off when they liked, so that it was not easy to know when the race was over. However, when

they had been running half an hour or so, and were quite dry
again, the Dodo suddenly called out "The race is over!" and they
all crowded round it, panting, and asking "But who has won?"

The analogy is not merely light-hearted. During the long haul
of the Viceregal Stakes from the autumn of 1942 to the following summer different figures kept taking the lead, fresh
competitors appeared in the race as others fell out, and such
uncertainty prevailed that only when the Great Dodo of
Downing Street announced his decision was the unexpected
winner's name confirmed.

By the beginning of October 1942 the front runners were
visible, the favourite being Sir John Anderson, Lord President
of the Council and a former Governor of Bengal. Another
ex-Governor (of Bombay) was often mentioned: Sir Roger
Lumley, the future Lord Scarbrough. Attlee wanted R. A.
Butler, the Minister of Education, and Butler wanted himself.
(In his autobiography *The Art of the Possible,* he wrote that 'all
my adult life this had been my greatest ambition'.) Indeed, it
was about this time that Brendan Bracken sounded Butler out
on Churchill's behalf – or so he alleged. To others it seemed
that Lord Halifax, the former Viceroy, might well be returned
to the throne: a fine solution, indeed, to the problem of what to
do with Lord Halifax. Then there was Oliver Stanley, once a
War Minister, and a fancied candidate in the shape of Oliver
Lyttelton. Even Lloyd George's son Gwilym, the Minister of
Fuel and Power, briefly took up the running.

In the pure spirit of Alice's caucus-race, however, it was
Eden who created the greatest confusion, for as the winter
turned into spring the direction in which he was heading was
not clear even to well-informed spectators. Was it towards or
away from the finishing-line? The comedy and the *angst* of
Eden's communing with his soul and his friends – 'Will you?
Won't you?' – are mercilessly displayed in his Private Secretary's diaries, for Harvey, though loyal, was not blind.
There was a Gordian Knot. Part of Eden yearned for a position
which matched his peacock vanity, yet the experienced politician, another element in that febrile character, warned him
that to spend five years abroad might destroy the virtual
certainty that he would become the next Prime Minister.

Churchill, for his part, was equally ambivalent: at one moment wanting Eden to go, at another afraid of losing the Crown Prince on whom (when he felt like it) he had so often leaned, the favourite son among his potential successors. How could the knot be cut?

It was always Churchill's way, when he himself was undecided, to keep even the closest among his advisers on tenterhooks or in the dark. Certainly Wavell, on his arrival in London, had no more than an intelligent inkling that changes were being considered, and his first session with Churchill cannot have suggested that his own name was on the list. The Prime Minister concentrated on being 'very critical and unpleasant about the Arakan operations', and when at the Cabinet meeting next day, 29 April, Wavell suggested that a mission ought to visit Washington to discuss a new Far Eastern strategy – since *Anakim* and the Stilwell plan were now in ruins – Churchill, as *The Viceroy's Journal* records, 'said he did not think he would trust me to discuss plans alone with the Americans'. There was frost in the air.

Churchill was taking no risks. The result of Wavell's proposal was the embarkation in the *Queen Mary,* on 4 May, of an impressive contingent including the Prime Minister, the Chiefs of Staff, and the three Indian Commanders-in-Chief, Peirse, Somerville, and Wavell himself, who by now had been consulted by Leo Amery (as Secretary of State for India) about Eden's suitability as Viceroy and had visited the Foreign Office to answer anxious questions from Eden himself – whose candidature Wavell readily endorsed. Neither the voyage nor the landfall were cloudless.

While they were on the *Queen Mary* Churchill continued to be cantankerous, circulating among the staff a paper in which he again criticized the Arakan operation with phrases like 'complete failure' and 'deep disgrace'.* Infuriated, Wavell wrote a letter of protest which he only withdrew on the advice of his friend the CIGS; nevertheless, he boldly faced Churchill

---

* Philip Mason records in his autobiography that during the voyage Ismay told him in confidence that the new Viceroy would be 'a man of a military background'. But at this stage Churchill's hostility was so evident that Wavell can hardly have been the preferred candidate – except as a last resort.

himself. The Prime Minister diplomatically professed to have complete confidence in Wavell (an evident terminological inexactitude) and called in his paper, thus drawing more attention to it. He also fired off some salvoes about the Indian Army and its unreliability:

> He accused me of creating a Frankenstein by putting modern weapons in the hands of the sepoys, spoke of 1857, and was really almost childish about it. I tried to reassure him, both verbally and by a written note, but he has a curious complex about India and is always loth to hear good of it and apt to believe the worst.

'I did not see much of the PM in Washington,' the diary continued, ' and he was not very cordial when I did.' At a private luncheon with Roosevelt, attended only by Wavell, Churchill and the faithful Harry Hopkins, Arakan and the deficiencies of the Indian Army were again embarrassingly condemned – the sort of mindless irresponsibility of which the *gamin* in Churchill was capable even in the presence of another Head of State whose confidence in the credibility of the Indian Army, at that particular moment, needed to be restored rather than undermined. Far more serious was the proposal, on which Churchill correctly sought Wavell's views, that a Supreme Commander for South-East Asia should be appointed by the Allies, analogous to Eisenhower in North Africa and MacArthur in the Pacific. This Wavell strongly supported: and then, to his surprise, was ordered to return to London rather than to Delhi, and to await there Churchill's return from the extension to the Mediterranean of his Washington visit.

Of Wavell's thoughts and actions during the weeks that followed it would be charitable to say that they illustrated a sublime failure to understand the delicacy of his personal position and a strange inability – unworldly, innocent or simply naïve – to exercise the *tact des choses possibles*.

For reasons mainly but not entirely beyond his control he had not, in the eyes of London and Washington, been a successful Commander-in-Chief in South-East Asia. Seen from a distance, his regime had been distinguished by stagnation and defeat. Only Wingate's venture had struck a spark to be compared with the glow of Alamein and Stalingrad. If the verdict was one that could reasonably have been carried to a court of appeal, it stood unchallenged in the minds of those who mattered. For Churchill, who relished his slang, Wavell was now no more than 'a busted flush', and it would not be inaccurate to affirm that even his oldest friends and admirers, Dill, Ismay, Alan Brooke, felt a growing sense of reservation: he seemed to be slipping. In terms of the future his past record was unpromising, for the essential function of a Supreme Commander in South-East Asia would be to unify and harmonize where, at present, only doubt and dissension seemed to reign. Nothing had so far demonstrated that Wavell was capable of concerting a combined and effective strategy with Stilwell and Chiang Kai-Shek. Roosevelt and his Chief of Army Staff, General Marshall, could not fail to be impressed by the cacophony of voices in Washington's corridors of power which savagely censured the performance of the British in India and the competence of the Commander-in-Chief. They echoed through the White House and the Pentagon. Yet in 1943 it was evident that so far as any new arrangements for a Supreme Commander might be concerned, the increasing dominance of the Americans must give them the casting vote.

These *nuances* were beyond Wavell's grasp. He understood Churchill's hostility but, for the rest, he was in a kind of coma, convinced that on all other grounds he was the man for the new job. This is not mere speculation. Soon after his return to London he discussed the proposal for a Supreme Commander with the Chiefs of Staff and their joint recommendation of the project was formulated in an official paper. At this point Wavell wrote in his journal, 'Without vanity, I could consider that I was the obvious choice for Supreme Commander.' Indeed, his speculations strayed further. Churchill returned to London on 6 June and as Wavell brooded about the decisions which must obviously soon be taken he 'considered, rather vaguely', as he put it in his diary, 'the possibility that the PM might intend to bring me home to take charge of the Forces for the invasion of the Continent, but thought this improbable as it would be a waste of my Eastern experience.' Nevertheless, he added, 'I did not quite see how the PM could avoid the conclusion that a Joint Command and a Supreme Commander was the right solution for the East Asian theatre; or that I was the obvious choice as a Supreme Commander.' It seems cruel to record such self-delusions – at a time when Churchill was seriously toying with the idea of burying Wavell as the next Governor-General of Australia.

It was only during the early evening of 14 June, as he drove up from his old school at Winchester to answer the Prime Minister's summons, that Wavell's dreams of a military future were dispelled:

> For the first time . . . I really began seriously to consider the possibility of the Viceroyalty being offered to me, and to wonder what I should do about it . . . It would mean that Eden had finally declined; and that the PM had decided that I would be of more value to the side as Viceroy, than as Supreme Commander of SE Asia, which was what I had hoped for.

What Churchill had actually decided was that Wavell had better be put on the shelf. As to the post of Supreme Commander, though this fortunately went in the end to Mountbatten, the first and ludicrous British suggestion was Air Chief Marshal Sir Sholto Douglas;* Tedder and Admiral Sir Andrew Cunningham were subsequently proposed,[2] but in spite of his imaginings Wavell's own name was never entered on the candidates' roster. Indeed, it was merciful that the truth was withheld from him. As he dined alone with Churchill that night at 10 Downing Street, to learn that he was in fact to be the next Viceroy and that 'you will have to become a civilian, and put off your uniform', it certainly made acceptance easier for a man who was unaware that his days of uniformed distinction were already, to all intents and purposes, ended.

Perhaps nothing throws a harsher light on the unworldly side of Wavell's nature than the company he kept during the long frustrating weeks in London before his wife arrived. In a sense he was a man at sea. Nearly four years of war had transformed the social scene and the social attitudes of which,

---

* Nevertheless, as Wavell himself shrewdly notes, there was a powerful lobby among the airmen to get a senior RAF officer installed as Supreme Commander on the dubious grounds that air power was of outstanding importance in South-East Asia.

even before 1939, he had only been a transient observer. Now, like so many who came home from the battlefield, he felt at a loss. Many of his old friends and old colleagues were serving abroad. Since he went out to Cairo as Commander-in-Chief, even before hostilities began, he had rarely returned – and then only for hectic consultations. His wife and his familiar ménage were in Delhi. He was weary, worried and very lonely. At the same time he was eager as a boy to refresh himself by meeting the intelligentsia, the luminaries in the realm of arts and letters from which he had so long been an exile, the bright talkers and the elegant ladies – for though he was bored by conventional conversation, and closed down the shutters, a pretty woman with a quick intelligence soon opened them.

It was not surprising, therefore, that from early May until mid July (excluding the Washington visit) he installed himself as the guest of the anglicized American and Conservative MP, 'Chips' Channon (whom he had met earlier in Egypt, and liked) in what Harold Nicolson described in his diary as

. . . his house in Belgrave Square next door to Prince George, Duke of Kent, and Duchess of ditto and little Prince Edward. The house is all Regency upstairs with very carefully draped curtains and Madame Récamier sofas and wall-paintings. Then the dining-room is entered through an orange lobby and discloses itself suddenly as a copy of the blue room of the Amalienburg near Munich – baroque and rococo and what-ho and oh–no-no and all that. Very fine indeed.

These simple home comforts provided an agreeable camping-site for a disorientated Field Marshal.[3]

There is more than a feeble pun behind that strong adjective. Channon was a climber. Not uncomfortably off in his own right, he had tapped into the great wealth of the Guinness family by marrying, in 1933, the eldest daughter of the Earl of Iveagh. Lavishly ostentatious as a host, with a cosmopolitan charm and an active intelligence, Channon had made it his business to know 'everyone who mattered' in high society and all the political coulisses: silent as an MP in the House, he nevertheless had the ear of the men in power – and of their powerful ladies. That brilliant surface, however, unsuccessfully covered other and less acceptable qualities. He was

volubly a diehard, a Chamberlain man for whom Munich had
been an apotheosis, an arrant snob from the extremities of the
right wing. His open friendship with the suspect Prince Paul of
Yugoslavia did not endear him to the informed and the
responsible. Moreover, there was another matter: something
*mondaine,* something perhaps epicene in the atmosphere. Not
for nothing had he dined between Proust and Cocteau or noted
in 1944 that he had deposited in the British Museum all his
diaries 'that I did not destroy, though gone are all the Proust
letters which in my youth and folly I burnt'.

In sharing Channon's roof, relishing his hospitality and revel-
ling in the dazzling society paraded for his entertainment,
Wavell was behaving like a man who had lost his bearings. Wise
friends felt a deep concern that a soldier of this distinction,
shining in his integrity, should allow himself to be used – for
though Channon sincerely admired Wavell he was certainly
using him – as a pawn in the social progress of a man of straw.
Ismay, well aware of all the implications, could not act directly
but saw to it that private warnings were conveyed. Wavell's
son, the gallant Archie John of the Black Watch, tackled the
father with whom he had a close bond.[4] But Wavell's response
was indifferent: they say, what say they, let them say.

Yet what is of profound interest, as much perhaps to the
psychologist as to the historian, is the fact that while Wavell
was so eminently capable of deceiving himself about his personal affairs – for how could he sensibly have thought of
himself as potential Supreme Commander, South-East Asia,
or as the head of the British armies in *Overlord*? How could he
have failed to size up the Channon situation? – nevertheless
almost from the moment that he was appointed Viceroy he
identified, and identified correctly, the course that he must
follow. Major-General Brown, who was Wavell's chief
survey officer in the Middle East, recalled that when he was
demonstrating to the Commander-in-Chief a new stereo-
scopic device for producing maps from air photographs
Wavell considered it and then observed, gravely, 'But I see
quite well with only one eye.' Now, suddenly, his vision
cleared and once again he saw things quite well: saw, in fact,
the real issues.

The precise moment of illumination cannot be indicated, but a rough guess is possible. After referring in his journal to various discussions with Amery and other informed persons Wavell made a simple, cryptic entry. 'August 4–17. I spent this fortnight in Scotland at St Andrews and Dalmeny.' But thereafter, on his return to London, he is to be observed tackling in head–on confrontation with Churchill and the Cabinet the two main themes which would dominate the whole of his period as Viceroy: India must be given a fresh start along the road to independence, and India must meanwhile be fed. Early on in *Seven Pillars of Wisdom* T. E. Lawrence described how the prophets of the Arab tribes would feel an urge to withdraw into the solitude of the desert and clarify their faith by contemplation: 'thence they returned with their imagined message articulate, to preach it to their old, and now doubting, associates'. If the Royal and Ancient at St Andrews and Lord Rosebery's princely demesne at Dalmeny can scarcely be described as a wilderness, something of the same kind seems to have happened to Wavell.

Indeed – to adjust the analogy slightly – he came back from Sinai bearing inscribed tablets in his hand. Following his custom as a commander, he sat down and drafted a paper for his Chief of Staff. At the time this officer was known as PSV (D) or, less obliquely, as Private Secretary to the Viceroy Designate – but the future Sir Evan Jenkins (educated at Rugby and Balliol, a member of the Indian Civil Service since 1920 and ultimately Governor of the Punjab) was – horses for courses – in a higher class than any of Wavell's previous henchmen.

As one examines this 'thinking-aloud' document it is heartwarming to see Wavell reviving that spirit of calculated originality which characterized his early ideas about *Compass* in 1940 and, indeed, flickered to life intermittently during his reign as Commander-in-Chief, India. The opening paragraph of his Note, dated 20 August 1943, established its tone.

I have been turning over in my mind how I should approach this question of finding a solution of the Indian problem if I discarded all normal methods and trusted entirely to my own common sense (such as it is) and my previous experience and training. As a result

I have evolved the following scenario, on which I invite your opinion. It will certainly appear to you as fantastical, impossible or inadvisable;

'I have always,' Wavell ended, 'been in military matters an upholder of unorthodox methods when orthodox methods have failed, as I think .they have in India.' Already he was distancing himself from the man who, in 1942, had rigidly resisted the implications of the Cripps Mission. Jenkins, drawing on his vast experience of the Indian political scene, advised that the chances of success for Wavell's proposals were five to one against, but that an effort would be justified.

The gist of Wavell's proposition was that he should personally invite a carefully chosen group of ten leading Indians (including Gandhi, Nehru and Jinnah) to confer with him at Viceroy's House, Delhi, under conditions of extreme secrecy. 'I believe,' he intended to say to them, 'that a vital decision in matters of government – and I am asking you to make a vital decision for India – can be arrived at only by a few selected men of wisdom and good faith, not by counting votes.' He would offer a definite pledge that His Majesty's Government was prepared to give self-government to India as soon as possible, subject only to the conditions that the war must be successfully concluded and that the British would be handing over to a government as capable as their own of ruling and enforcing its decisions. 'I leave you,' he intended to say, 'to devise your own procedure and methods of debating the problems of India's future and advising me on it.'

But Churchill wanted nothing like this. It was he, now, who seemed like a Frankenstein, faced with an emerging monster. Not unreasonably, in view of Wavell's record, the Prime Minister had assumed that his new Viceroy would be conservative in attitude and malleable over policies: in cricketing terms, a 'night watchman' inserted to stonewall until the end of the war offered fresh options. Churchill wished, in effect, to do nothing about India, and here was Wavell suggesting radical and *immediate* measures. What had happened, and happened irrecoverably, was that the man who joined the army class in his last year at Winchester was re-affirming the classical humanism of his earlier youth, the sense of history, of mutual justice and of social order which, in spite of years of constricting service and wartime command, had never been entirely overlaid. Wavell was ceasing to think merely as a soldier. He was on his way to becoming a statesman.

But he had to deal with 'old, and now doubting associates'. His own journal and the Cabinet papers make it clear that on the secondary issue – the problem of increasing India's food stocks, which he had diagnosed as urgent – he met not only a refusal to make substantial deliveries to supply the necessary shipping, but also an indifference amounting to what he felt to be incomprehension of the realities. On the central question, his project for a secret conference with the Indian leaders, all the high-level discussions in Whitehall that followed left him with no more latitude than a general formula, instructing him to advance the war, maintain internal peace, and vaguely seek for political progress. 'You are wafted to India,' said Amery, 'on a wave of hot air.' Wavell's last meeting with Churchill, on 8 October, was bleak. He said, Wavell recorded, that only over his dead body would any approach to Gandhi take place. 'I resented this and I am afraid rather replied in kind.' It was a disillusioned Viceroy Designate who set off for the East next day. That single eye had spotted how, in the Prime Minister's mind, the fear of splitting the Conservative party overrode any notions of a forward policy in India. Wavell's final journal-entry for the 8th reads: 'I have discovered that the Cabinet is not honest in its expressed desire to make progress in India; and that very few of them have any foresight or political courage.'

Retrospect reveals a miscellaneous variety of reasons for the diehard attitude adopted by the Churchill administration – an attitude, as Wavell noted, fundamentally meretricious in that the soothing noises it uttered from time to time were never backed by the intention, or indeed the will, to act positively about India's independence – at least until after the war: and even then, Churchill obviously hoped, further means of stalling would be found. Neither of the leading political parties in Britain was solid on the issue. An ugly note of racialism is to be observed in the private, unguarded conversation of the Prime

Minister and his circle. There was a strong reaction against American pressure, by no means disinterested, to shed the imperial cloak. The old man was determined, at all costs, to hang on. A reforming Viceroy was in for a rough ride. Even Wavell's stolid predecessor saw this. When they reached Delhi on 19 October the Wavells dined at Viceroy House, and he noted Linlithgow's judgement that 'the chief factors of the problem of Indian political progress were the stupidity of the Indian and the dishonesty of the British: we should not be able to get away with it much longer'.

But statesmanship, like military command, is subject to the pressure of events and the selection of priorities, and it happened that Wavell's return to India as Viceroy coincided with a period when, for millions of Indians, food was more important than freedom. The problems of plain living, rather than high thinking about the future, became his immediate concern, for Bengal was starving. When he dined with his predecessor on his arrival in India, before being sworn in as Viceroy next day – October 20th – Linlithgow warned him that 'in July he expected that deaths in Bengal might be up to 1,000,000 or 1,500,000, and that we looked like getting off better than we had thought possible'. ('Better than we thought possible' equalled about twenty times the casualties of the whole of Bomber Command in the Second World War!) Gandhi's absurd cry, 'I tell the British, give us chaos. I say in other words, leave India to God,' had been answered by yet another practical demonstration of the way that, left to the mercies of Providence, India was prone to decimation by natural disasters – famine, flood, drought, epidemic disease. Wavell's reflex reaction was to see what the British could do to prevent, rather than to produce, chaos. He flew down to Calcutta immediately, cross-questioned Ministers and officials, explored the streets by night to see how the destitute existed, and toured the country regions most devastated. 'Fight forward' was still his principle. Dalhousie, Curzon, Hardinge, Irwin, Linlithgow . . . which of the previous Viceroys would have made his own reconnaissance without the slow ponderous mechanism of the special train, the myriad staff, the cohorts of servants?

Like the economies of some modern societies or Mr Micawber's financial position, the province of Bengal could have been saved from disaster – the effect of a universal shortage of food-stocks – by the difference of a marginal percentage.* Japanese control of the great rice-bowl regions and the selfish hoarding of cereals by farmers and entrepreneurs, assisted by an inefficient Bengali administration, had created deficiencies in the staples of life which, in the main, the more fortunate or far-sighted areas of India avoided. Wavell could not produce a miracle, since the fatal processes were already in train. But his stringent and authoritative grasp of an amorphous situation, and his robust handling of the officials responsible, certainly turned the tide. Moreover, it is evident that his personal involvement in famine relief reinforced in his mind the imperative need to fight the government in London over the issue of food-ships for India. In mid November he made his next unorthodox move, summoning a two-day conference in Delhi for the eleven provincial Governors: an event which had not occurred since 1930. 'We had a whole day,' he recorded, 'on the Food problem.' His persistence throughout his period of office is frequently registered in the documents. Perhaps it is most vividly expressed in a letter he sent to the CIGS, his friend Alan Brooke, on 11 August 1944. The letter itself is in typescript. But there is a post-script in his own graceful calligraphy. 'Our food problem is acute so please continue to support me.'

But the accurate and unpleasing picture he had formed in London of the attitude in Westminster and Whitehall towards Indian independence did not deter him in what might be described as his last great campaign: even though he had no illusions about Churchill, whose dead slow march in that direction reminds one of Karen Blixen's observation that elephants walk as if they had an appointment at the end of the world.† Yet the powerbase from which he might have launched himself rapidly into a policy of reform had been

* The estimate of the shortfall in food-grains that might be significantly dangerous was about 5 per cent.

† 'The Prime Minister passionately hopes that any solution involving the fulfilment of our pledges can still somehow or other be prevented, and with that in view naturally makes difficulties at every stage.' Amery, letter to Wavell, 16 August 1944.

denied him by the Prime Minister's rejection of his bold and
imaginative proposal for a secret summit meeting with the
Indian leaders. Had it actually been permitted, of course, such
an initiative would very probably have failed, either through
the refusal of essential representatives even to attend such a
conference, or through their inability to reach an agreed
agenda for submission to the Viceroy. Still, it would have been
an initiative, and a positive, undeniable gesture of British
intent. But in this respect Wavell's power, indeed his very
freedom for manoeuvre, was severely restricted. Nothing
illustrates this basic truth better than Nehru's famous inter-
change with Mountbatten in 1947. 'Have you by some miracle
got plenipotentiary powers?' 'Why do you ask?' 'You behave
quite differently from any former Viceroy. You speak with an
air of authority as though you were certain that what you said
would never be reversed by HMG in London.' 'Suppose I have
plenipotentiary powers, what difference would it make?'
'Why then you will succeed, where others have failed.'

Moreover, for Wavell the parameters were defined not
merely by the apathy of the British government, but also by
circumstances within the sub-continent itself. An anonymous
review of his *Journals* in *The Times Literary Supplement*
summed up the state of affairs graphically:

> Apart from being out of tune with London, Wavell entered the
> Indian political scene when it was at its bleakest and most sterile.
> The Congress leaders were in jail. Mr Jinnah plugged, relentlessly
> and uncompromisingly, the case for Pakistan. Famine had devas-
> tated Bengal, and, incidentally, irretrievably damaged the British
> reputation as efficient and considerate administrators.* The
> Japanese still pressed on the eastern frontiers. As the months went
> by and the Allied cause began to prosper, the political and com-
> munal volcano showed every sign of being ready to erupt.

Nor, indeed, did the Vesuvius of communal passion remain
dormant in Wavell's time. The Calcutta massacres of August
1946, with their 20,000 dead or seriously wounded and the
streets strewn with corpses, provide the most terrible example
and other instances abound, localized but ghastly. But they

---

* A comment presumably not intended to apply to Wavell. In any case, Bengal
happened to be one of the provinces under an Indian administration at this time!

were mainly post-war, and, *pace* the reviewer, this was – in part at least – the result of a prospering cause: of the increased Anglo-American commitment to India which followed the appointment of Mountbatten as Supreme Commander in 1943, the growing military presence, the visible aircraft, the flood of stores and then, in 1944, the victory at Imphal. In part, too, the greatly expanded opportunities for employment and manufacture and profit-making surely had their tranquillizing effect, as well as the mint of money sent back to poor village homes by the Indians under arms, whose total was rising to over 2,000,000 (2,500,000 by 1945, as well as 8,000,000 working on defence tasks and at least 6,000,000 drawn into the war industries and the expanding railways). But Wavell's patient, fair-minded, self-imposed quest for conciliation and compromise unquestionably was a major factor. During one of his many private moods of doubt and disillusion he confided to his journal: 'Continual hard work, and almost continual failure. No rest, no success.' Few historians would accept that as a final verdict on his achievement.

But whatever it was – and it was certainly *something* – any success, however incomplete, was achieved in spite as well as because of his own character. Lacking Mountbatten's open hand and easy smile, his showman's instinct, his youthful thrust and eager ambition, Wavell had to set about making friends and influencing people with such social assets as he possessed – and they were not always enough. Those abrupt silences, a stiffness of manner that seemed like *hauteur,* a sense of inaccessibility that could be glacial . . . the leopard could not completely change its spots. The chi-chi of the minor politicians bored him, and he misjudged at least one major figure, for though he released Gandhi he was surely wrong in thinking of him as 'malevolent' and 'malignant' (yet malevolent was the actual word he used in reporting to the King on 8 July 1946).★ Maulana Azad, the Congress President, wrote to him on his departure that he felt the loss of a personal friend, but Wavell told George VI that 'put up against Gandhi he was as a

★ Even so, when Gandhi was released, on the ground that he was liable to die in captivity, Wavell requested that he might be allowed to talk politics with him and was prevented from doing so by the Secretary of State for India.

rabbit faced by a stoat'. Jinnah he disliked but tolerated, 'a curious character, a lonely, unhappy, self-centred man'. It would be fair to say that among all the Indian figure-heads whom he so conscientiously cultivated he never found one with whom he truly felt at home.

It would be wholly wrong, nevertheless, to imply that this apparently frosty exterior did not conceal an instinctive warmth and a genuine relish for human relationships. As in the case of many commanders, his public *persona* seems disconnected from the private Wavell. In the recollections of those who saw the unofficial figure *en pantoufles* – recollections scattered through Connell's biography and the memoirs of such officers as Bernard Fergusson, Philip Mason or Peter Coates – a visible and immensely likeable human being is to be discerned, a man so different from Churchill's 'chairman of a golf club' that one seems to be examining photographs of a different person.

Nothing illustrates this better than a vignette relating to the precise period when Wavell was so conscientiously but, it must be said, awkwardly striving to achieve a *rapport* with the Indian politicians. Rosalind Chenevix-Baldwin, niece of the Commander-in-Chief Sir Claude Auchinleck, was serving at Mountbatten's headquarters in Ceylon. She came up to Delhi on a short visit to her uncle and found herself plunged into a world of protocol and ceremony wholly strange to her. She recalled:

> At the time I was very very young, just out of the schoolroom and terribly shy. I was entirely surrounded by Generals, Viceroys, Chiefs of Staff, Lord Mountbatten, the whole affair! No women, because my aunt was ill. Lord Wavell was about the only one except for my uncle whom I knew. Somehow or other he made it clear, without saying anything really, that this must be a terrifying ordeal for me, and he was an extra uncle. . . .
>
> Personally I have always looked upon him as a warm, kindly and friendly person who, although he never said a great deal, managed to convey his sensitivity without words.
>
> The stereotype he has acquired, of the reverse, is because many people are too self-interested to pick up the hand that is offered to them. If you don't put flowers in water they wither.

Yet conscience drove him on (a man not given to diplomacy and winning ways, a masterful soldier whose natural style was authoritative rather than persuasive), to infinite hours of discussion with the politicians. The impression that he reigned from afar, aloof and monolithic, is wholly unfounded. Nobody, except Evan Jenkins and a few others, knew how inaccurate this image was until *The Viceroy's Journal* was published in 1973: nobody thereafter could possibly be in doubt. Or, for that matter, could possibly doubt that though Wavell never got as close to the Congress leaders as did Cripps, and though he never evoked so warm and wide a response as Mountbatten, he won unfeigned respect. If he just lacked the indefinable qualities which any man would have needed to achieve a decisive settlement, it is evident that he carried the Indians with him a far greater distance than Linlithgow did, and that if he had received, like Mountbatten, the virtually unconditional support of the Government in London he might have carried them a great deal further. His victory over circumstances and the limitations of his own temperament, seen in this perspective, was not only remarkable, it was unexpected: for who, watching Wavell in that troubled spring of 1941 or fumbling over Arakan, could have guessed that by his liberal policies he would build the launching-pad for India's independence?

Yet this is the true measure of his achievement. Perhaps it would not have seemed so unexpected to anybody who had read and reflected on his life of Allenby, for much that anticipates Wavell's conduct of affairs as Viceroy is to be found in the final volume – which covers Allenby's service, from 1919 to 1922, as High Commissioner for Egypt. Wavell had worked on this volume while he was in Cairo: as he confessed in the preface, 'It was written in spare hours or half-hours, often separated by days, weeks, or even months, during two years of intense military work. Some of it was written in my frequent aeroplane journeys. On being transferred to India nearly two years ago I laid the manuscript aside.' Thus it was that the book did not appear until late in 1943, a 'progressive' account of a 'progressive' proconsul. When on 10 September 1943 Sir Edward Grigg asked to see an advance proof, because he feared the criticism that it might cause in Conservative circles, Wavell noted in his diary, 'I don't think I mind if it does, I am not very much in sympathy with the right-wing Conservative.'

One thing was certain: Churchill, who had been Colonial Secretary during Allenby's regime in Egypt, was not in sympathy with Wavell's presentation. In fact he was so shocked that he nearly cut the dinner given to Wavell by the Cabinet before he flew off to India. Would a publication earlier that year have caused Wavell to be 'sent to Coventry' as Governor-General of Australia – Churchill's original idea? The question is not idle, for undoubtedly Wavell's published views about Allenby made him, from the Prime Minister's viewpoint, even more suspect and diminished his small chances of reaching a reconciliation in India.

Nevertheless, slowly but steadily he tested the possibilities. There were so many obstacles in his path that to hurry would have sent him headlong. He felt the temperature, assessed the personalities, clarified his own ideas. And over one question, central to the whole theme of conciliation, it may be asserted that this non-political soldier with his one eye saw more clearly than the experts in London, than some of his own advisers, and even than the sophisticated Nehru himself. Since the failure of the Cripps Mission Jinnah and the Muslim League had extended their power-base so far and so effectively that any idea of treating with them other than on the same level as Congress was doomed. This was the reality whose truth was ratified by the final split. In London they were desperately slow to sense what was happening: the India claque in the Labour party, dominated by Cripps, inevitably looked on Congress through rose-tinted glasses, and by Nehru's contemptuous rejection of the Muslims' *locus standi* Congress itself increased the illusion. Wavell was locked in a situation where compromise could only be achieved by altering the terms of the debate, and none of the participants was willing to budge until, in 1947, the British themselves made a crucial adjustment, so that Mountbatten could wield the sword that cut the knot.

For that adjustment Wavell cleared the ground and set out

the sign-posts pointing in the right direction. The process is not easy to chart, because false steps, diversions, impasses and reversals mark its course. But there are three salient features, generally known as the Simla Conference, the Cabinet Mission and the Breakdown Plan. Of these the last sounds like the beginning of the end, but it was really the end of the beginning.

Yet even the first was a long time a-coming. It took prolonged effort, many written exchanges with Churchill and Amery and, finally, a special visit to London before, on 14 June 1945, Wavell was able to announce in Delhi his intention to summon to Simla on the 25th a large and broadly based selection of Indian leaders, the object being to discuss the formation of a politically representative Executive Council. In effect, he was setting up a re-vamped but watered-down version of the conference he had proposed when he first became Viceroy. That was to be secret: this was public. In the House of Commons Amery stated that it was founded on fact: that the 1942 Cripps offer still held good. Moreover, he declared that the new initiative owed everything to Wavell and to his deep sympathy with India's aspirations. Churchill, reluctantly accepting the proposal, grunted 'at any rate we aren't giving anything away'.

The Simla Conference reflected Wavell's fundamental principle, that a political settlement must inevitably be achieved but that it would be best achieved while the war was still being waged: while strong British authority was still available to control and direct the cross-currents. Churchill, of course, wished for everything to be pushed aside into a post-war limbo. In fact he still hoped that this would happen, for when Wavell called on him in London after his election defeat he 'revealed that the only reason he had agreed to my political move was that the India Committee had all told him it was bound to fail!' But Wavell himself was well aware of the shoals ahead. On the day that he broadcast his announcement of the Simla Conference he noted in his Journal:

And so is launched a fresh attempt to help India to political freedom, which I initiated with a note to HMG just nine months ago. I suppose it is something of an achievement to have got it thus

far, but whether it will crash on Indian intransigence, like the
Cripps and other proposals, remains to be seen. I have certainly
got a very difficult time ahead and I do not pretend to be a
diplomatist.

Success would certainly have appalled the Prime Minister, for
in the new representative Executive Council which was anticipated the only British members were to be the Viceroy and the
Commander-in-Chief. Never before had responsibility in the
three vital areas of defence, finance and home affairs been
offered to Indian members. And the question of how to reach
agreement on a new constitution – a constitution for *Indians* –
was high on the agenda. But there was no agreement.
Churchill's hopes and Wavell's premonitions were fulfilled:
the conference foundered on the rocks of intransigence. If
Congress killed the Cripps Offer, Jinnah was the hatchet-man
at Simla, for it was his sustained and rigid insistence that the
Muslims' share of the new political cake was less than their
entitlement which brought the conference to a fruitless close
on 14 July. 'So ends my attempt,' Wavell noted, 'to introduce a
fresh impetus and a fresh spirit into Indian politics.'

For long afterwards he reflected on whether the failure was
his own fault: whether he should have called Jinnah's bluff.
But his only weapon would have been a threat that he would
nevertheless go ahead with setting up a new Council, which in
the circumstances must necessarily have been dominated by
Congress. And that, surely, would have made Churchill burst
a blood-vessel. On a practical view, it seems inconceivable
that the Cabinet, in whose hands the ratifying power lay,
would have authorized a Council controlled by a party many
of whose leaders had just emerged from the prisons where
they had languished since the August 1942 insurrection. The
Prime Minister who called Gandhi a baboon and was furious
when he heard of his release from his cage could never have
supported such a proposition. It was still true that the terms of
the debate would have to be altered.

Others besides Wavell thought and think that he failed. The
most austere criticism of his performance is perhaps to be
found in H. V. Hodson's *The Great Divide: Britain, India,
Pakistan*. Hodson was an experienced eye-witness. Yet it is to

be noted that his book, published in 1969, preceded *The Viceroy's Journal* by four years, and only then were Wavell's thoughts disclosed. The editor of those journals, Sir Penderel Moon, whose service in the ICS from 1929 to 1944 gave him a work-span in India more than ten times longer than Hodson's and whose subsequent editorship of the India Office Records on the Transfer of Power lends him a special authority, judged that 'the Simla Conference, though it ended in failure, may be regarded in some ways as the greatest achievement of Wavell's Viceroyalty. The idea of holding it, undoubtedly a right one, was entirely his, and it was his dogged persistence that overcame the resistance of HMG.' The Congress President, Maulana Azad, wrote to Wavell that by calling the conference he had rendered India and Great Britain a service which had few parallels in history and that the new possibilities of Indo-British friendship were due to that step. *Quot homines, tot sententiae.*

Within weeks, however, those new possibilities had to be assessed in a different context and the first major change in the terms of the debate occurred. On 9 August the final results of the British General election were declared, and Churchill resigned his premiership. On 6 and 9 August atomic bombs (about which the Viceroy of India had received no forewarning) were dropped on Hiroshima and Nagasaki. With a Labour government in power and Japan defeated, the affairs of India entered a new dimension. 'I think,' Wavell wrote after the first news of the election landslide, 'Labour is likely to take more interest in and be more sympathetic towards India, but they will have some weird ideas about it.'

Yet what might have been a honeymoon looked, at first, like ending in a tragedy. Wavell perhaps never realized how, in Attlee, he had a Prime Minister who distrusted him as Churchill had done. What he soon appreciated was that the ideas of the government were not so much weird as wrong. Cripps, who since 1942 had looked at him askance, was now the moving spirit over Indian affairs on whom the grasp of Congress never relaxed. Thus the basic fact that the Muslims were a power to be reckoned with as much as the Congress party – a fact self-evident to Wavell and fatally demonstrated at

Simla – was shrouded in Westminster by Congress propaganda consumed too easily and perhaps too avidly. It seems, for example, inconceivable that Nehru could have written to Cripps as late as 27 January 1946 that 'if the British Government made it clear that it would in no way encourage Pakistan, then agitation for it would rapidly collapse, and that the Muslim League leadership were incapable of any form of direct action or of instigating any real trouble'. Still less is it easy to understand why Cripps, with his quick lawyer's mind and his long experience of the Indian scene, did not dismiss such a claim as balderdash.

The consequence was a policy of dither. Since Congress was the favourite child, Wavell found himself restricted in his negotiations with Gandhi and Nehru while the stance of impartiality which he had always tried to retain became less and less credible in the eyes of the Muslims. All these impalpable and imponderable factors coalesced at the end of 1945. In November Wavell sent to London a long, carefully reasoned document drawing attention to the strong indication that the disturbances of August 1942 were about to be repeated on a much larger scale:

> The object of the rising the Congress leaders have in mind would be the expulsion of the British. . . . I must accordingly, with the utmost gravity, warn HMG to be prepared for a serious attempt by the Congress, probably next spring, but quite possibly earlier, to subvert by force the present administration in India.

The classic response of all British governments to unpalatable news from the man on the spot, particularly when he is under a cloud of distrust, was immediately adopted. A parliamentary delegation was despatched.

The fate of the Cabinet Mission, as it was called, might have been predicted from its composition and its remit. Amery's successor, the worthy veteran Lord Pethick-Lawrence, was at its head, his colleagues being Cripps and A. V. Alexander, a sound First Lord of the Admiralty short on the *tact des choses possible* for navigation in the strong seas of Indian politics.*

---

* Nevertheless, it was Wavell's judgement that by the end of the Mission Alexander was the member who had best appreciated the realities.

But even less promising was its status and its object. 'They were not enjoined to impose, or to recommend for imposition, any solution; nor were they to be concerned with the details of a future constitutional structure. They were not principals but mediators. . . .' This lack of normative, still less of executive authority, which kept Wavell in fetters and was only dispelled by Mountbatten, undermined an already ill-balanced Mission.

Between 24 March, when what Wavell called 'the three Magi' arrived, and the end of June when they departed, discussions and wrangles were more or less continuous, forming a skein of such complex ramifications that only a specialized historian could disentangle it. The arguments as to whether there should be a sovereign Pakistan or a 'truncated' Pakistan, and over the form that an interim government and a final constitution might take, remind one in retrospect of the metaphysical hair-splitting at one of the great religious conclaves of the Middle Ages.

Wavell carried the whole load on his back, as well as the routine responsibilities of a Viceroy: even Cripps praised in the House of Commons the 'amazing way' that he had functioned. But it was to no avail, for in the final stages Gandhi withdrew Congress from co-operation in an interim government. Then Jinnah, sensing an advantage, quickly persuaded the Muslim League to accept the terms proposed, assuming that this would result in a Muslim-dominated government. Instead both Wavell and the Mission interpreted the texts as requiring them merely to institute a caretaker government and await fresh negotiations before anything was finalized. Thus Gandhi was left to gloat over the wreckage while Jinnah felt that he had been conned. 'A chapter of false hopes', as H. V. Hodson put it, 'raised by equivocal formulae compounding basic conflicts, and doomed to disappointment, was ended when the Cabinet Mission left India on 29th June.'

Nevertheless, in the course of these weary weeks (during which, at one point, he was near to resignation) Wavell formulated the idea – and it was *his* idea – which altered the terms of the debate so radically that at last Mountbatten was given those essential, decisive, plenipotentiary powers without which argument might have continued for ever, or at least until it was drowned in seas of blood even wider and deeper than those released by the Great Divide in 1947. The idea had a name: the Breakdown Plan. It was described graphically by Wavell himself to Mountbatten when the latter took over:

> I am sorry for you, you have been given an impossible job. I have tried everything I know to solve the problem of handing over India to its people; and I can see no light. I have only one solution, which I call Operation Madhouse – withdrawal of the British province by province, beginning with women and children, then civilians, then the army. I can see no other way out.

But the Breakdown Plan was saner than its author admitted, for built into it was the revolutionary feature from which so much was to flow – the notion that the British should actually name a date on which power would be irreversibly handed over. And the date he had in mind was March 1948. At the time it seemed wishful thinking and yet, astonishingly enough, it was on 13 August 1947, the Raj's last full day, that Mountbatten announced 'Tomorrow two new sovereign States will take their place in the Commonwealth . . . this is a parting between 'friends.' Such was the policy that Wavell carried to London on 3 December 1946, and such the policy for which, after many but desultory discussions, he requested an affirmation as his last act before returning to Delhi on Christmas Eve – and was refused.

Like Shakespeare's 'poor cat i' the adage, letting I dare not wait upon I would', Attlee and his colleagues superficially accepted but, throughout his visit, refused to ratify what Wavell proposed. They could be manoeuvred to the brink, but dare not – at this stage – jump. By the time Mountbatten was appointed, of course, their desperation – perhaps particularly their fear of the pent-up violence in India – had so increased that what Wavell formally requested, his successor's peremptory demands obtained. It does not erode the last Viceroy's supreme achievement to make plain that Wavell had acted as his John the Baptist: yet it was due to Wavell that the famous concept of a 'final day' was born, was ventilated in London, and was so implanted in the government's mind that when it was finally seen to be inevitable familiarity had made it digestible.

From the journal-entries which Wavell made in London, however, it is obvious that his personal relationship with Attlee was strained and uneasy. At the time he did not understand the reason, for he was allowed to return to Delhi and function normally – until, on 4 February, he noted, 'Just after lunch I had a letter from the PM by special messenger, dismissing me from my post at a month's notice. Not very courteously done.' The fact is that Attlee had already decided to replace Wavell while he was still in London, but had failed to face him with the decision. Possibly he was too embarrassed, for the Major Attlee who had served at Gallipoli was not lacking in moral courage, or, at other times, tender in his sacking.

In any case, this particular evasion can be at least partially excused. The immense problem of finding a successor had not yet been overcome: scarcely, perhaps tackled. And nobody recalling how Churchill, having already determined that Wavell must go, continued to spur him on to undertake the *Battleaxe* operation, and how he took to Washington a Commander-in-Chief from India who, in his eyes, was already 'on the toboggan' and suitable for an Australian burial, could condemn Attlee out of hand for his silence. But his dismissal of the Viceroy was of a different order. Only a full transcript of his letter will convey its flavour.

PRIVATE AND PERSONAL                     31st January, 1947

My dear Viceroy

I have your letter of the 19th in reply to mine of the 8th. It is clear from what you say with regard to Government policy that there is a wide divergence of view as to the course which should be followed during the interim period. I had hoped that it would have been possible for you to have returned here during January to discuss the situation which has arisen.

I am very conscious of the heavy burden which you have carried and of the great service which you have rendered during this difficult period. I know that you undertook this task from a high sense of duty.

You were, I understand, informed that your appointment was a war appointment and that while the usual term for a Viceroy is five years, this might not apply. I think that three years was

mentioned. This has now expired. I know, of course, that prior to
your appointment as Viceroy you had had the heavy strain of high
commands in war and, as you say in your letter, you have had no
rest. I appreciate that you desire a month or two's leave at home.

But the Indian problem is entering a new phase, which will be
very exacting and may be prolonged. The next few months are of
great importance.

In view of all these circumstances and of the fact that it is
specially necessary that the Viceroy should be in full agreement
with the policy of His Majesty's Government, I think that you
may agree that the time has come to make a change in the Viceroyalty.

I recall that you expressed your readiness to retire in the event of
disagreement on policy and this would seem to me to be the
appropriate course to follow.

An announcement should be made with as little delay as possible in order to allow time for the appointment of your successor
and for him to take over at the end of February or early in March.
The normal announcement about your successor would be pre-
faced with the statement 'Field Marshal the Viscount Wavell who
accepted the Viceroyalty as a war appointment is now retiring.' I
have not looked into details, but if as a result you are denied any
leave of absence which you normally would have had, you may be
sure that you will not suffer financially.

I should like to submit your name to His Majesty for the dignity
of an Earldom in recognition of the self sacrificing and loyal
service which you have displayed in your long and distinguished
career in India both to the Indian people and to this Country and
the Commonwealth.

> Yours sincerely,
> C. R. Attlee

To this bleak document, at once apathetic and icy, Wavell
replied with appropriate decorum. After pointing out the
Prime Minister's error about a three-year term (for Churchill
had never specifically limited his tenure to less than the normal
five years) he added: 'I think, however, that I am entitled to
observe that so summary a dismissal of His Majesty's representative in India is hardly in keeping with the dignity of the
appointment.' Six months previously, he pointed out, he had
suggested that Attlee might wish to replace a soldier by a
politician but had received no reply. 'Whether my conduct of

my office since then has deserved dismissal at a few weeks' notice is for others to judge.'

The Field Marshal who, whatever his errors, had served his country with the heart of a lion was to be expelled like a dog. Attlee's reference to petty financial matters, in a document of this nature, was the equivalent of treating his Viceroy as though he were some time-served barrack-room private bleating about his outstanding pay and allowances. It is ironical to think that, *mutatis mutandis,* Churchill would have known what to do. With all the history of the Raj in mind, with memories of Clive and Warren Hastings, of the Mutiny, of the long line of warriors and men of affairs who had carved out a place for the British in India – and conscious too, that the letter he was writing would be laid before the eyes of posterity – he would have put aside all past differences and written gracefully, magisterially, appropriately. When Wavell's dismissal was announced in the House of Commons it was Churchill who rose to protest at the manner of his going. It had been a long war. The scarred veteran, in his magnanimity, did not forget how Wavell, 'that brilliant chief, irregularly great' had done his best, in Robert Browning's words,

> Through a whole campaign of the world's life and death
> Doing the King's work all the dim day long
> And, now the day was won, relieved at once.

# 9

## Postscript: *Other Men's Flowers*

Few, but roses
*The Garland of Meleager* (c. 90 BC) on the poems of Sappho

Generals tend to win their reputations at the cost of other men's lives. By an anomaly unique in military history Wavell's own reputation has reached its widest range – certainly in the English-speaking world – not because of his prowess as a soldier or a proconsul, but because of his identification with a small miscellany containing a selection of other men's verses. Historians, members of the armed services or old hands from the Mediterranean and the Far East are in a special class: they remember Wavell in his leading roles. But a mention of his name to the ordinary citizen still evokes, almost as a reflex, the reaction, 'Ah! *Other Men's Flowers.'*

In one sense this is not surprising, for whilst the names of defunct Commanders-in-Chief or Viceroys are rarely recalled this little anthology, since it first appeared, has been in continual circulation. Grahame C. Greene, the managing director of Wavell's publishers, Jonathan Cape Ltd, kindly arranged for a check on the book's history and its sales to be carried out in March 1979. He wrote: 'I find that they amount to 119,898 plus 8000 for the Book Society. I think it is fair to say that the book has been continuously in print since 1944. The only gaps I can find are short ones while awaiting the arrival of a reprint.' During that post-war period when publishers and Fleet Street fought for the memoirs of wartime leaders Field Marshal Slim once observed, sardonically, that 'we soldiers are accustomed to sell our lives dearly'. Yet in terms of mere commercial success few of these prestigious volumes (Slim's is a remarkable exception) can compare with *Other Men's Flowers* for longevity and

and width of appeal. Nevertheless – like more than one famous child – the book had a difficult and almost disastrous birth.

In 1942 Peter Fleming, as has been seen, was serving on Wavell's staff in Delhi, enjoying a special and envied position because his laconic master not only approved of Fleming's unorthodox approach to war but also found in him a civilized companion who, utterly unabashed by rank or status, could talk on equal terms about literature or that life-outside-war which was Wavell's preferred domain. They shared a wave-length. And so it was Fleming who suggested to Wavell that a personal anthology might be assembled from the many poems which he had by heart. The original impulse to make a note of them had arisen, with no thought of publication, from discussions with his son about their preferred styles of poetry. This new proposal, that they might be shaped into a book, struck Wavell as being an agreeable relaxation from the tortuous manoeuvres of Gandhi's Congress Party or his more insistent preoccupation with the Japanese. An initial text, therefore, was dispatched in due course to Fleming's publishers in London, Jonathan Cape – for Cape had handled in the thirties the books that made Fleming famous: *Brazilian Adventure, One's Company* and *News from Tartary*.

Events now took a serio-comic turn. Wavell was working far from home and books of reference. His memory, though prehensile, was not minutely exact, and the text he submitted was naturally blemished by incorrect quotation, doubtful attribution and other imperfections. It was examined in Cape's headquarters at 30 Bedford Square in London by the resident editorial adviser, Daniel George, a man whose mastery of English literature was formidably comprehensive and who combined an academic's ferocious passion for precision with a diamond-merchant's unerring eye for a flaw. His report, written as a private privileged document – as all publishers' reports should be – was inevitably adverse and, Daniel being the man he was, scathing.

Unfortunately Jonathan Cape, one of the greatest publishers of his day, had risen to that eminence from the launching pad of a bookseller's errand boy through qualities sometimes characteristic of a rogue elephant, and his occasional displays of elephantine tactlessness were the joy and despair of his colleagues. He now excelled himself, writing to Wavell a chilling dismissive letter as though this world-famous figure was some unknown scribbler from the suburbs who had submitted an unsolicited manuscript. Moreover, he made the fatal and unpardonable error of enclosing Daniel George's uninhibited report. Fleming was furious and Wavell, not unaccustomed to dealing with publishers, was wounded perhaps more deeply than his stoicism allowed him to disclose. Those poems, many of them absorbed decades ago, were the journey-money on which he had drawn throughout his career: a stimulant in good times, a consolation in defeat. Wavell's comment in the anthology on Francis Thompson's *The Hound of Heaven* is explicit:

> I had it by heart in a very few readings and from that day I have used the magic of its imagery in my times of stress, to distract my mind from peril or disaster. I have repeated the words of this greatest of all lyrics under fire, on a rough Channel crossing, in pain of body or mind.

The phrase 'greatest of all lyrics' may seem an extraordinary judgement. Still, this is what the poems meant to Wavell: they mirrored his inner life. It would not have been surprising if he had immediately baled out.

But there was a Blücher at this Waterloo. Peter Fleming's closest friend, from Eton and Oxford days, was Rupert Hart-Davis who, before becoming a post-war publisher in his own right, had in the latter thirties been the junior member on the board of Jonathan Cape Ltd. Like Fleming he was now an officer in the Guards, but unlike Fleming he was at that time stationed in London – and still a director of Cape's. Fleming swiftly sent him a *cri de coeur,* and Hart-Davis, whose pre-war board-room style had no doubt been stiffened by a captaincy in the Coldstream, first assaulted Jonathan Cape on the telephone and then reinforced with an uncompromising letter in which he pointed out that both Wavell and Fleming (a valued Cape author) were piqued by Cape's communication whose inadequacies he pointed out as firmly as if his Chairman was a delinquent private on Defaulters' Parade.

Further, to a man who is probably a bit shy about knowing and liking poetry at all, to describe his poetic treasures as 'familiar school recitations advancing in close formation' is tantamount to a sock on the jaw. Frankly I'm quite surprised he didn't try to cancel the arrangement right away. You see, he looks on the book as a lifelong treasure, which doesn't require much work on it. We know there's a lot to be done, but really that's quite a minor point. The important thing is, surely, that we have the complete bones of a tremendously saleable book. Your letter and memorandum rather give the impression that if the book is any good at all it will be due to the work of D. George (you mention his name seven times). This of course is balls, and to my way of thinking puts the matter out of proportion. . . .

Common sense now prevailed, and arrangements were made for publication of what did indeed prove to be 'a tremendously saleable book'. But the serio-comedy continued. Cape was notoriously close-fisted, sometimes to a point of absurdity. And it was surely absurd to dun the Commander-in-Chief India with a demand for £50 as a fee for the editorial work carried out by Daniel George. Wavell's telegraphed response of 24 March 1943 had the terse authority of a military signal: 'PARAGRAPH EIGHTEEN AGREEMENT FEE GEORGE NOTHING TO DO WITH AUTHOR . . .' So it was a happy chance that when Wavell had to spend some time in London later in the year Hart-Davis was still available to nurse him through various tricky but essential problems of book production. There was a day, for example, when they met at the Army and Navy Club to consider how Wavell's name should be printed on the book-jacket. Field Marshal Sir Archibald Wavell? Or A. P. Wavell? 'My friends,' said Wavell in a marvellous moment of inno-cence, 'my friends call me Archie.'

When *Other Men's Flowers* finally appeared in 1944 Wavell had other things to think about. The Japanese were at the gates of India – in Arakan and at Imphal and Kohima. He was now Viceroy, and even these military realities were only a menacing background to the problem which increasingly became his prime concern – how to reach some viable political accommodation with the main Indian pressure groups, Con-gress and the Muslim League. But in London his book was producing a nightmare for his publishers.

Its instant success – for which it is not difficult to account – had taken these shrewd gentlemen by surprise. An anthology of accessible, undemanding and familiar poems, selected and annotated by a famous soldier who had something of a war hero's status, was opportune and direct in its appeal during those days of 1944 when hopes were rising and readable new books were rare. The quality of this response was captured by Wavell himself in his introduction to the revised edition of 1947:

> A tribute which I greatly valued came in the form of an annotated copy which a friend of mine sent me. The annotations had been made by a soldier who read *Other Men's Flowers* during the period of his training for D-Day in Normandy. As he read each poem he put the date on which, and sometimes the circumstances in which, he had read it; and added his comments of enjoyment, indifference or dislike. He finished the volume while crossing to Normandy and had fallen in battle shortly afterwards.

People came to feel, quite simply, that Wavell and his chosen poems 'spoke for England': a dream of England, perhaps, something to do with tradition and racial memory, with the old values which they believed they had been fighting for and would still face death to preserve. Whatever the reason, *Other Men's Flowers* astonishingly matched a mood, and the constant flow of orders for the book created formidable problems for Jonathan Cape's. A strong effort of historical recall is necessary to envisage the circumstances of wartime publishing: the universal shortage of paper, the complicated licensing mechanism by which stocks were obtained, the lack of staff, the printing delays, the difficulties of distribution. Production was in the hands of Cape's fellow director, Wren Howard, whose herculean efforts and skill in exploiting to the full (and perhaps bending) the rules of the game kept the anthology alive. In its upbringing, as at its birth, *Other Men's Flowers* had an uneasy passage which was not smoothed by the war's ending. Rationing still prevailed. In January 1946 Howard was writing to Wavell to say that he had managed to produce 24,000 copies, *'almost all of which are now being despatched to fill orders on hand'*, and as late as December of that year he reported that 'you may be interested to know that I received this morning notification that a permit had been granted us to enable us to buy paper for a further 20,000 copies'.

For the student of Wavell's performance as a commander, however, statistics and sales figures are of far less significance than the extent to which his choice of poems for *Other Men's Flowers* illuminates his own mind: a mind which, on his own confession, drew on them for sustenance in battle, in perplexity, in times of stressful decision. Cromwell and Montgomery may have turned to God for inspiration but amid the tensions of war it is evident Wavell sought comfort among the Muses. And the first point to establish is that though there are over 250 quotations in the anthology (many of them substantial) they were indeed part of Wavell's mind, held there by an exceptional gift for verbal retention which, like Macaulay's, did not glue the words automatically in the memory but kept them on hand for instant use. Over this point Wavell was proud – and firm with his publishers. When there was a question of cutting FitzGerald's *The Rubáiyát* he wrote, in March 1943: 'I have gone on the principle throughout to include what I knew by heart; and I knew, and still know, the whole of Omar by heart; so I think it should be included in full.'

The most striking impression made by the poems is their quality of straightforward and frequently simple statement. They are compositions, on the whole, that might be expected to appeal to a man with a direct, a lucid and uncomplicated mind. The poets included are as indicative as those excluded. 'Practically all the verse in this collection is capable of being declaimed, it seems to be a function of poetry that it should be so.' Wavell's note in his introduction is supported in his selection by a wealth of Kipling and Browning, by Scott, Macaulay, Chesterton, Belloc. Yet some of the exclusions are baffling. 'Wordsworth's and Tennyson's verses,' he wrote, 'have never registered an impression on my memory. They seem to me to belong to a limbo which is earthy without being quite human and star-gazing without being inspired.' It is better to move on: but as we move on to the section called 'Good Fighting' we find the usual 'Into Battle' by Julian Grenfell (which Wavell curiously described as a nature poem!), one

Sassoon – his conventional 'The General' – Seeger's
'Rendezvous', and 'Magpies in Picardy'. None of the best
Sassoon: no Wilfred Owen, or Sorley, or Rosenberg, the most
memorable voices of Wavell's first great war. There is no sense
of an alert and questing discrimination. Perhaps the most
important revelation about Wavell in this section is that during
the early years of the Second World War he carried with him a
pocket edition of Malory, for his affinity was, above all, with
the knightly spirit and the *beau geste*.

Nevertheless it would be superficial, though easy, to dismiss the contents of *Other Men's Flowers* as merely an amalgam
from popular assemblies like *The Golden Treasury* and *The
Oxford Book of English Verse:* as 'familiar school recitations
advancing in close formation'. Wavell knew his own limitations and worked within them. In 1948 his publishers sent him
a slim new volume and Wavell replied, 'Lilian Bowes Lyon's
poems are I think very good of their kind, but it is not my
kind, they are all poems of contemplation': perhaps this is why
he could shrug off so dismissively the authors of 'In Memoriam' and the ode on 'Intimations of Immortality' as 'earthy
without being quite human and star-gazing without being
inspired'. It is surely better to ask not what he left out but what
he put in, and to add a question which perhaps tells one more
about Wavell's cast of mind than any niggling over his list of
titles: for among his peers in the war – Alan Brooke, Alexander, Montgomery, Tedder, Eisenhower, not to mention
opponents like Rommel, or Kesselring or their fellows of the
*Generalität* – who in the slightest degree kept himself going as a
soldier by recourse to the central core – if not always the most
exquisite or intense expression – of his nation's poetry? The
man of action enjoyed verse that embodied the spirit of action:
but he *enjoyed* it, memorized it, and found it a *vade-mecum*. This
is why so many thousands of readers, perhaps not very sophisticated in the main, have devotedly kept *Other Men's Flowers* in
print for over three decades.

Wavell's preference for the poetry of statement rather than
the poetry of contemplation, which is illustrated on virtually
every page of *Other Men's Flowers,* conforms in a striking way
to his performance as a commander. Certainly it is true that he

was a prophet and practitioner of deception, a student of surprise. What he had learned under Allenby he taught as a trainer of troops and applied as a general. Nevertheless, in action he was essentially pragmatic and, like the classic theorists, understood well that finesse is essentially the embroidery of war and that results are finally achieved by concentration on and direct effort at the vital point. For all his experience of Allenby's famous deception of the Turks, he did not budge in believing that the First World War had to be won on the Western Front. Two comments give the flavour of his thought. In his Lee-Knowles lectures of 1939 he remarked that Lee was 'possibly too much a gentleman for the ungentle business of war. A sterner man would surely have driven Longstreet into battle hours earlier at Gettysburg, which might have won the day, and perhaps the war, for the Confederate cause.' Anybody who has examined the battlefield of Gettysburg will understand the quality, the ruthless practical quality, of this judgement. And while he maintained so long and so close a relationship with Liddell Hart he was not, as might have been thought, seduced by the doctrines of 'the Captain who taught Generals'. When he was in the Pacific during the desperate phase of his ABDA Command he sat down one day and wrote to his old friend, having just read Liddell Hart's *Strategy of Indirect Approach,* 'My main conclusion was that with your knowledge and brains and command of the pen, you could have written just as convincing a book called *The Strategy of Direct Approach'.*

His own fundamentally direct approach, to poetry and to war, is well illustrated in a letter he wrote to Anthony Quayle in 1948. He had just visited Stratford where Quayle was then Director of the Shakespeare Memorial Theatre.

You started some interesting remarks the other night about Iago and military ambition for promotion, especially in the non-commissioned ranks. Iago was, I take it, a 'ranker', who had made his way up by hard fighting and also by some hard and unscrupulous intrigue against rivals. I can imagine his disgust at finding Cassio preferred, "with unhatched rapier and on carpet consideration". And Cassio does much to justify Iago's poor opinion of him as a soldier. He gets drunk on guard, an unpardonable offence on active service; and then tries to work through the women to get his pardon, instead of going straight to the general, as a strong character would have done. And when wounded in the last Act, not very severely, he makes a most unsoldierly fuss about it, crying out for help repeatedly; this is in contrast to Iago's defiant facing of the prospect of torture at the end.

I imagine that Iago's resentment against Othello was largely due to the feeling that O., previously a camp and field general, had been now 'nobbled' by the drawing-room dowagers and politicians, and that Desdemona was the cause; and that her partiality for the Cassio type may have been the reason for his preferment. So that Iago's hatred and revenge are understandable on these premises, especially to the Elizabethans, who were much rougher and tougher and probably more unscrupulous intriguers.

On this matter of the analysis of Shakespeare as if he wrote for the study and not for the stage, I have been thinking of the deaths in Hamlet and Othello, and what nonsense medical comment could make of them. If Hamlet had been dying from a poison-tipped rapier, he would have been writhing in knots, quite unable to speak, at least connectedly. And death by smothering causes people to go black in the face, I believe, and their eyes to pop out of their head and other unpleasant symptoms; Desdemona would not have been a pretty sight, and would have been quite unable to utter a word before death. But we accept these deaths as part of the stage convention. So I fail to see why commentators should deny to Shakespeare other stage conventions, e.g., a certain vagueness as to date and place – Hamlet's exact age for instance – which no audience in the theatre would notice.

There is something in that letter which explains why Kipling, the committed poet of the practical, is a dominant figure in *Other Men's Flowers*. And Kipling, curiously enough, was an interest he shared with the greatest poet of his time who became his friend and admirer even though, in his anthology, Wavell had written that 'much of the work of T. S. Eliot has obvious dignity and beauty, and is a pleasure to read as long as one makes no effort to solve his cryptograms; but some of it seems deliberately ugly as well as cryptic'. Yet after Wavell's death and the publication of Bernard Fergusson's memoir, Eliot wrote to its author, on 13 September 1961:

I do not pretend to be a judge of Wavell as a soldier; although I accept the opinion of yourself, and other competent authorities, that he was a great soldier. What I do know from personal acquaintance with the man, is that he was a great man. This is not a term I use easily; there are very few men whom I have met in all my years in two continents, and amongst all the variety whom I have known, who seem to me great men. But about Wavell I feel not a doubt whatever.

# Notes

## 2 A Thing of Shreds and Patches
(pages 30–61)

1 John Connell, *Wavell: Scholar and Soldier* (Collins 1964), p.220.
2 The wartime references from Shearer's memoir are taken from an autobiography prepared privately for his family records.
3 Lord Boothby, *Boothby: Recollections of a Rebel* (Hutchinson 1978), p.147.
4 W. B. Kennedy Shaw, *Long Range Desert Group* (Collins 1945), p.47.
5 David Mure, *Practise to Deceive* (Kimber 1977), p.21.
6 Wavell/Liddell Hart correspondence file, the Liddell Hart Centre, King's College, the University of London.

## 3 The Enemy Encompassed
(pages 62–91)

1 O'Connor papers.
2 I.S.O. Playfair, *The Mediterranean and the Middle East* (HMSO 1954), vol. I, p.263.
3 Correlli Barnett, *The Desert Generals* (Kimber 1960).
4 O'Connor papers.
5 John Connell, *Wavell: Scholar and Soldier* (Collins 1964).
6 O'Connor papers.
7 The full texts registering O'Connor's disquiet are in his papers.
8 See Michael Carver, *Harding of Petherton* (Weidenfeld & Nicolson 1978).

## 4 The Hounds of Spring
(pages 92–116)

1 F. H. Hinsley *et al.*, *British Intelligence in the Second World War*, vol. 1 (HMSO 1979), p.357.
2 John Connell, *Wavell: Scholar and Soldier* (Collins 1964). p.239

3  Wavell/Liddell Hart correspondence, the Liddell Hart Centre.
4  Connell, p.357.
5  Private letter to Major-General David Belchem.
6  Stephen E. Ambrose, *The Supreme Commander* (Cassell 1971), p.641.
7  Miles Reid, *Last on the List* (Cooper 1974), p. 132.
8  Reid.
9  Private communication from Major-General Belchem.
10 John Hetherington, *Blamey* (The Australian War Memorial 1973), p.136.

## 5  Things Fall Apart
(pages 117–146)

1  F. H. Hinsley *et al.*, *British Intelligence in the Second World War*, vol. 1 (HMSO 1979), p.391.
2  Original text in O'Connor papers.
3  Signal quoted more fully in Winston S. Churchill, *The Second World War*, vol. 3 (Cassell 1950), p. 175.
4  See John Connell, *Wavell: Scholar and Soldier* (Collins 1964), p.384.
5  Michael Carver, *Harding of Petherton* (Weidenfeld & Nicolson 1978), p.65.
6  Private communication from O'Connor.
7  I. McD. G. Stewart, *The Struggle for Crete* (Oxford University Press 1966), p.53.
8  Hinsley *et al.*, p.418.
9  Stewart.
10 Stewart.
11 Private communication from Norman.
12 Private communication from Norman.
13 Major-General Sir John Kennedy, *The Business of War* (Hutchinson 1957).
14 Kennedy, *The Business of War*, p.119.
15 John Connell, *Auchinleck* (Cassell 1959), p.237.

## 6  The Wind from the East
(pages 147–183)

1  Hutton, private memoir, '*Rangoon 1941–42*'.
2  Pownall (ed. Brian Bond), *Chief of Staff* (Leo Cooper 1974), vol. 2.
3  John Connell (ed. Michael Roberts), *Wavell: Supreme Commander*

(Collins 1968), p.94.
4 Pownall.
5 Field Marshal Lord Slim, *Defeat into Victory* (Cassell 1956).
6 See *inter alia*, Brigadier Sir John Smyth, *Leadership in War 1939–1945*, p.153.
7 See also Appendix 19, 'State of Training of Reinforcing Formations from India', in Kirby, *The War against Japan* (HMSO 1957), vol. 1.
8 Personal communication from Hutton.

# 7 Shaking the Pagoda Tree
(pages 184–214)

1 Philip Mason, *A Shaft of Sunlight* (Deutsch 1978), p.166.
2 R. J. Moore, *Churchill, Cripps and India 1939–1945* (Oxford University Press 1979), p.52.
3 Christopher Thorne, *Allies of a Kind* (Hamish Hamilton 1978), p.157.
4 Moore, p.62.
5 Moore, p.135.
6 Barbara W. Tuchman, *Stilwell and the American Experience in China* (Macmillan 1971), p.329.
7 Ronald Lewin, *Slim the Standard-bearer* (Leo Cooper 1976), p.96.
8 See Duff Hart-Davis, *Peter Fleming* (Cape 1974), and Bernard Fergusson, *Wavell: Portrait of a Soldier* (Collins 1961), p.74.
9 Hart-Davis.
10 Wavell's correspondence with Alan Brooke about *Error* and *Purple Whales* is in a file still reserved.
11 See Ronald Mckie, *The Heroes* (Angus & Robertson 1960), for the full story of *Jaywick*.
12 Kirby, *The War against Japan*. vol. 2, p.237.
13 The relevant papers, including Wavell's letters, are in PREM 4/84/4.
14 *The Army Medical Services*, vol. V, p.678.
15 Personal communication to author from Lieutenant-General Sir Reginald Savory, who put up Wingate on his return across the Chindwin.

# 8 Quite a Respectable Position
(pages 215–241)

1 John Harvey (ed.), *The War Diaries of Oliver Harvey, 1941–1945* (Collins 1978).

2 Michael Howard, *Grand Strategy* (HMSO 1970), vol. 4, p.578.
3 Harold Nicolson (ed. Nigel Nicolson), *Diaries and Letters 1930–1939* (Collins 1966/7), entry for 19 February 1936.
4 Private information.

# Bibliography

Apart from private papers referred to in the prefatory acknowledgements the main sources employed – apart from relevant volumes in the Official Histories, and Wavell's own Despatches – are:

AMERY, JULIAN, *Approach March*, Hutchinson, 1973.

ASTLEY, JOAN BRIGHT, *The Inner Circle*, Hutchinson, 1971.

BARKER, ELISABETH, *Churchill and Eden at War*, Macmillan, 1978.

BARNETT, CORELLI, *The Desert Generals*, Kimber, 1960.

BELCHEM, MAJOR-GENERAL DAVID, *All in the Day's March*, Collins, 1978.

BIDWELL, SHELFORD, *The Chindit War*, Hodder, 1979.

BOND, BRIAN (ed.) *Chief of Staff: the diaries of Lieut.-General Sir Henry Pownall*, vol. 2, 1940–4, Leo Cooper, 1974.

BRYANT, SIR ARTHUR, *The Turn of the Tide*, Collins, 1957.

BRYANT, SIR ARTHUR, *Triumph in the West*, Collins, 1959.

BUTLER, LORD, *The Art of the Possible*, Hamish Hamilton, 1971.

BOOTHBY, LORD, *Boothby: Recollections of a Rebel*, Hutchinson, 1978.

CALLAHAN, RAYMOND, *Burma 1942–1945*, Davis-Poynter, 1978.

CALLAHAN, RAYMOND, *The Worst Disaster: The Fall of Singapore*, University of Delaware Press, 1977.

CARVER, MICHAEL, *Tobruk*, Batsford, 1964.

CARVER, MICHAEL, *Harding of Petherton*, Weidenfeld & Nicolson, 1978.

CHANDOS, LORD, *Memoirs*, Bodley Head, 1962.

CHURCHILL, WINSTON S., *The Second World War*, vols 1–6, Cassell, 1948–1954.

CLARKE, DUDLEY, *Seven Assignments*, Cape, 1948.

CLARKE, DUDLEY, *The Eleventh at War*, Michael Joseph, 1952.

CONNELL, JOHN, *Auchinleck*, Cassell, 1959.

CONNELL, JOHN, *Wavell: Scholar and Soldier*, Collins, 1964.

CONNELL, JOHN (ed. Michael Roberts), *Wavell: Supreme Commander*, Collins, 1969.

CRUICKSHANK, CHARLES, *Greece 1940–1941*, Davis-Poynter, 1976.

CRUICKSHANK, CHARLES, *Deception in World War II*, Oxford University Press, 1979.

CUNNINGHAM, ADMIRAL OF THE FLEET VISCOUNT, *A Sailor's Odyssey*, Hutchinson, 1951.

DAVIN, D. M., *Crete*, Oxford University Press, 1953.

DE GUINGAND, MAJOR-GENERAL SIR FRANCIS, *Operation Victory*, Hodder & Stoughton, 1955.

DE GUINGAND, MAJOR-GENERAL SIR FRANCIS, *Generals at War*, Hodder & Stoughton, 1964.

DILKS, DAVID (ed.), *The Diaries of Sir Alexander Cadogan*, Cassell, 1971.

EVANS, LIEUTENANT-GENERAL SIR GEOFFREY, *The Desert and the Jungle*, Kimber, 1959.

FERGUSSON, BERNARD, *Wavell: Portrait of a Soldier*, Collins, 1961.

FERGUSSON, BERNARD, *The Trumpet in the Hall*, Collins, 1970.

FERGUSSON, BERNARD, *The Black Watch and the King's Enemies*, Collins, 1950.

GOLANT, WILLIAM, *The Long Afternoon: British India 1601–1947*, Hamish Hamilton, 1975.

HART-DAVIS, DUFF, *Peter Fleming*, Cape, 1974.

HARVEY, JOHN (ed.), *The War Diaries of Oliver Harvey 1941–1945*, Collins, 1978.

HENDERSON, G. F. R., *Stonewall Jackson*, Longmans, 1898.

HETHERINGTON, J., *Blamey*, The Australian War Memorial, 1973.

HINSLEY F. H. (*et al.*), *British Intelligence in the Second World War*, vol. 1., HMSO, 1979.

HODSON, H. V., *The Great Divide*, Hutchinson, 1969.

HOWARD, MICHAEL, *The Mediterranean Strategy in The Second World War*, Weidenfeld & Nicolson, 1966.

IRVING, DAVID, *The Trail of the Fox*, Weidenfeld & Nicolson, 1977.

ISMAY, GENERAL THE LORD, *Memoirs*, Heinemann, 1960.

JACKSON, GENERAL SIR WILLIAM, *The North African Campaign 1940–43*, Batsford, 1975.

JAMES, ROBERT RHODES (ed.), *Chips: the diaries of Sir Henry Channon*, Weidenfeld & Nicolson, 1967.

KENNEDY, MAJOR-GENERAL SIR JOHN, *The Business of War*, Hutchinson, 1957.

KIPPENBERGER, MAJOR-GENERAL SIR HOWARD, *Infantry Brigadier*, Oxford University Press, 1949.

KOLIOPOULOS, JOHN S., *Greece and the British Connection 1935–1941*, Oxford University Press, 1977.

LEWIN, RONALD, *Rommel as Military Commander*, Batsford, 1968.

LEWIN, RONALD, *Churchill as War Lord*, Batsford, 1973.

LEWIN, RONALD, *Slim the Standard-bearer*, Leo Cooper, 1976.

LEWIN, RONALD, *Ultra Goes to War*, Hutchinson, 1978.

LIDDELL HART, B. H. (ed.), *The Rommel Papers*, Collins, 1953.

LIDDELL HART, B. H., *The Tanks*, Cassell, 1959.

LIDDELL HART, B. H., *Memoirs*, Cassell, 1965.

LOUIS, W. R., *Imperialism at Bay*, Oxford University Press, 1977.

MASON, PHILIP, *A Matter of Honour*, Cape, 1974.

MASON, PHILIP *A Shaft of Sunlight*, Deutsch, 1978.

MCKIE, RONALD, *The Heroes*, Angus & Robertson, 1960.

MOORE, R. J., *Churchill, Cripps and India 1939–1945*, Oxford University Press, 1979.

MURE, DAVID, *Practise to Deceive*, Kimber, 1977.

NICOLSON, HAROLD (ed. Nigel Nicolson), *Diaries and Letters 1930–1939*, 2 vols, Collins, 1966 and 1967.

NICOLSON, NIGEL, *Alex*, Weidenfeld & Nicolson, 1973.

POGUE, F. C., *George C. Marshall*, 2 vols, Viking Press, 1966 and 1973.

REID, MILES, *Last on the List*, Leo Cooper, 1974.

ROMANUS, C. F., and SUNDERLAND, R., *Stilwell's Command Problems*, Office of the Chief of Military History, Department of the Army, Washington DC, 1955.

SCOTT, PAUL, *The Raj Quartet*, Heinemann, 1978.

SHAW, W. B. KENNEDY, *Long Range Desert Group*, Collins, 1945.

SLIM, FIELD MARSHAL LORD, *Defeat into Victory*, Cassell, 1956.

SMYTH, BRIGADIER SIR JOHN, *Before the Dawn*, Cassell, 1957.

SPEARS, MAJOR-GENERAL SIR EDWARD, *Fulfilment of a Mission*, Leo Cooper, 1977.

STEWART, I. McD. G., *The Struggle for Crete*, Oxford University Press, 1966.

STILWELL, GENERAL JOSEPH W. (ed. Theodore White), *The Stilwell Papers*, New York, Sloane, 1948.

SYKES, CHRISTOPHER, *Orde Wingate*, Collins, 1959.

TEDDER, MARSHAL OF THE RAF LORD, *With Prejudice*, Cassell, 1966.

THORNE, CHRISTOPHER, *Allies of a Kind*, Hamish Hamilton, 1978.

TUCHMANN, BARBARA W., *Stilwell and the American Experience in China*, Macmillan, 1971.

TULLOCH, MAJOR-GENERAL DEREK,' *Wingate in Peace and War*, Macdonald, 1972.

VERNEY, MAJOR-GENERAL G. L., *The Desert Rats*, Hutchinson, 1954.

WAVELL, FIELD MARSHAL EARL, *The Palestine Campaigns*, Constable, 1928.

WAVELL, FIELD MARSHAL EARL, *Allenby*, Harrap, 1940.

WAVELL, FIELD MARSHAL EARL, *Generals and Generalship*, Times, 1941.

WAVELL, FIELD MARSHAL EARL, *The Good Soldier*, Macmillan, 1948.

WAVELL, FIELD MARSHAL EARL, *Other Men's Flowers,* Cape, 1944.

WAVELL, FIELD MARSHAL EARL (ed. Penderel Moon), *The Viceroy's Journal,* Oxford University Press, 1973.

WILMOT, CHESTER, *The Struggle for Europe,* Collins, 1952.

WOODHOUSE, C. M., *The Struggle for Greece 1941–1949,* Hart-Davis, MacGibbon, 1976.

WOOLLCOMBE, ROBERT, *The Campaigns of Wavell 1939–1943,* Cassell, 1959.

# Index

fallacy of direction by remote control, 209–10, 210n
Commandos, arrival in Middle East, 86
Connell, John, *Wavell,* 230
  quoted, 21n, 23–4, 32, 102
  on Ulster Crisis, 23
  and Churchill/W. relationship, 24–5
  on Dorman-Smith/W. meeting, 88
  and Greek expedition, 102
  on Morshead/W. meeting, 125
  on W. in Malaya, 163
  and W.'s responsibility for Singapore, 169
  on Japanese advance in Burma, 173
  *Auchinleck,* 141
Coupland, Sir Reginald, and Indian constitution, 189
Cowan, Brigadier 'Punch', 17 Indian Division, 181
Creagh, Maj.-Gen., and *Compass,* 58
Crete, 15, 59, 78
  problems of reinforcement, 40n
  Galloway and, 110, 120, 130
  Churchill and, 116, 128, 129
  motley garrison of refugees, 127–8, 131
  D-Day, 128–9
  W.'s responsibility for disaster, 129–34
  'second Scapa' concept, 129–30
  succession of COs, 130
  Italian prisoners of war, 131
  absence of defence preparations, 131–2
  German victory, 131, 132–4
  W.'s worst hour, 134–5
  evacuation, 134
Cripps, Sir Stafford,
  and Labour Party, 232
  and Indian affairs, 235–6
  and Cabinet Mission, 236, 237
Cripps Mission, Draft Declaration on transference of power, 187–8, 231
  and responsibility for defence (paragraph (e)), 188
  on W.'s ignorance of Indian people, 189n
  failure, 189–90, 202, 224, 232
Cruickshank, Charles, *Greece 1940–41,* 96n
Cunningham, General Alan, 74
  and Kenya, 69, 71, 73, 165

  failure in command of 8th Army, 165
Cunningham, Admiral A. B., first Viscount Cunningham, 220
  C-in-C Mediterranean, 33, 42
  and *Lustre,* 103, 113
  belief in superiority of RN, 114
  evacuation of Greece, 127
  evacuation of Crete, 134
  *A Sailor's Odyssey,* 113
Cyrenaica (Operation *Compass*), 35
  W. and, 46, 48, 57–9, 64 ff
  exercise of secrecy, 48, 58, 59–60, 66
  role of cryptanalysis, 56
  to be kept from Churchill, 58, 59–60, 68
  dilemma after Italian ultimatum to Greece, 59–60
  reception of plan by Defence Committee, 60–61
  apportionment of credit, 62–4
  use of tanks (Matildas), 65–6, 67
  role of *Apology* convoy, 65
  exercise of deceit and surprise, 66
  O'Connor/W. agreement, 66–7
  W.'s declaration of intent, 67–8
  use of Desert force, 68–9
  switch of Indian Division to East Africa, 76, 77
  milked by demands of Greece, 78, 82, 120
  re-alerted after Greek refusal, 84–5
  tactical advantages of Mechili and Derna, 88–9
  O'Connor's final coup, 87, 88–9
  compared with *Lustre,* 111
  Neame in command, 120, 121
  army deprivations, 120

de Gaulle, General Charles, 23, 141
de Guingand, Sir Francis, 150
  and W.'s responsibility for Greek disaster, *Generals at War,* 80
Delhi, 20, 47, 148, 190
  and W.'s Burma command, 154, 155
  his state of mind as C-in-C, 179–80, 184–5, 193, 210
  Wingate at Army HG, 212
  W. as viceroy (*see under* Wavell), 224
  conference of provincial governors, 227.
Dentz, General, and Syria, 138, 139, 141

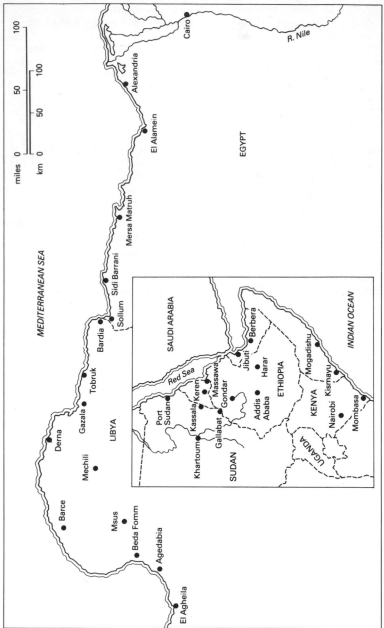

Map 1. The 'Compass' Theatre and East Africa

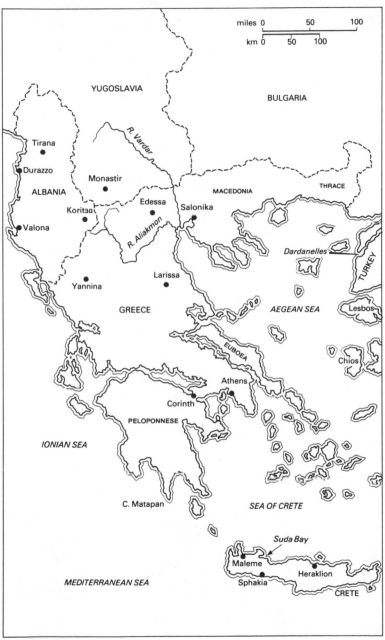

miles 0     50     100

km 0   50   100

YUGOSLAVIA

BULGARIA

Tirana

*R. Vardar*

Durazzo

Monastir

ALBANIA

MACEDONIA

THRACE

Koritsa

Edessa

Salonika

Valona

*R. Aliakmon*

*Dardanelles*

TURKEY

Larissa

Yannina

GREECE

*AEGEAN SEA*

Lesbos

EUBOEA

Chios

Athens

Corinth

PELOPONNESE

*IONIAN SEA*

C. Matapan

*SEA OF CRETE*

*Suda Bay*

Maleme

Heraklion

*MEDITERRANEAN SEA*

Sphakia

CRETE

Map 2. The Balkan Stage

282

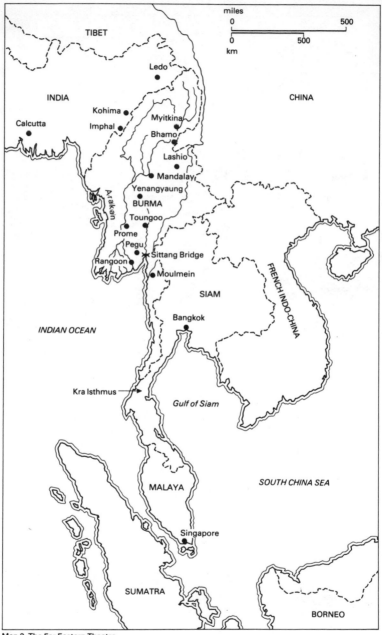

Map 3. The Far Eastern Theatre